Step by Step

The Life in My Journeys

Simon Reeve

HODDER &
STOUGHTON

First published in Great Britain in 2018 by Hodder & Stoughton
An Hachette UK company

4

Copyright © Simon Reeve 2018

All photos are from the author's collection

A CIP catalogue record for this title is available from the British Library

Hardback ISBN 9781473689107
Trade Paperback ISBN 9781473689114
eBook ISBN 9781473689138

Typeset in Bembo by Hewer Text UK Ltd, Edinburgh

Printed and bound by CPI Group (UK) Ltd, Croydon, CR0 4YY

Hodder & Stoughton policy is to use papers that are natural, renewable
and recyclable products and made from wood grown in sustainable forests.
The logging and manufacturing processes are expected to conform
to the environmental regulations of the country of origin.

Hodder & Stoughton Ltd
Carmelite House
50 Victoria Embankment
London EC4Y 0DZ

www.hodder.co.uk

For Jake

Contents

CHAPTER ONE

The A-Team

Everything felt wrong. I was damp with sweat, my head was thumping, my limbs were aching as if I'd run a hard race, and I was lying face down on a bed in the early hours of the morning wearing my clothes and muddy boots. I opened my eyes. The room began to spin. I turned on my side and an overpowering sense of nausea welled within me. I staggered to my feet and half-fell against the wall of the hotel bedroom, my limbs now shaking and the room turning over and over in my head. I knew this was serious. Not a hangover, not the flu, not food poisoning, but much worse.

It was 2006, and I was in Gabon, West Africa, filming *Equator*, my first major television series and biggest adventure. For most people, the equator is just an imaginary line running for 25,000 miles around the middle of the world. But the equator is at the heart of the tropics, home to both the richest collection of wildlife on the planet and the greatest concentration of human suffering. Following the line would take me to utter extremes and parts of the world rarely seen on television. The journey was supposed to transform my life. Not end it.

This leg of my series had started on a beach on the coast of Gabon in the middle of nowhere, bang on zero degrees latitude. I had followed the imaginary line across Gabon to the remote east of the country, the wild forest home of impoverished communities and diseased apes suffering from Ebola, a desperate, eyeball-bleeding contagion that sounds like the stuff of science fiction. Now my limbs were aching, shaking and burning. I was feverish and sick. I knew I had to make it to the bathroom before my insides came tumbling out.

With one hand pressed to the wall I fixed my gaze on the outline of the bathroom door and tried to take a step. My feet wouldn't move. I was requesting movement, but nothing was happening. Deep within my brain I was processing my thoughts, but other physical controls were shutting down. The inside of my mouth was burning, and the thudding in my temple was reaching a crescendo. I knew the only way to create momentum to reach the bathroom was to push off from the wall like a rock climber.

I swayed back and forth, fell against the bathroom door, collapsed onto my knees in front of the bath and vomited dramatically. Through the haze of sickness, the dim light and my spinning brain, my mind was still able to flash a stark warning signal. There was blood in my vomit. My first thought was a moment of complete clarity: it must be Ebola. Ye gods. I was screwed. Then I passed out.

It was hours before I came to, slumped on mouldy lino on the bathroom floor. I was shaking, my temperature was rising, and I was scared. But I was still alive. I remember thinking that if I hadn't died, then I had to get up, and I had to carry on. Not make some noise, or call for help, or something sensible like that. Not drag myself back to my bags and my phone and try to ring one of my colleagues or the BBC safety number for a doctor. But get off the floor, rinse out the bloody bath, and get downstairs to see my colleagues, and carry on with my journey. We were supposed to be leaving little-known Gabon and heading east, flying across the neighbouring country, Congo-Brazzaville, and on into the vast Democratic Republic of Congo (DRC). There was an outbreak of Ebola, a viral haemorrhagic fever, on and around the equator in Congo-Brazzaville. There is no cure and a mortality rate of up to 90 per cent. Some victims bleed from every orifice until they die. It is horrific, terrifying, and international medical teams were being attacked by desperate villagers who accused them of spreading the disease. I had been keen to head along the equator into Congo-Brazzaville, but the BBC said it was too dangerous. So instead we were supposed to board a small plane that would leapfrog the insanely dangerous zone, and deliver us into the DRC, scene of perhaps the most violent conflict on the planet since the Second World War. So still not exactly safe, and lacking in advanced medical facilities to treat anyone suffering from Ebola.

Lying there on the bathroom floor, I half-knew all this. I should have called for a doctor. But this was supposed to be the beginning of a whole new chapter for me in television. The few series I had made for the BBC before *Equator* had been fascinating, life-changing and mind-altering, but they had been budget trips shown in the so-called graveyard shift after *Newsnight*, when people were switching on the telly after coming home from the pub. *Equator* had been a bigger idea, a more ambitious proposition, as TV people say, and we had more resources, planning time and dedicated, exceptional cameramen. The end result was supposed to be shown in a primetime slot on BBC Two.

I couldn't let everyone down. The planning for our trip across the DRC alone had taken weeks. And I was excited about the journey. Following the equator around the world – who gets to do that? It was an adventure money could not buy, with the clear purpose of exploring the centre of the tropics, the most beautiful and benighted region on the planet. I might have Ebola, but I was still alive. If I was still alive I wanted to continue. I tried pushing myself away from the tub so I could get to my feet, but my hands wouldn't work, let alone my feet. My mind was swimming in and out of consciousness. I could feel my temperature going through the roof.

With a monumental effort I managed to get up, but my head felt like it was on a spin cycle. Using walls, handles and banisters to remain upright, I dragged my bag out of my room and across the corridor to an ancient lift. When the doors opened I started dry-retching, to the alarm of a couple already inside. My eyes caught theirs and I glimpsed horror, then fear. Everyone in Gabon knew what was happening in Congo-Brazzaville. People were terrified of Ebola. They rushed out of the lift as I stumbled inside. How selfish of me to think only of my journey, or my programmes. If I was a walking Ebola petri dish I should have stayed in my room. Instead I spilled into the hotel lobby, where Sophie and Sam, director and cameraman on this leg of the *Equator* series, were waiting with our Gabonese guide Linel. They saw me sliding along the wall, pulling my bag along the floor, and I could see their mouths drop. I wasn't sweating so much as dripping. Every millimetre of skin was alive with perspiration and yet I was shivering.

'My God, Simon.' It was Sam who spoke first. 'You look like death.'

'Bad night,' I muttered. 'I was sick in the bath and I slept on the floor. I didn't have the strength to climb into bed.' I was swaying back and forth, nothing in my legs but jelly. 'I'll be fine. What time is the flight?'

Sophie took a look at me then exchanged a glance with Sam. Taking my arm, she told me the only place I was going was back to bed. By this time I was shivering so badly my teeth were chattering. I was on the point of collapsing again, but the three of them managed to half-carry, half-drag me back upstairs to my room.

'It's Ebola, isn't it?' I mumbled. 'You shouldn't be touching me. You need to get me into quarantine.'

We had been travelling in Gabon for just over a week. Before starting research for the programme I knew next to nothing about the place, other than it was small, formerly French, and blessed − or cursed − with massive oil reserves. But the BBC team had found me an excellent guide. Linel was a local teacher with a patient but enthusiastic air.

I felt a real thrill filming the opening scenes for the series. We had hired a boat in Libreville, the capital of Gabon, and chugged down the coast. Using a GPS unit and a handful of satellites orbiting the Earth, we found a beautiful and unspoilt beach of pristine sand and palm trees. Yet it was unremarkable. There was no plaque, sign, beach bar or monument marking the point. But it was the stretch of land where the equator made landfall in Africa. It was the middle of the world.

The idea behind the series was simple. I was going to follow or track the equator line through a unique region of the planet, and countries suffering from war, poverty, disease, deforestation and corruption. Following the line would force us to go to remoter areas, to places rarely visited by outsiders, let alone TV crews.

Beyond Gabon months of travel were supposed to take me across Africa to Uganda and Kenya and on to the lawless border with chaotic Somalia. Indonesia, the Galapagos, Colombia's interminable civil war and the vast Amazon all beckoned ahead.

We were expecting endless problems while following the equator. Even chugging to the start point had been eventful. Initially the captain ignored the plan we had agreed and tried to fob us off with a sightseeing trip into a huge lagoon.

'Perhaps we can get to the sea and the line that way,' he said, gesturing vaguely towards a peninsula that clearly offered no through-route. 'Isn't this good enough for you?'

He only agreed to turn back and out to sea when we at first politely and then sternly insisted we wanted to brave the ocean. Checks on the fuel reserves and life jackets he had assured us were stowed in bench seats revealed he had neither. Two hours were lost fuelling and finding jackets. Linel tied his tight. So did the two crewmen on the boat. None of them could swim, they much later admitted. We headed out to sea towards the zero degrees. The sea was certainly choppy, but the speed at which the boat started to take on quantities of water surprised me. I have a bad reputation among my colleagues for being a bit of a Jonah. Half the boats I travel in while filming seem to nearly sink. By the time we reached the equator we were bailing furiously using buckets and our own water bottles, and I was relieved to be first off the front, leaping into the water, reaching dry land and officially starting my journey. There was no bunting (there is never any bunting), but it was a moment to savour.

Tides and the wind were in our favour on the return journey, and we were soon out exploring Libreville, which boasts casinos, musty hotels, miles of sandy beaches and a handful of handsome seafront buildings with a passing resemblance to those of South Beach. Prior to independence in 1960, Gabon had been ruled from Paris as one of four territories known as French Equatorial Africa. The continuing presence of French soldiers had helped keep Gabon relatively stable, while oil had made a few well-connected locals extremely rich. At one point in the 1980s Gabon had the highest per capita consumption of champagne in the world.

Everywhere I looked the face of President Omar Bongo beamed out from billboards and posters. In power since 1967, he was the longest-serving leader in Africa, and globally second only to Fidel Castro. Critics would point out that perhaps Bongo had not spent Gabon's vast oil revenues entirely wisely or fairly. But he seemed to wield absolute power from a vast and hideous presidential palace. Linel told us nervously that filming it might cause problems, particularly for him, so instead we turned the camera in the opposite direction and I just made sarcastic comments about the leader and the architecture.

Later that day as the team were filming elsewhere in the city, I was wandering the seafront with Linel when a phalanx of motorcycle outriders raced along the main road closing side streets. Five minutes later the President came down the road in a huge convoy of armoured cars, limos, army trucks and an ambulance as medical back-up. I counted forty-five vehicles. Even the US President manages with less. A French attack helicopter swooped low overhead, machine-gunners at the open doors, providing security and a clear sign the autocratic leader still had the backing of Paris. Gallic influence was pervasive in the former French colony. Restaurants were full of oil industry ex-pats drooling over young locals, while pricey supermarkets were stuffed with French wine and *foie gras*.

Linel told me Libreville was one of the most expensive cities to live anywhere in Africa. He took me to a local supermarket where I was amazed by the number of expensive cars parked outside. Mercedes, Lexus and Land Cruisers all had their slots.

Inside the store was fruit imported from France and sold at exorbitant prices.

'Isn't this mad?' I said to Linel. 'We're in Africa. The sun shines and fruit grows everywhere here.'

He shrugged his shoulders. 'When you have oil, you can do anything,' he said wryly.

But even for those rich enough to afford the supermarket prices, the party was coming to an end. Supplies of Gabon's black gold were dwindling. After Bongo took power the once rich and profitable farming industry had slowly but surely collapsed. There was desperate poverty in Gabon and the super-market had armed itself with three guards carrying pump-action shotguns to protect against robbery.

We headed to a more traditional street market just a mile from the supermarket, with basic stalls and hungry dogs running loose and hustling for a treat. It was risky for people to talk to us, but one brave middle-aged woman who had been shuffling along the street carrying a basket of vegetables on her head stopped to bemoan the state of the country and the dictator, as she called Bongo with disgust.

'We have nothing. I pray for him to die,' she said, before paus-ing. 'But perhaps whoever follows will be worse.'

Such was the reality of Gabon. Some of the supermarkets might be stocked with French delicacies. But most people endured dirt roads and tin-roofed shacks.

Back in our dilapidated hotel I had a moment of terror stuck in the lift while the metal cables groaned and strained. Then I wandered outside and a battered Citroën racing along the coast road suddenly turned sharply and slammed into the thick wall right next to me, demolishing the front of the car, and the wall. The driver slid out of his seat, dusted himself with a dramatic flourish, and calmly walked into the hotel. 'I'm fine, thank you, there is nothing to worry about,' he said. I gave the car a wide berth as it began to smoulder and hailed a taxi. We drove 40 metres before hitting another car. My driver had been distracted by a completely naked man carrying a bicycle into a shop. Gabon was a weird place.

We packed our kit ready to continue the journey east and made a beeline for the train station. Three times a week trains would leave Libreville and head east, parallel with the equator, on the Transgabonais railway towards Lopé National Park, home to a large population of mandrills and several thousand western lowland gorillas.

With the oil running out, Bongo had decided to tap tourist dollars by exploiting other national assets. With apes, hippos splashing in the sea, pristine rainforest, and nearly 700 species of birds, Gabon is a paradise for naturalists. Absolute power can clearly speed decision-making. The President had recently ordered that 11 per cent of Gabon should be converted into national parks – almost overnight. It was a bold move: Voila! Gabon was being touted and promoted as the 'Costa Rica of Africa', an unspoiled high-end destination for wealthy eco-tourists.

I doubt they travelled on the railway. Our carriage was old, wooden, but charming and surprisingly empty. 'It's not cheap, and anyone with money drives,' said Linel.

The train grumbled and rattled as we rolled slowly along, following, skirting and then crossing the equator in a narrow gulch surrounded by a blanket of bright-green foliage. Ahead was a rickety bridge with a pathetic barrier on one side and nothing but a void on the other. The driver slowed to a crawl. The stanchions sagged under the weight of the train and hairs climbed on my forearms. Linel whispered the obvious.

'The bridge is very unstable,' he said.

An elderly man in a suit sitting alone a few rows ahead crossed himself. I stopped breathing. The whole train seemed to sigh and exhale as we reached solid tracks.

At a remote stop called Lopé we left the train and clambered into four-wheel drives for a journey into the rainforest. Roads were terrible, and time and again we had to push and winch the vehicles out of muddy holes.

Eventually we found a place to camp deep in the forest. As darkness fell, it was spell-binding. Light from the moon or stars could not penetrate the canopy, and the forest was pitch-black and filled with a cacophony of nocturnal life. I drifted off, snug in a sleeping bag, hearing the eerie wild cry of primates in the distance. The whole area was riddled with Ebola. Apes had been badly affected and Ebola can spread from primates to humans. Over the previous decade a third of the world's entire gorilla population had succumbed to the awful disease.

When I poked my head out of the tent in the morning the drivers were already up. They looked downcast and embarrassed. Their boss had been on the phone overnight. If we wanted them to take us any further we had to pay an additional chunk of cash, nearly $2,000.

'What?' I said. 'Two thousand dollars, are you kidding?'

The driver shook his head. He held up his mobile phone. 'The boss,' he said. 'It's what he told us to tell you.'

It was outright blackmail. They took us another hour or so further along the track, but then one of them received a text message ordering them to get the money out of us or turn back. We refused to pay. So they helped us unload our gear and abandoned us, deep in the Lopé forest.

We knew that somewhere ahead was the Mikongo camp,

home to a team of researchers, and we set off towards it on foot, each of us carrying a heavy load of kit, clothes and equipment.

Surrounded by tall, dark trees I started to wonder whether we'd be spending a second night on our own in the forest, when researchers from the Mikongo camp appeared, alerted on a radio to our plight, and helped to carry and lead us towards their sanctuary, a scattering of wooden buildings in a sunny clearing.

Researchers at the centre were monitoring the impact of the Ebola virus on the local ape population. They showed us a stack of gorilla and chimpanzee skulls that were victims of the dreaded disease. I picked up a couple for a closer look before the researchers suggested they were best left alone. Washing my hands with disinfectant made me feel safer, but I couldn't shake a nagging feeling something awful from the forest had implanted itself in my brain.

The team based at Mikongo were also studying lowland gorillas in their natural habitat, and they suggested we could trek into the jungle with their researchers. We plunged into the trees led by wiry local tracker Donald Ndongo and began to explore.

Lowland gorillas can wander several miles a day, so in the dense forest the odds of a sighting are not great. Between June and November more than a thousand mandrills can also congregate in the jungle, thought to be the largest non-human gatherings of primates anywhere in the world. I had dreams of an Attenborough-style encounter with huge primates in the jungle. Unfortunately, it was April and we couldn't even find droppings.

But tracking in the jungle was endlessly exciting. The entire ecosystem is alien and surprising. Donald was a mine of information on trees that bled red, and plants used for fighting fever, even as he clucked away noisily to alert gorillas to our presence.

'A surprised gorilla is a frightened gorilla,' Donald said sagely. 'And a frightened gorilla is not something you want to stumble across. Far better that we let them know we are coming. Then they can decide if they want to say hello.'

Pushing through the jungle was a challenge, but after a few hours we finally spotted, followed and filmed putty-nosed monkeys. It was an incredible treat. Sam, our cameraman, had been lugging a heavy camera while we took it in turns to carry the tripod. Long shots of our distant cousins flitting through the trees made the entire experience memorable and a joy – even if we sweated buckets in the equatorial heat and all of us were bitten to pieces by ferocious mosquitoes and insects the size of small sparrows.

Gabon clearly offers both more and less than a standard safari. More, in the sense that, after trekking and sweating through the rainforest, there is the chance of genuine and spontaneous wildlife discoveries. Compare that with a traditional safari in South or East Africa, where you can find yourself watching a bored cheetah on the open savannah while sitting in a jeep with honeymooners from Texas and Bavaria. And Gabon offers less, in that much of the country is thick green jungle, and you might only catch a rear-end glimpse of a mandrill or a gorilla as it heads in the wrong direction. In the rainforest there are no guarantees of a wildlife encounter.

Donald, whose father was a proud hunter ('never a poacher', he added quickly), explained how life was changing since the President decided to target wealthy tourists. Villagers who live in and around national parks had suddenly been banned from hunting in the forests.

'It's been a big shock for them,' he said. 'We try to explain that it's for the benefit of the country, but they need to eat, so they need to see the benefits of tourism quickly.'

Donald took us to the village of Makoghé, on the outskirts of the forest, where Jean Jacques, the energetic headman, had been struggling to hold his community together since the hunting ban. Overnight traditional hunting grounds had been taken away and an entire way of life had gone. Jean Jacques told me that as an alternative income for the community he had started organising traditional dances for paying foreigners.

Men from the village started drumming and some of the women started singing and dancing while a small group of visitors watched politely and snapped away with their cameras. It was clearly all very new to the villagers. More than once I saw a lady nudging another and reminding her to lead the next move. But this was their new economy. One young man used a clenched fist as a microphone to announce the dancers while others passed among us collecting payment.

I had a moment with the chief and he asked me to make sure people in the outside world knew they were welcome in Makoghé.

'Tourism is all we have now,' he said.

His message was clear: if you want us to stop hunting the wildlife, someone needs to provide us with an alternative means of putting food on the table.

Wildlife across Africa must be protected. But what about the humans? The Lopé forest is a lush wilderness, but it is also a home to thousands of Gabonese living in villages scattered around and in the middle of the new national park area. With a bit of guidance and training, the villagers of Makoghé and other small communities nearby could be helped to make money from guiding, hosting and feeding tourists. But often conservationists, even the most well-meaning, think that villagers, with their live-stock and human diseases, should be forced to move so that national parks can be protected as natural wilderness.

'Now that hunting is forbidden we have animals hunting our cattle and eating our crops,' said Jean Jacques. 'And if we do anything about it we get into trouble.'

I have heard this story in several forms on my travels. Across sub-Saharan Africa, populations are expanding but natural resources are scarce, so humans and animals compete for land, food and water. Villagers find themselves on land that govern-ments or conservation groups want to earmark for animals and exploit for tourist dollars.

Everyone knows that evil corporations push native peoples off their lands for oil or timber. But across the world, some conservation groups have occasionally done much the same, wrecking lives and cultures to create national parks. Bernhard Grzimek, who helped create the Serengeti National Park, and Joy Adamson of *Born Free* fame were both accused of expelling locals from land they wanted for animals.

National parks should be a powerful protection for Gabon's wildlife, but I wondered what would become of Jean Jacques and Makoghé.

We left the community and headed back to the station. Our journey further east was blocked by the Ebola outbreak in Congo-Brazzaville, and our incoming train back towards Libreville was late. A herd of drunken elephants had wandered in front of the train deep in the Gabonese jungle. Four of the elephants had been killed, and the engine and two carriages had been derailed. The line was completely blocked.

The stationmaster sweated profusely as he explained the prob-lem to our small group waiting on the Lopé station platform.

'It's the iboga fruit they keep eating,' he grumbled, apparently annoyed at the herd's failure to obey railway regulations. 'They get intoxicated and stagger around on our lines.'

It was another day before the line was cleared and we arrived back in the capital, Libreville. By the time I made it to bed that night my muscles were aching. I dreamt of sickly gorillas. Then woke in the early hours to my very own medical nightmare.

After Sophie, Sam and Linel had half-carried me back to my room they had a hurried chat. We had all been on remote medical courses and were travelling with a trauma kit for injuries and packs of pills for dealing with pain, fevers and infections. We had our common sense but none of us were paramedics and this was clearly something serious. Sophie rang London for advice and help. An expert was lined up on the phone.

My temperature was rising: 39.7, 39.8, 39.9. The room was warm, I was feverish, but I was also shaking and cold. Linel rang a local doctor and asked him to jump in a taxi. Sam remembered that on our delayed returning train we'd briefly met a young German doctor who was working at the nearby Albert Schweitzer Hospital, one of the best research centres on the continent for tropical diseases. It was a chance encounter that ultimately helped to save my life. Sam could remember the doctor was called Jenny but couldn't get through to the hospital on the phone. He jumped in a car and sped off to find her.

I was drifting in and out of consciousness, with a temperature that left me just a shade off brain impairment, and I was hallucinating. I thought Mr T from the A-Team was in the room helping to look after me, with his Afro Mohawk and gold jewellery. It took a while for Sophie and Linel to work out what I was talking about while I mumbled incoherently to my childhood hero. Sophie was able to laugh about it. Linel remained baffled until much later when we had a chance to explain. The A-Team weren't big in Gabon.

Linel's doctor arrived first. I came round in time to find him examining me. I was terrified. I was still convinced I had contracted Ebola.

'Where we were planning to go next,' I mumbled. 'My brain's not working. I feel so rough.'

The doctor spent a few minutes checking me over before he was ready to deliver his verdict.

'What do you think it is?' I asked.

'Malaria.'

I've never felt such an immediate relief. Malaria. Thank God. Not Ebola. My eyeballs wouldn't bleed. I wouldn't haemorrhage internally. Anything was better than Ebola.

Then there was a dawning realisation.

Hang on. Malaria isn't good.

Sam arrived back at the hotel with Dr Jenny. She gave the same diagnosis. A medic in London ticked off a checklist of symptoms and also confirmed the judgement.

But Jenny offered some practical help. She had brought a packet of Artemether with her, a newish drug derived from Vietnamese sweet wormwood that was not regulated or allowed in the UK, but was showing great promise as a treatment for malaria in Africa and Asia.

'Look, you will have to check with your people in London whether he can take it, but I think it could really help,' she told Sophie and Sam. 'The journey is over, at least for now, but this could save his life.'

Linel's doctor agreed. The London medic told Sophie the two doctors standing in my room were the best source of advice.

While I had a moment of clarity the team called my partner Anya, at the basement flat where we lived together in North London. They told her what was happening and the drugs Jenny had brought. We talked down the line, or at least I mumbled. I told her Mr T was there looking after me. Anya remained calm. She was cradling the phone and scanning the internet at the same time.

'I think you should take it,' she told me. 'Simon, can you understand? I think you should take the drugs. It won't be easy. It says here that roughly four hours after you take the pills World War Three will break out in your body.'

Artemether works by persuading malarial parasites to launch their attack before they are fully armed and ready. I had no choice. I took the pills. Six chunky tablets, braced with a cocktail of other drugs and paracetamol to get my temperature down. Four hours later I was doubled up with the most intense sickness I had ever experienced. I had a full-blown malarial assault and my temperature leapt around like the bearing in a pinball machine.

The attack went on for twenty-four hours. I was so weak, I could barely lift my head. I spent the next few days just sleeping before I was able to get out of bed. The sickness was a key turning point in my life. Before I had malaria I felt fit, energetic and just a little bit immortal. I've never felt the same since.

Throughout history, malaria has been our greatest enemy. It's thought that up to half of all the humans who have ever lived have died of malaria. Millions of Africans are still infected each year and thousands of children on the continent die every single day from the disease. The mosquito-borne virus is one of the great curses of the tropics, a disease found almost entirely between the Tropics of Capricorn and Cancer. We might have forgotten about it in the temperate West, but in Africa especially it can still dominate life. I have been in some areas of Africa where the incidence of malaria is more than 200 per cent. How is that possible? People are infected more than once a year. How can you have a fully functioning society when you are permanently dealing with that sort of catastrophe? Malaria is a spectre that haunts the continent. But if malaria still affected Europe, I have no doubt drug companies and governments would be working around the clock to find a way to beat the disease.

I was lucky. As a privileged, foreign TV presenter travelling in Africa I had swift access to qualified help and rare drugs. I was also stupid. I knew I was in a danger zone but had forgotten to take my anti-malaria drugs. It is not a mistake anyone makes twice.

My recovery was slow and in stages. After a few days I was able to lie on some bedding outside in the rough garden of our dodgy hotel. I still felt awful inside, and desperately weak, but I could open my eyes and my brain had started to function.

There was time for reflection, a bit of self-pity and then gratitude. I'd had a good run, I decided. I never thought TV presenting would be much of a career. If it ended then I would have already banked memories to last a lifetime. I had travelled through some of the most remote and beautiful areas of the world. I tried to tot up how many countries I'd visited. It was scores. I lay there in that grotty hotel garden and chuckled away to myself. I was sick and drained of energy. But I was in Gabon. I had been a teenage delinquent who left school without qualifications and went on the dole. I suffered from depression and mental health issues and was a whisker from suicide. But I had overcome my fears and failings, written books, travelled the world and met some of the most inspiring and extraordinary people on the planet.

How on earth had I been so lucky?

CHAPTER TWO

Mystery Tours

I grew up in Acton, West London, the hinterland between the inner city and the suburbs. We lived in a far corner of the otherwise leafy borough of Ealing, but on the edge of gritty Shepherd's Bush and White City. With my younger brother James, I had a childhood that was small and simple in a modest three-bedroom semi, which our mum and dad bought through years of grafting.

My father Alan was a strong, competitive man who grew up in rural Norfolk as an only child. A champion tennis player in his twenties, he lost a crucial match that would have put him into the Wimbledon championships, and still played tennis hard for the rest of his life. He was young when his father died and his mother had raised him on her own. It can't have been easy, but he struggled and studied, and eventually made it to college, trained and became a maths teacher at a tough comprehensive school in North-West London. Dad was one of the last teachers to qualify without a degree, a huge achievement. But the lack of a university education held him back, which riled him as years ticked by and he was passed over for promotions. Dad never earned vast sums, but he was careful with money and took on private students to supplement his income and pay for our home, the only one I ever knew. My mum Cindy still lives there. She survived a similar start in life to my dad. Her father died when she was young, just nine years old, and she was brought up in a single-parent household by my Grandma Lucy. Mum studied domestic science and then worked in restaurants, kitchens and sold sausages in a supermarket around the time she met my dad. It wasn't the most glamorous of starts, but they look blissfully happy in their wedding photos.

I was born in 1972, and my earliest memory is pain. Extreme pain. At four years old I was sick for a few days and the GP said I had sinusitis. Mum was not convinced. When my condition took a turn for the worse she called the hospital and was put through to a sympathetic specialist.

'That doesn't sound like sinusitis,' said the doctor. 'That sounds like a serious case of meningitis. Put the phone down, call an ambulance and get him here right now.'

It took a doctor, two nurses and my mum to hold down my wriggling, screaming little body while I was given a lumbar puncture to diagnose and confirm meningitis. It is an excruciating procedure where fluid is extracted through a large needle shoved up your spine. Deep within me I still sense the pain and shudder and squirm at the memory. The deadly meningitis was easy compared to the puncture, and after a few weeks I recovered from that only to have tonsillitis. My tonsils were whipped out quickly, just in time for me to contract pneumonia, and I nearly died all over again. It hadn't been spotted by the doctors. I'm only here today because Mum knew something was wrong and wouldn't take no for an answer. I ticked through a few of my nine lives as a tot. I hate to think how many I have left now after years of adventures.

Ours was a small family. Both my parents were only children. James and I had no first cousins, no uncles, no aunts and no grandfathers. When I was five my dad's mother Delsie died. But my Grandma Lucy was a rock of love through my early life with a cosy home nearby in West London that was a loving refuge. Gran was large, cuddly and always ready with a hug and some home-made cakes, especially when life was challenging or things were difficult for James and me at home.

I don't come from a connected family. I didn't grow up in wealthy Westminster or Chelsea. I didn't go to private school or Oxbridge, and I wasn't commissioned in the forces. Nobody in my immediate family has ever gone to university. Go back just a couple of generations on my dad's side and they were fish-hawkers traipsing door to door. One generation further and they were child labourers with no education at all.

Some of my earliest adventures were when my grandma, who for years wore a caliper on her leg due to childhood polio, and always found walking a struggle, would take James and me on magical mystery tours in her adapted car. My gran inspired me when I was a child and her memory remains with me and guides me as an adult. James and I would sit on booster seats and direct her left or right down one street after another. It was completely thrilling, exploring exotic areas like Hounslow, or Park Royal Trading Estate. Gran loved the freedom to drive, and for me, directing a car at the age of six was a real power. I can still remember the sense of excitement as we peered out of the window and discovered the McVitie's biscuit factory from the back of Gran's converted Ford Escort. I don't think I've ever quite lost that thrill of discovery, of seeing what lies over the hill, or round the next corner. I have my gran to thank.

My second favourite treat as a kid was our monthly family meal out. All dressed up in Sunday best, we'd go to our local church, then drive to a huge Makro cash and carry, stack the boot of the car with wholesale quantities of potatoes, baked beans and toilet roll, then troop to the Makro canteen where plates of chewy beef and two veg had been waiting, possibly for a while, behind Perspex pull-up windows. Sunday was bulk-buy day for the small-store and corner-shop owners in West London, and we must have looked ridiculously out of place, but it was what we could afford, and the lemon meringue pie was delicious. A proper Harvester restaurant or Berni Inn was reserved for really special occasions.

My early horizons were local. I had a parochial view of life on the periphery of the most exciting city in the world. I went to the school near the bottom of our road at first and then a couple that were just a bus ride away. Holidays took me a little further. Year after year we went to Studland Bay in Dorset, where the waters of the English Channel lap a sandy shore that drifts for mile after mile. It was almost a pilgrimage. Dad had seen an ad in a magazine for a house rental near Studland in the small market town of Wareham. The owner was offering it ludicrously cheaply. He only advertised once, and he never raised the price, so we just went back again and again. Every day was the same: we would make a packed lunch, climb into our old Volvo and race down roads packed with holidaymakers. Dad loved overtaking. Once he managed to zip past eight cars in one go on a long straight. That was his record. What was he thinking? No wonder the engine blew up. We'd get to the beach and put up our deckchairs in the same place on the beach, every day, every year, as if it was our patch of sand. James and I spent hours exploring every inch of the dunes, and we were in the sea so long our skin was as wrinkled as wizened old men. At the time it was idyllic. Studland was a gorgeous bit of coast, and we went crabbing, swimming, climbing and digging. It was the 1970s.

People didn't travel abroad the way they do now. We went across the Channel once when I was a child – on a camping holiday to France, Switzerland and Italy. I didn't get on a plane until I started working.

My parents had travelled a little further before they had us kids. They went on a cruise on the Med, and Dad took a party of children from his school skiing in the Alps in the late 1960s. Taking state school kids from a poor area of London abroad, let alone to the slopes, was almost unheard of at the time, but Dad was stubborn and determined to make it happen. A first-timer himself, he spent an age lecturing them on the dangers of skiing and how they needed to take it slowly and carefully. He was on the slopes for less than twenty minutes before he fell badly and snapped his leg in two places. The break was so bad he needed a thick metal pin almost a foot long inside his leg to hold it together. We still have it in a drawer in the house in Acton. After it was taken out of his leg Dad used the pin to stir the sweet home-made fruit wine he would make every year from cheap powdered kits you could buy in Boots the chemist. Huge old pots steamed on our cooker, then glass demijohns full of Chateau Reeve sat on top of the kitchen cupboards, popping as they fermented. Bottling and labelling the wine was a ritual, creating cheap and cheerful presents for Christmas. Dad swore his metal rod gave the wine an extra kick.

If there was anything specific that really helped to inspire my adult love of discovery and my interest in the wider world and our billions of stories, it was our local church when I was a small child. We weren't a particularly religious family, and I don't go to church now, but there's no doubt the exposure I had to life at Acton Hill Methodist Church shaped me. But initially it was just a playground. As a tot I was fascinated by a steep cast-iron spiral staircase that led up to the organ loft. Every Sunday I would scale and play on the steps until I finally plucked up the courage to swing down on one of the support poles. Nobody stopped me, nobody worried, it was completely fine for kids to have the run of the place, because it was a community centre and extended family.

By the time I was five Mum says I was a thoughtful lad who would take a knife and chop individual Smarties into four pieces to share among my family, which perhaps suggests my parents had a lax approach to knife safety and I didn't have enough sweets.

From the age of six or seven I was an inquisitive little soul asking tricky questions about the biblical books we were given in Sunday school. My parents passed me on to the minister, an enlightened man who told me he didn't have all the answers and that it was OK to ask questions. There was never any sense of submit and obey. The church gave me the confidence to query. So when religion told me that anything was possible if your faith was pure and absolute, that if you believed something fervently enough it could happen, I decided to put it to the test.

On our next holiday at Studland I stood by the sea screwing up every ounce of belief I could muster, telling myself that if I believed hard enough I would be able to walk on water. I took it seriously. Eyes closed fast, I lifted a foot and let it dangle above the lapping waves before trying to take a step. I told myself I could do this. I could walk on water.

I stood there for an hour. Sadly gravity was against me. It was shattering. No matter what I'd been told, belief was not enough and never would be. It was a mad thing for a seven-year-old boy to do, but that was the day I lost my faith and it has never returned. It was important, a moment when my sense of child-hood wonder cracked. I couldn't walk on water, so I never really listened when people at church talked of faith. But I had never really been interested in the service anyway. It was the playtime, friends and stories from the congregation that I loved.

Compassionate and constructive, the church was more like a gathering of UN volunteers than a congregation. Acton was almost ludicrously diverse, and the church doors were open to all. Dozens of countries were represented and national day, when the congregation wore national costumes and clothing, was as colourful as a carnival.

When I was young Mum and Dad would regularly invite lone visitors to the church over for Sunday lunch, so we had a procession of people sharing their stories. George, a research scientist from Ghana, stood out. He was studying the best vegetables for growing in sub-Saharan Africa and was championing the sweet potato as the best option for reducing poverty and hunger. I remember him holding a gnarled old chunk up to the light as if it was sacred and talking about the desperate suffering he'd seen travelling in West Africa. He had me spell-bound. Sweet potato became a staple in family meals for years after.

Our house was never full of friends. By the time I was in my teens I was at war with my father and most people stayed away. But when I was still a child other teachers from Dad's school would visit. There was Uncle Ian my godfather, Uncle Eddie the art teacher, a wild-haired Aussie with a glint in his eye who would tell James and me tales of his travels in the outback, and Uncle Angelo from Sri Lanka, a bull of a man. He told us about tensions, uprisings, and what the Brits had done to his country. He brought tales to our table I had never heard before.

There were also talks in the church that somehow my parents persuaded me to sit through. In one a couple of white aid workers and their young son came to visit and described the wonderful colour blindness of children. Their son was blond-haired and blue-eyed and he had been educated in an African school where every other child was black. His mother described to us how one day when he was roughly five years old he told her they had a new teacher.

'Mum,' he'd said. 'I was just sitting there when the new teacher came in and none of us had seen him before. He looked straight at me and said, "You must be Peter." Well, how did he know my name? Nobody told him. How did he know I was Peter?'

Of course, Peter had been the only white face in the class. I was nine when I heard the story. Even at that age I could see how funny this was but also how profound. I was growing up among every creed and colour and hearing horror stories about racism and discrimination. The wonder and the beauty that skin colour never occurred to younger Peter struck a huge chord. I see it now in my own son Jake, who will mention what people are wearing to identify them rather than their skin colour. We're not born racist. As kids we're all just human.

Other talks and sermons at the church focused on natural disasters, war or suffering. Much of the world was represented in the congregation, and whenever something awful happened elsewhere there was usually someone with a personal connection to the issue or area. Speeches were given. Tears flowed. Money was raised. Then every year we'd have a dedicated week of fund-raising where my family of four would stuff charity envelopes through doors in streets near our home for a specific campaign. James and I would work each side of a street, ducking in and out of gates and crawling through hedges in a race with the other. The envelopes came with mini leaflets that I'd read and studied. They gave me an understanding and appreciation of my own good fortune. I was raised to be mindful and I'm grateful for it. No doubt it sounds worthy, even cheesy, but even at a young age, before I was ten years old, the church, the congregation and fund-raising helped me to realise there was a huge, extraordinary world out there often haunted by an immense amount of suffering.

My mother says I was eight when I told her about global warming. I doubt I could have grasped that concept at such a young age, let alone described it. It's more likely I was telling her about the hole in the ozone layer. TV programmes and teachers were talking about the issue by the very early 1980s. Whatever the issue, Mum says what struck her most wasn't the fact I knew about it, but that I cared about the consequences. I've tried to keep that sense of concern and empathy and not allow the world and its endless horrors and cynicism to strip it away.

I can't claim to have many skills, but when it comes to engaging with people I hope I'm able to empathise without being patronising. When someone tells me their story I really feel what they're going through and can work myself into a complete state internally. I feel it viscerally, deeply. I don't know if that empathy was born of talks in church or wiring from birth, but it was certainly shaped at a young age, and then fed further by hurdles and challenges later in life. I never want to lose it. That early awareness helped to teach me a person's plight or circumstances at any one time should never serve to entirely define them.

By the time I was ten I told my mum I wanted my life to mean something. That I wanted to count. But we were an ordinary, hard-working family and I grew up with no idea of what

I would do with my life and no real horizon beyond my corner of Acton. My main ambition was to be a van driver. Then I thought about being a policeman. I was getting serious. Maybe a bit too serious. But then I was given a BMX as a birthday present and I became a little tearaway.

CHAPTER THREE

Mr G. Raffe

Historians say one of the most significant developments in the lives of ordinary Brits was the invention of the bicycle. Suddenly farm workers and villagers had a cheap way of moving large distances, widening their eyes, their world, and our gene pool. Bicycles transformed Britain.

Nothing broadened my horizons as a child faster than my BMX. By the age of eleven I was on two wheels and exploring Acton and the parks and estates of White City. At the same time James and I were taking the 207 bus every morning from Acton to our school in Ealing Broadway, a 20 minute journey away, with a huge group of other kids, many of them older and infinitely naughtier. The bus journey became like crime academy, with the older kids teaching and encouraging my brother and me how to skive off, muck about and misbehave. Bunking the bus fare was the entry-level game. Those were the days of the old Routemaster double-decker with a conductor and an open deck at the back with a grab pole.

A conductor would approach for a fare and I quickly learned how to glance around completely innocently, with perfect timing, and smile with my eyes. I had just the right air of confidence. He or she would pause for a second and more often than not suddenly seem to remember I'd already paid. Among our group of kids who took the bus together I became one of the best at bunking the fare. I was disarming, and I became a good liar. Even if the wiliest conductors made it past my smile they could still be fooled.

'Ticket?'

'It's right here.' I'd fumble confidently in my pocket, then wear an expression of utter bemusement. 'Well it *was* here. Hang on a minute, I must've dropped it on the floor.' I'd be on hands and knees among discarded sweet papers and cigarette butts.

'All right, if you dropped it you dropped it. Sit down, son. It's not a problem.'

If all else failed and a fare was demanded my brother and I could always just leap up, push past the conductor and jump off the bus. Even at speed you could hold the pole and start running in the air, and that would dramatically reduce your chances of going head over heels under a following lorry. Once or twice I had my ears boxed by conductors during a scuffle. And once or twice we leapt off at speed and landed badly. James went into a bus shelter. I went into a bin. But we usually saved our 15p and walked the rest of the way to school, and then just lied about why we were late and got away with it, day after day, which just emboldened us further.

Initially we were just skipping bus fares, playing chicken by lying down on the dual carriageway near our house as cars whizzed close, or making hoax calls from phone boxes to the operator or calling London Zoo and asking to speak to Mr. G. Raffe who was needed urgently at home. The operator on the other end would generally fall for it and we'd hear the request blasting out over the Tannoy. They were just silly pranks for my brother and me, but we soon had a little gang with a few other kids from the same area, and every feral victory was addictively exciting.

Soon we gravitated from bunking bus fares to petty vandalism. We would smash milk bottles, fill car locks with glue and shoplift. For years I held my school record for stealing Kinder Eggs from W.H. Smith in Ealing Broadway: twenty-seven eggs in one go. How I managed it, at eleven, while wearing school uniform, I still don't know. It was ridiculous, of course, and childish. But for me it was completely intoxicating. My poor old mum had no idea what we were up to. James and I told her we were having extra recorder lessons.

At twelve I moved to a high school nearer home with older kids who weren't just thieving sweets. We'd be out late into the evening playing football in the park or causing trouble. One day during the summer holidays a group of us broke into the Barbara Speke Stage School in Acton, which has had soap stars, celebs and Phil Collins as students. For a few years we had butted heads with kids from the private school and in truth we were delighted a fire had broken out and the school had been closed for renovation. Before the work began a group of us decided to see if we could make the builders' job a little bit harder.

We broke in easily enough and then quite literally smashed it to pieces: windows, doors, water pipes and dance mirrors. I ripped a long piece of piping off the wall, watched the water flooding out and then used the pipe to smash the huge floor-to-ceiling mirrors in the hall. Shameful now, but utterly thrilling at the time, gifting a feeling of power and destruction. We broke everything and flooded the rooms. We were out the back playing in a couple of old wheelchairs on a fire-damaged waste dump when the police arrived. We were disarmingly young, and told the police we had seen a bunch of older lads smashing the place and then legging it. It's almost ludicrous with hindsight, but I told the officers 'they went thataway', and they believed me. Astonishing. We went back several times to create more mayhem, and other groups of kids did the same. Within a few weeks we were told the damage was so bad the school could no longer be repaired and they had to move to another building further down the road.

Phil Collins kept his link with the school. I met him when we were both guests on the *Chris Evans Breakfast Show* and apologised. To his eternal credit he drummed on an empty box of photocopier paper and let me sing backing vocals to 'In the Air Tonight' live on the radio. Perhaps that was punishment.

Time and again as a kid I got clean away with pranks and crimes. Before too long I found myself in stolen cars. I wasn't driving and I didn't steal the cars. I was only twelve or thirteen. But I'd hang out with friends on Acton Vale Estate causing trouble, and then on White City Estate which at the time had a tricky reputation. Cars were regularly set on fire on the estate and the area was considered a major riot risk. This was the mid-1980s, with the Brixton riots a fresh memory, Margaret Thatcher in power and many inner-city areas tense or on a knife-edge. I didn't burn any cars but I knew the young guys who did. More than once they stole a vehicle, set it alight, waited for the fire brigade to show up then lobbed petrol bombs at the firefighters. I don't remember feeling guilty at the time, but I certainly do now.

I was obsessed with fire, burning and explosives as a kid. One time I was by the side of the main road in Ealing setting fire to a rubbish bin at dusk, in the rush hour. There was a line of stationary traffic right alongside. A group of us poured a can of petrol into the bin before lighting it with matches. Nobody yelled at us from the cars. The traffic was nose-to-tail but nobody did anything, and nobody said anything, except for an incredulous young French couple walking by.

'What are you doing?' they said in thick French accents. 'Why are you doing this? Don't be so destructive.'

We would steal petrol from pumps and cars and start fires. We would nick fireworks from shops or steal money to buy them, then take bangers apart to make larger devices. I remember unscrewing the bottom of a CCTV camera in a stairwell of Ealing Broadway Shopping Centre and packing a small device inside and then watching it blow up before racing off laughing. Why? It was just a stupid, destructive thrill. We ran down the stairs and outside to the back of the shopping centre and I lined up a huge rocket I'd made to fire low across the ground. There was nobody around when I lit it, but at that exact moment a policeman came storming out of an exit looking for us. Everything happened in slow motion. I saw him and looked down at the fuse, which was burning. The policeman was perhaps 25 metres away. I tried to kick the firework away, but it launched. I watched in horror as it spiralled through the air towards him, fizzing and burning. The poor guy tried to leap out of the way, but it hit him in the leg, sickeningly hard, and he went down screaming. We took off, running as fast as we could. He must have put out an 'officer down' distress call, because within moments there were dozens of sirens wailing and the police swamped the whole area. I still feel terribly guilty about that moment. I hope to God he was all right.

I was a rebellious kid at school and on our streets, and at the same time at home my relationship with Dad was collapsing. I was cheeky and naughty, and he wasn't sure how to deal with it. I can't remember what had happened or what I'd done but one day during a row Dad was trying to get me to come out from around the table I was hiding behind.

'Come here, Simon,' he was saying through gritted teeth. 'I want to talk to you.'

I hesitated. I knew what a talking to from my father could mean.

'I'm not going to smack you.'

Still I hesitated.

'I said, I'm not going to smack you. I just want to talk to you.'

I crossed the room to him, and he whacked me.

I stood there staring at him, tears brimming, feeling a colossal sense of betrayal. My dad had given his word and broken it. Who do you trust after that?

Both my parents were only children brought up by single mothers. My dad had lost his father figure as a lad. With no role model to guide him, he only really knew how to relate to me as a teacher.

The school where our dad taught was one of the toughest in London. It had a terrible reputation as a place that was traumatising for the staff as well as the pupils. In those days teachers had more power than they do today. They were able to enforce discipline physically, and sometimes that was echoed at home. Dad was a competitive man, quick to anger, who often didn't think twice before ranting and shouting. His life was the battlefield of the classroom or the competition of the tennis court. Confrontation was often his parenting style.

It wasn't all bad, and I don't feel like I suffered terribly. Dad certainly had a softer side and when James and I were smaller he was fantastic at rough and tumbles. But the relationships in our family became hugely destructive. More than once James and I begged our mum to divorce our father.

At school Dad was used to being obeyed, but at home you can't so easily boss or control a stroppy, confused thirteen-year-old. You have to guide and inspire. Dad wasn't the easiest person to get along with and ours was a tense and sometimes violent relationship. Throughout my early teens we were at loggerheads. We fought verbally and sometimes physically and it was pretty one-sided. Perhaps I would do something stupid or not do something helpful and my dad would fly off the handle. But it wasn't just my father. We all fought. Mum turned the kitchen table over. I had a fiery temper and put my foot through a door and my fist into a wall. The house bore the scars. I bashed my brother and he threw knives at me. There was endless shouting, lots of crashing and banging, and a few times it was so violent we or our neighbours called the police to come and break us up.

As a child the rows were all incredibly upsetting. They dominated my feelings and emotions. Over the years of my middle teens the arguments and upheaval at home fed a sense of despair and depression that slowly grew within me. Now I'm an adult, I blame Dad less, of course. I feel sorry for him. I just think he lacked the skills of compromise and resolution. We fought because we didn't know how to communicate. Too much time, and too many opportunities for happiness, were completely wasted with pointless rows and arguments.

Only later did James and I realise our childhood experiences made us better communicators in relationships as adults. Dad didn't have the wiring to talk issues and arguments through to resolution, but gradually, through the mistakes of others, James and I learned the skills.

My immediate response to our family rows was to skulk upstairs to my room, close the door and simmer and sulk on the bed. Above me was a poster of Whitney Houston, the usual Lamborghini and Ferrari car posters that were obligatory for kids in the 1980s, and on the ceiling directly above my pillow was a poster of an idyllic tropical beach, fringed by palm trees. Whenever I rowed with my dad, which was often, I'd lie on that bed afterwards and immerse myself in the poster, sensing the sun, feeling the sand between my toes. It was a place to escape. That poster was the ultimate contrast with the grey streets of West London. I never imagined, in my wildest dreams, that my feet would ever crunch onto a beach anywhere similar.

Dad's response to our arguments, and me staying out late and sometimes coming home a little blood-stained, was to buy me a couple of books that were supposed to encourage me to stick to the straight and narrow. First the autobiography of my hero, Mr T, which was a jaw-dropping account of his life in a neighbour-hood that made mine sound like Windsor. Almost every page was littered with extreme swearing. Dad can't have even opened the book.

The second was *Run Baby Run* by Nicky Cruz, a famous account of gang life by a man who found Christianity and turned his life around. Cruz spent much of his childhood locked in a pigeon loft. His dad would shut him in and leave him with the birds flying around his head. It terrified him to the point that birds dominated his nightmares for years to come. He fled to New York to live with his sister and joined the notorious Mau Maus, rising to become president of the gang. I will never forget the details of his gang initiation. Cruz and another guy were offered the choice of either a savage beating from three or four gang members or they could stand against a target wall, not moving a single muscle, while a knife was thrown. If anyone chose the knife and then so much as flinched they would be jumped and thumped. Nicky decided to take the beating. The other initiate plumped for the knife, but then flinched and cowered in tears against the wall. As a consequence, the Mau Maus grabbed him, spread his arms out in a crucifix, and stabbed him in both armpits. I was just starting my teens when I read that and I couldn't imagine anything worse. I developed a complete phobia of anyone touching or stabbing anything into my armpits. My wife thought I was joking about it when we met, but to this day only my son can tickle me under the arms without fearing an involuntary attack.

I was thirteen when I started carrying a knife. As a kid in Acton hanging out on the streets and even walking home from school I often felt at risk of a random act of violence. Over a few years I was mugged for pocket money, was punched hard in the face by a youth wearing a knuckleduster medallion ring, and was chased by a gang of older boys who threatened to kill me. I was also nearly lured into a car by two men, threatened by another boy with a knife, and had my beloved bike stolen by a gang. My school and streets certainly weren't the most dangerous, it was just an average part of the city. But we were in competition and rivalry with others close by and kids from my school would organise fights with youngsters from nearby Acton High School that would turn into mini brawls. I bought a small flick knife from a friend for pocket money and carried it for protection, or so I thought. It was more for bravado and a sense of power.

Back then you could buy ludicrous weapons by mail order just by ticking a box to say you were over sixteen. I stole money from my dad, used some more cash from a paper round I was doing for less than £2 a week, bought postal orders and sent off for a small combat blade I had seen advertised in a classified-ad paper called *Gun Mart*, even enclosing a letter saying I was a squaddie about to be deployed abroad and so needed it immediately. They wrote back a few days later saying my choice was out of stock, but they thanked me for serving and enclosed an alternative Rambo blade the size of a machete that only just fitted in my school bag.

What the hell was I doing? Right now the news is full of horrific stories of knife crime in London and kids stabbing each other in petty feuds and drug deals. Parents and victims are pleading with youngsters to see sense. Back then, for me, it was mainly about ego.

I revelled in the secret feeling of power and respect carrying a knife gave me. Nobody looks up to a thirteen-year-old. At that age you're on a path to adulthood but you're not respected. People hardly listen to you. Nobody takes you seriously. I thought carrying a knife would give me authority. In the years since I've been held up at chaotic guerrilla checkpoints abroad by kids the age I was back then, carrying Kalashnikovs rather than knives. I've seen the look in their eyes and sensed how they gloried in a feeling of power. It's terrible, and it can result in tragedy. I was a young fool who thought a weapon helped to make me a man. If we want to stop teenagers carrying knives we need to devote resources, school and community attention, to boosting their confidence, self-belief and self-worth.

I also carried a knife partly because of consequences. Or the lack of them. My parents never found my weapons because I was clever at hiding them. I was never stopped and searched by the police, even when I was once caught in a stolen car. Teachers at school never checked our bags. And I never found myself in a situation where I pulled a knife in anger. Thankfully. Because more likely than not it would have been turned around and used against me. There were no dramatic or dire consequences for me. I was never caught carrying a knife. I got away with it.

Many, many others were not so fortunate. People I knew ended up committing a crime, were sucked into a serious gang, stabbed someone, or had their own blade pushed into their chest, and bled out in a street and died pathetically early. I was lucky. I used to hang out near a community centre in Acton that was a notorious dive for dealers and trouble. I started smoking at eleven and used to sit around outside on the periphery, puffing away and trying to look hard. Then a bouncer at the centre was shot in the head by a drugged-out guy he turned away at the door. Even I realised it wasn't a good place for a kid to spend their spare time.

I was never a gang member, or a really bad lad, I don't think. I was never a brutal, hard kid. I was never deliberately violent and nobody feared me. I was never hungry, cold, or without a shelter or a bed. But I was very aware of poverty in the lives of friends from broken families, junkie homes, and kids who had fled from towns up north devastated by unemployment. I knew people living seven or eight to a room. My life, even my family life, was cosy by comparison. But ultimately I still managed to sink pretty low.

I'm not proud of everything I did in my early teens, but I mention it now as evidence of what I was and eventually where I was able to get to. In many ways the teenage me is a far cry from the guy on TV. But I'm still much the same person, with most of the same failings and still some of the old fears. I can still see how circumstances could have changed and pushed or led me down alternative paths. Too many people think it's just hard work, study, mindset and focus that determines your journey in life. They're certainly all important, but just a small nudge can throw you off course and change everything. Life, often, is about luck.

The 1980s were a very different era. There were no camera phones, no social media, and our actions were never as visible or informed as they are now. I carried knives, and I'm sorry to say I also sold them to other kids. Then I used the money I made to buy a replica handgun and a covert holster by mail order. It was an identical heavy-metal copy, loaded with blanks, the sort of device that confuses armed police officers, and leads to the idiots and the unstable who are wielding it being shot. I was a child. It was ridiculous. The only time I ever remember pulling it out was when a group of us got into a fight with an older group of travellers in a local park. They were young adults, and fists and anything else were flying around. It was immediately madness. Everyone was screaming abuse, hurling stones and punches, but the other guys got the shock of their lives when I pulled the replica. They scattered, immediately. I might even have fired into the air. It was chaotic and I can't remember. I had an incredible rush of adrenalin. But again I got away with my stupidity. I ducked into a nearby estate, took a longer route home, and hid the gun back in a secret space I had hollowed out under my bedroom floorboards. Eventually I forgot it was there and years later, long after I had left home, my poor mum found it while redecorating.

'Simon,' she said calmly when finally confronting me. 'Do you have any idea what it was like for me to find a gun underneath the floorboards?'

CHAPTER FOUR

The Boy on the Bridge

Eventually I was caught doing something stupid. Finally. James and I were hanging around some abandoned tennis courts just a few streets from our home with a group of younger kids, when among the tall weeds and overgrowth we found a stretch of high brick boundary wall punctured by a small hole. Some of us had started kicking a ball around, and some were standing around chatting. One of us must have idly tapped their foot at the loose bricks in the wall and knocked one of them out. That inspired me to kick a few more of the bricks out as well. Then a few kids piled in and rather than talking or knocking the football around we began to completely focus on destruction. We kicked and pushed so more and more bricks came tumbling out. After half an hour or so all that remained was a huge, unsupported arch maybe 8 feet long. It looked precarious, and we stopped to admire our work. Then we crept close and kicked a few more bricks until, in a great cloud of dust, it came thundering down. The noise and dust were terrible. We cheered, knocked out some more bricks, and then wandered away to find our bikes and skateboards. Most of the wall had been knocked down. If any of us had been underneath when the arch fell we would have been crushed or badly injured, but we rarely thought about risk as kids.

For some reason it never crossed my mind that it was a wall

belonging to a garden. We left, went home, and I didn't think any more about it until there was a knock on the door. Glancing out of my bedroom window I saw a woman I thought I recognised and instinctively I knew it had been her wall. It was an awful moment. A real chill went through me, like a spider walking on my spine. I knew exactly why she was there and what it meant. After years of shoplifting, setting fires and selling knives, I had never been caught or had to fess up before. And I hated it.

Dad listened calmly to what the woman was saying, apologised, then made me come downstairs to say I was very, very sorry. I cringed. It was crushingly embarrassing. The woman said she would rather avoid calling the police, but we would need to pay to rebuild the wall. There was no bravado from me. Nothing gangster. It was the moment I realised that even if I was trying to be a tougher lad, it was all a front. I had been the oldest kid present when the arch came crashing down, so the burden of paying fell heavily on me. Rebuilding that bloody wall cost me £147, a fortune that I had to pay off with pocket money and cash I had under my floorboards from knife dealing. It wasn't just the money, though; it was the fact that I'd been caught and humiliated. That was what I really hated. I felt like an idiot. And rather than feeling like a big lad who could knock down a wall, I felt like a pathetic little boy. I thought everyone else would think the same, seeing me for what I really was. Ultimately it was the public wounding of my ego that helped bring me to heel, and a painful accident that then knocked my confidence sideways.

Just a few weeks after knocking down the wall I was playing around with my brother and friends in a park near our house. I was behaving a little better already, but some of the other kids were chucking grass at each other and then sods of earth and chunks of stone and rocks. One of the boys grabbed a handful of grass, came up with an old half-brick and lobbed it towards me. I was crouched and facing the other direction when my brother shouted a warning.

'Si!' he screamed. 'Look out!'

I stood up, turned around and at the last millisecond saw the half-brick as it hit me full in the face. The edge of the brick raked right across my pupil, scraping my eyeball. I was knocked out. When I came around my crying brother was cradling my bleeding head. In A&E at Hammersmith Hospital I spent a fearful few hours as doctors warned us I could lose my eye. The accident was bad enough, but specialists had to scrape and pick bits of brick, grit and stone out of my eyeball. The pain was excruciating. I had to lie, petrifyingly still, to avoid further damage, even while I could see what the doctors were doing to my own eyeball with tweezers and scalpels. I wince at the memory even while writing this now. For years after the accident anything that was pointed towards my eyes would make me physically recoil. I couldn't even face sitting opposite the corner of a table or a length of wood.

I already had poor vision in one eye, and reasonable vision in the other that just about compensated. The brick, of course, hit my good eye. After the bandages came off I tried to hide the fact that suddenly I couldn't really see, but after a month or two I had to admit reality and went for specs. Nothing designer, there was no money for that. It all happened at the worst possible moment. Testosterone was kicking in. I was suddenly gangly and awkward. My body didn't fit my clothes. Things were terrible at home. I'd revealed, to myself if nobody else, that I was still a silly little boy. And suddenly I had to put two thick bottle tops on my face in a pair of hideously uncool specs.

Then I suffered just about the grandest humiliation an adolescent boy can endure. It was ridiculous, ludicrous, but life-changing. After school one day I was trudging towards home in Acton past a bus stop on the other side of the road that was packed with perhaps 150 kids from the school waiting to head back west towards Ealing. I was wandering along, trying not to look self-conscious, when I spotted a girl I really fancied waiting near the front of the group.

'Adie!' I called out. She turned. I nodded to her and smiled awkwardly. 'All right?' I said, pointlessly. She shrugged sweetly.

I had no idea of the disaster, the catastrophe, that was about to befall me. Think of the prom scene in *Carrie*. That comes close. My attention was completely fixed on Adie across the road. I smiled gormlessly back at her, and then walked slap bang straight into a colossal lamp-post. It was a powerful impact. My face connected first, and I went down straight like a tree. My glasses buckled and landed nearby. I found myself sprawled on the pavement, feeling like a frog that had been whacked with a frying pan. I scrambled around to find my specs, and then became aware of the laughter. The entire bus stop of kids was having hysterics at my plight.

Thinking about this now, I feel sorry for the young me. A stronger, more confident, funnier kid could have styled it out. They might have stood up, laughed uproariously at themselves, bowed with style and sauntered off, smoothing themselves down. I did none of that. I struggled hopelessly to get my glasses back on, faffed around on the ground trying to pick up my bag and books, looked in utter horror at the kids opposite, some of whom were bent double at the funniest sight they had ever witnessed, and finally slunk away. It might be amusing now, but it was hideous at the time. Simple little moments in life can have profound consequences.

I was never a star pupil. School had not been going well for me for a while. I was uninspired and deeply uninspiring. I couldn't concentrate and I often struggled in lessons. I don't blame my teachers. They were all caring and thoughtful. Several were charismatic and keen. If there was any failing it was mine. I never really understood, at least until much later, that each of us has to choose life and decide to get involved and active. Rarely can anyone make us. I was too confused, stubborn and perhaps a bit lazy. I just fell through the cracks.

But one book really sparked my interest. Hilary Belden, my brilliant and passionate English teacher, gave our class *Schindler's Ark* to read, by Thomas Keneally.

'There is a chance,' she said, as she placed the books carefully on each table in front of us, 'that this book might just change your life.'

She was right. I didn't entirely realise it at the time, but the book and its story lodged in my mind. Oskar Schindler was a womanising factory owner and Nazi party member who directly saved 1,200 Jews from concentration camps and extermination in the gas chambers of Auschwitz and Gross-Rosen during the Second World War. Calling it an extraordinary story doesn't begin to do it justice. Based on fact and meticulous research, the book gave me a window into the most devastating and intense period of pure human evil. Every page shocked and surprised, yet it was very readable, even as Keneally described the full brutality of the Nazis. It won the Booker Prize and was turned into the movie *Schindler's List* by Steven Spielberg, itself a life-changing film for many viewers.

Up until I read the book my only real knowledge of the war had been gleaned from the pages of *Commando* comics where Tommies fought the Jerries. What I read in *Schindler's Ark* hit me in a way I'd never experienced before. It was an apocalyptic time and the story was uniquely gripping, because the reality of the book was infinitely more powerful and upsetting than any of the young-adult fiction I had read before. It was life, death, survival, and it was brutal, honest, affecting and horrifically emotional. I sobbed. I put the book down. I bit my nails. I picked it up again. Every tragedy I have witnessed around the world as an adult, every desperate act, every wicked demonstration of corruption or abuse is benchmarked against that book. Much later, whenever I worried how futile and pathetic my work was as an adult, I would remember the lives in the book, and feel humbled. Then I recall the moment when Schindler is chastising himself for not saving more of his workers. His accountant, Itzhak Stern, who Schindler protected, consoled him by quoting the Jewish Talmud: 'He who saves one life, saves the World entire.' It said to me then, and still says to me today, that even when we can't do everything, we can still do something.

The book itself was exceptional, and the story behind it was fascinating, even for me, even as a teenager. Keneally was an Australian writer on a book tour in the US, nearly four decades after the end of the war. He popped into a shop in Beverly Hills to ask about a briefcase in the window. The owner of the store, a Holocaust survivor, heard that Keneally was a novelist and bent his ear trying to persuade him to take the story of Schindler and turn it into a book. The entire astonishing tale had never been told. Only a chance encounter set it free.

Within six years of reading *Schindler's Ark* I would be writing a book of my own. Keneally made me realise that truth and our collective, hidden stories could be not just stranger than fiction, but infinitely more moving and powerful. Yet I cannot say that Keneally's masterpiece inspired me to write as a teenager, or that the dark tragedy of the book encouraged me to accept the privilege of my simple world in my mid-teens and embrace education. I finished the book and my focus shifted quickly back to my own problems.

Life for me felt like it was taking a quick turn for the worse. Dad and I were continually at odds. I had been caught destroying the wall, then nearly lost an eye, and had been humiliated in front of the school. I was also desperate for a girlfriend, but I had completely lost my social confidence. It was maddening. As a young kid I had always been great with girls. When I was in first school I was so naughty I was moved from the table where I sat with my friends and onto a table with three girls who were supposed to keep me in order. It was some sort of punishment, but I thought they were great. It was one of my happiest years at school, and gave me a self-assurance around girls that many other boys envied. In my early teens I was still able to chat happily with girls at school and on holiday. By my mid-teens, though, when I needed it most, my confidence was completely and utterly shot.

I remember going to the annual school disco when I was fifteen or sixteen, and was so low I should have stayed at home. There is surely nothing like a teenage party to broadcast inadequacies and then amplify and ram them back down your own throat. Everyone but me appeared to be dancing. Everyone but me appeared to be snogging in a dark corner. When the music was really blaring my limbs wouldn't move to the tunes. When the slow songs came on I couldn't summon the courage to ask anyone to dance. It's weird and actually a little frightening how that evening is still seared into my mind. I've been around the world, three times, but I can still recall the cheesy 1980s tunes, the crappy striped shirt I was wearing, and how desperately I wanted to chat up a girl called Lisa. I am one of millions scarred by a school disco and that evening I decided dancing was not for me. By the time I resolved my issues and fixed my mind it was a little too late. To this day I do not dance. If there's a party I'm the guy getting the drinks in at the bar, or sitting at a table maybe tapping just one foot. I've faced many fears and been on *Celebrity Bake Off*, but *Strictly*? Forget it.

To add a final layer of topping to my social shame, my parents decided to buy a mustard-coloured Reliant Kitten, the tiny four-wheel fibreglass version of the van driven by Del Boy in *Only Fools and Horses*.

'I mean, come on,' I shouted at them, 'who would inflict a car like that on their children?'

Of course, much of my downward spiral was self-inflicted and self-indulgent. Pathetic, even. I have since met people around the planet who have suffered, endured and survived astonishing tragedy. I knew that terrible things were happening in the world, and I had only just read *Schindler's Ark*. But everything is relative. I was a fifteen-year-old adolescent with raging hormones and a confused mind, and in just a few short months of bad luck my confidence dripped away.

I went from puffing on light cigarettes to smoking Capstan Full Strength, cancer sticks that carried a picture of a salty sea dog on the front, clearly trying to kill himself as an alternative to the loneliness of the ocean. I began drinking more, sometimes slipping out of school at lunchtime. Being tall, if baby-faced, I could get away with buying booze in off-licences, and I could drink in a few pubs in Acton back then while wearing school uniform, even a stone's throw from the police station. I went with friends, but I'd always drink more, and as a complete light-weight I often went back into school worse for wear. There's a photo somewhere of me slumped and slurring in the corner of a classroom. Once I fell asleep drunk in the school library, and some of the kids painted my glasses with Tipp-Ex. When I woke up I thought I had gone blind.

I fell further and further behind at school. Then came exams. I struggled, panicked, and refused to take some of the papers. I scraped a single GCSE, I think, and was somehow accepted to take A-levels. But I rarely appeared for lessons.

Then Mum noticed my fingers were starting to turn blue. I went for tests, had a tube stuck into my heart and iodine pumped through my body so my arteries would show-up on an X-ray, and was eventually told smoking was furring the veins in my neck. If I didn't stop puffing away I would lose my hands. It was all too much for me. I became depressed and withdrawn.

I had already been going for weekly counselling for a year or so at a children's mental health clinic in South Acton. Our GP was concerned about me. On his advice my sessions were upped to two a week. I went for counselling for almost three years from the age of fourteen, with a series of NHS mental health profes-sionals who helped to keep me going and relatively stable just by listening and giving me the space to open up about my feelings and fears. But the counsellors and their centre were woefully underfunded. The building itself was dilapidated concrete, with a dark interior, and grim, grey, empty, dank rooms, like something out of Orwell's 1984. My heart and spirits sank every time I stepped inside. The staff themselves were stretched. My therapist once broke down in tears as we talked, and I had to comfort them with a pat, a chat, and a box of tissues.

One of my teachers could see I was falling behind. She called me into an office. Far from chastising me, she wanted to know what was wrong. I didn't tell her. I couldn't tell her. I couldn't begin to articulate it myself. She reached out, extending a hand of friendship.

'I can see you're in a bad way. I know things aren't easy for you at home,' she said. 'I've met your father. I know he can be very . . .' she paused meaningfully, '. . . difficult.'

I had started to blub. But now I just looked at her. I was shocked that she could see through me. But at the same time I was also angry with her for talking about my dad behind his back. He wasn't the only one in the family at fault. He was far from perfect, but he was still mine. He was my dad.

If even the teachers knew I was having a tough time, that felt like final proof everyone knew. With the self-regard you only have as a teenager, I thought I must be the butt of every joke. With my specs and the lamp-post disaster, the fact I was getting drunk and stoned on dope – far from making me seem cool – just made me feel even more pathetic. I vaguely remember a school coach trip where I was so spaced out I did nothing as the boy in the seat behind flicked my earlobe every mile of the way.

My final months at school are a bit of a blur. I wasn't studying or preparing for the exams. The thought of sitting down to take tests terrified me, and I had absolutely no idea what I was going to do with my life afterwards.

'What are you doing to do when we leave, just sit in the pub?' one of the lads in my class asked with a sneer.

Going to university never entered my head. Other kids were lining up college and jobs, working in a trade with their father. My only ambition was still to get a job as a delivery driver. But to me even that seemed unlikely. I was becoming seriously depressed and sinking into self-pity and despair. Looking back now I can track how it all happened. A run of apparently insignificant events can turn a life upside down, to the point where you become a shadow of the person you were, and a fraction of the person you should be. My bad luck had left me feeling completely inadequate. One minor perceived humiliation followed another, coming at me from all directions. I started thinking I couldn't go on.

I managed to hold out at school until my final exams but dropped one of the subjects with weeks to go. By the time the actual papers came around I was having panic attacks and I didn't show up to take a couple of exams. I made it into the hall for another one but when I sat down and stared at the questions panic started to well. I was in a complete state. The room began to spin, my mouth flooded with saliva and I knew I was going to be violently sick. I pushed the table away and stood up.

'Simon, are you OK?' shouted one of the teachers in concern. I ignored her, grabbed my bag, rushed through a side door and threw up all over the floor. I walked out of school right then, and I never went back.

My heart breaks for other kids who slip through the net and don't get career or life guidance. Leaving school was an exceptionally difficult time for me. With nothing to do I spent most of my time skulking in my room, watching a tiny, tinny black-and-white TV and ignoring my family when they knocked on the door to check on me. They had no idea how low I was falling. I would get out of bed and wander to the shops to pick up a few cans of Special Brew, then sit in my bedroom alone drinking booze strong enough to stand a spoon in. I felt I had nothing. No education, no girlfriend, and nowhere to go. Within just weeks of fleeing school my thoughts of suicide grew and trans-formed from passing thoughts to a stronger desire.

Today, the single biggest cause of death among younger men in the UK is suicide. Thousands are killing themselves every year, the equivalent of perhaps sixteen a day. Men aged twenty to forty-nine are more likely to die at their own hand than from road accidents, heart disease or cancer. If any other, more obvious issue caused such tragedy, surely we would be researching it more, studying it harder, and talking about it more openly. We are experiencing a mental health crisis, and we need to spend more time discussing the causes and consequences. Personally I think suicide needs to be thought of like a virus. It can infect through emotions, ego, or as a result of bereavement, failure or loss. Men and lads like me, who are known to the mental health system, are obviously at risk, but so are those with no contact with therapists or a counsellor. Confident, tougher blokes are often less likely to open up when life takes a downwards turn. Women suffer as well, of course, but suicide kills three times as many British men as it does women. Nothing completely explains why. But we know that young men are shockingly vulnerable.

In my case I felt depressed, helpless and hopeless. My family were reaching out to me, but negative feelings and a sense of pessimism about my future were overwhelming. It felt as if a dark weight was hanging around my shoulders, physically hold-ing me down and taunting my mind. Nothing could get through to me and convince me I had a future.

Just a few streets from my house was a footbridge across the Western Avenue, an endlessly busy artery in and out of Central London. For twenty-four hours a day traffic thundered along four lanes. The bridge had been a feature of my life as long as I could remember, a link across what was effectively a dividing motorway.

Occasionally we would troop up there as a family at night to watch fireworks over Central London. I would grip the railings as the whole bridge shook when heavy articulated lorries rumbled past below. From when I was a young child my mum had warned my brother and me about playing up by the road and made us swear we would never muck about on the bridge itself.

There was no single moment of disaster that pushed me to the edge. No catastrophe. Just a nudge here and there can shift some of us from what passes for stability to a state of maddening despair.

I thought for weeks about using a kitchen knife on myself, about taking handfuls of pills. I thought about stepping in front of a train, or a tube. Then I thought about falling in front of a lorry. One night I found myself wandering towards the bridge. It was familiar, comforting somehow. I climbed the steps, hopped the railing and shuffled along until I was facing out of London, above traffic heading towards the suburbs. It was windy, noisy. There were no pedestrians to talk me out of it. I looked at the sky. I remember teetering slightly, like a diver on a high board. I was serious, but scared. I looked down just as a heavy lorry passed underneath and a huge horn sounded. Had he seen me from behind? I will never know. It jerked me out of my moment. I started to wonder whether dropping from this low height onto the road would really work. Would I be able to time it so I landed in front of a lorry? Yet the thought of what a heavy vehicle would do to my body was horrific. It was reality, and that might have saved me. In that instant I started to fear the pain of dying more than life. I gripped tightly, nervously. I shuffled back along the side of the bridge and hopped back to safety, shaking with fear. I was choosing life.

*

It was a turning point for me, of course, but at first nothing changed. There was no euphoria, there wasn't even a sense of relief. I just climbed back over the rail and stood there feeling almost as wretched as I had before. I went home, crept indoors, slipped into bed and had a cry. I had no money, no job and no prospect of getting one either. I'd screwed up my schooling and walked away from my education. I still had no girlfriend; I could see no future. It all looked bleak.

It was a hard time, a painful time, and it is still troubling for me to revisit and admit it all now. But if I hadn't gone through it no doubt I wouldn't be who I am as an adult, or doing what I do today. From the relative comfort of older age, every trauma and darkness that I suffered as a teenager now looks like part of my journey to get to where I am. But I have never stopped to look back, to try to understand my past. Sharing it now is humbling and cathartic.

Every story is unique, every life so frighteningly specific. There is peril in offering further thoughts or advice to others. But perhaps, perhaps, if you are suffering from depression, try to tell yourself there is hope. Try to drown the whispers in your head that are negative with the knowledge, with the stronger and louder certainty that you are wonderful, inspiring and interesting, both now and into your future. Find voices that comfort you and people who hug and help. If you are caring for a young me, just listening is a huge support, but perhaps also remember the human mind is a powerful machine. Many years later I was with a young French special forces captain, in the most dangerous place in the world, on a base under attack from suicide bombers: 'People don't change when others tell them they should. People change when they tell themselves they must.'

He was talking about countries, but the same thing applies so often to us, as individuals. Sometimes we have to walk our own path, wherever it takes us. In my case I had love around me. I had hugs. But still the darkness was too powerful and overwhelming. It took me to the brink, to a moment from the end.

The days dragged past after I stepped off the bridge and I managed to drag myself along with them. I hadn't changed, I wasn't suddenly brimming with confidence or filled with a zest for life and I had no idea what I was going to do. But I had to do something. Anything. If I wasn't going to kill myself then I needed alternatives. My relationship with Dad improved, to the point that he was able to give me driving lessons without us killing each other. Then he started checking classified adverts and leaving them out for me, but I was nowhere near confident enough to apply for a job. James said I should sign on. I was desperate for a bit of money, so I took a bus into Ealing. From the top deck, I had an elevated view of my world and it felt small and stifling. I wandered over to the DSS office, down a side street opposite the Town Hall, telling myself I was just going to check where it was, but I saw other lads heading inside and followed them in. It had a depressing air and there was a long queue for the counters. But just as I walked inside a man who had been talking to an official near the entrance stood up from her desk. He moved out of the way and she looked straight at me. She had a kindly, wise face and an open smile. She must have dealt with scores of tragedies and desperate souls every single day, but there was no judgement in her eyes.

'Can I help?' she said warmly.

I hadn't really planned to sign on for benefits, but she put me down for Income Support. At £26 a week, I think, it was even less than the dole, but the only option for a seventeen-year-old who had never had a full-time job. I went home and mooched around for a few weeks, still depressed and unsure what to do next. But then I passed my driving test and an idea popped into my head that I can honestly say changed my life. A simple thought that, perhaps more than anything, connects my adult self with that troubled teen. I decided to go on a journey.

CHAPTER FIVE

The Lost Valley

It just came to me one morning. I felt like I had to face my fears and push myself just a little. But knowing that and doing anything about it were two different things. I would go somewhere, and I would do something. But where? What? I had been so low for so long I wasn't even entirely sure what my specific fears or even my strengths were any more. I was wracked with self-doubt and low self-esteem. Thoughts of doing anything adventurous were frightening.

Initially I had no idea where I would go, or what I would do. Although I had a bit of money from benefits, I wasn't exactly flush. But my mum was desperate for me to get up and out of the house, in the best sense, and she lent me some cash. I bought a cheap train ticket to Scotland, inspired, I think, by nothing more than watching the movie *Highlander*.

Whatever the reason for choosing Scotland, even thinking about going there was a few tentative steps towards recovery. I had been a whisker from suicide, and I knew there was a risk I would be back there again. What if I had a panic attack on the train? What if I couldn't handle it?

I thought back to the lady in the DSS office. I was used to therapy, and even in my brief fifteen minutes with her I had talked openly. I told her I'd left school, with no real qualifications, and that I was pretty low and had no idea what to do next.

As I write these words I can feel myself back there, sitting opposite her, as if I have passed through a portal in time, with my hands on her desk as I explained some of my fears. I can remember the sharp raised voices around us, the smell of stale cigarettes and disinfectant in the office, the screw-down chairs in the waiting area, and – most of all – her patient air. I can remember everything about that moment because she gave me simple advice that guided me then, and still does to this day.

'If it's difficult for you,' she said, 'just take it all slowly. Take things step by step.'

I latched onto those words as wisdom. Even in my hopeless state I realised that was the answer. I was no longer a child. I could start behaving like an adult. Everyone seems to think that childhood is without responsibility, but actually you are forever told where to be, what to do and what to study. Now I could claim the freedoms of an adult. If I didn't like something, or didn't want to do something, I could just say no. If I started a journey and changed my mind, I could just turn back. It was OK. I would just take it all ... step by step.

So, off I went, my first real adventure by way of a train to north of the border. I'd never been anything like that distance on my own. I'd never even been out of London on my own.

As the miles ticked by, I became more and more aware my journey mattered. I got off the train, spent the night in a cheap B&B then hired a car in the morning. A tiny red Peugeot took almost all of the money I had but it got me to Glencoe, which was my jumping-off point. For what, I don't know. I'm not sure what was guiding me, but I like to think it might just have been a bit of fate. By the time I arrived in Glencoe it was far too late in the day to set out anywhere and all I was wearing as outer layers were jeans, a pair of trainers and an old Adidas cagoule. I'd just go for a quick hike, I told myself. I left the car in the car park and ambled up the mountain.

When I started my journey I was an insecure teenager. But the climb changed me. I wasn't conscious of anything as significant as that at the time, but I know it now. Deep within me I must have realised that I had to conquer something. That's what this was about, setting myself a task that seemed unlikely and making sure I achieved it. It would be a tonic, even a cure. Perhaps, deep down, I knew that evening that if I was able to stand on a summit somewhere I would prove something to myself. But initially I just set out, not thinking any further ahead than the next step. I crossed a river, scrambled up a slope and trotted through a wood. I found myself becoming a little bolder. I started selecting specific points in the distance that I promised myself I would get to.

'Step by step,' I muttered to myself. If I can reach that tree over there I'll stop and turn back, I thought. Then when I reached the tree I saw an outcrop of rocks. 'I'll just get to them,' I said out loud.

Soon it was early dusk. I passed hikers and climbers on their way down. More than one raised an eyebrow when they saw me. I said I was just going to see how far I could go before nightfall.

'Be careful, it's dangerous,' one guy in breeches and walking boots told me severely. He was carrying a walking pole and gestured up the way he had come. 'It'll be dark before you know it. You're not dressed properly. You've no pack and no sleeping bag, someone will be calling out mountain rescue.'

No, they wouldn't, I thought. I hadn't told anyone I was up here.

I promised to turn back, but pressed on, passing others on

their way down. I didn't care. I was on a mission. Every step gave me an increased sense of self-worth and purpose. Only I could understand and I wasn't about to explain it to anyone.

I followed a track up rough steps and crested a summit and was initially gutted to realise I had only reached a long flat glen. I now know it was Coire Gabhail, The Lost Valley, where the Clan MacDonald used to hide their cattle, or any they had rustled. It's a rough and rocky walk; all the guides tell you great care is needed and you shouldn't be up there in twilight, never mind darkness. But I didn't think about that.

I looked along the valley and knew I should turn back. There were boulders the size of houses. The glen was surrounded by peaks, but right at the back directly in front of me, I could still see a fold in the mountainside leading up to a high ridge. I wasn't thinking about a summit. I just wandered to the end of the valley to have a look, and then, almost absent-mindedly, I started to climb. Step by step. I didn't think about how I would get down if I made it to the top; I concentrated on taking each step, focusing on targets nearby: a rock, a bush. Onward and ever upward, one foot in front of the other, scrambling on my hands and knees up loose scree, until eventually I was completely committed to the climb and was focused on reaching the ridge above me. I didn't care how dark it got, this was something I was determined to accomplish.

I reached the ridge in darkness, and I stood there feeling euphoric and a tiny bit brave, aware I had really accomplished something. Above me loomed higher peaks, but for the first time in years I felt a sense of physical success. I stared at the stars, lost in the moment and delighting in a sense of achievement. This wasn't how the government wanted me to spend my benefits, but it was a complete tonic. I'd completed a journey, the very first one I had taken alone and the furthest I had ever been. Suddenly Acton seemed small and faraway and the distance offered perspective. With it the panic that had been haunting me seemed to slip away. Then, of course, reality kicked in.

'It's bloody dark,' I thought to myself. 'How the hell am I going to get down?'

I started back the way I had come but it was really dark and cold. I couldn't see where I was going and it wasn't long before I discovered it was harder to go down the mountain than climb up. I scrambled from side to side on the loose scree until the clouds thinned and I was able to see rocks and holes. I made it back to the valley unscathed and spent a freezing night alone in the car. I didn't care. I was elated.

A day or two later I was back on a train heading south, and, to my amazement, realised I was chatting confidently with a young woman sitting opposite. That climb up the mountain taught me that no matter how bad things might have looked for me, there was hope. When you're a youngster struggling to come to terms with life, it's easy to slip into a trough of despair. But if you can pick yourself up just enough to take a few initial steps, sometimes, just maybe, you can start to climb out of your situation. Life advice often consists of people saying you should 'aim for the stars' and plan where you want to be in a year or even five years, but for me that was completely unrealistic. I could hardly see beyond the end of each day. So I set much smaller goals. It worked for me. I had climbed a mountain and my life began to improve.

It wasn't easy and things didn't change overnight. People talk about 'getting their mojo back', and mine had been missing for a while. But I could feel a gentle rise in my confidence. I took things slowly. Step by step. My income support helped, as did the sympathy and support of my parents. Dad was calmer, more willing or able to love and compromise, with all of us. He suggested I try for a temporary job, and I managed to get a part-time role collecting trolleys and stacking shelves in a Waitrose supermarket. I loved it. But I still couldn't get a full-time job, so during the week I started volunteering in charity shops. It kept me out of the house, taught me how to negotiate tricky relationships and made me feel like I was actually doing something. It was my job to organise the roster, a role fraught with difficulty. Imagine organising forty occasional volunteers of a certain age. It was a diplomatic challenge to rival negotiating with Pyongyang. Each week I'd figure out what I thought would work in terms of staff then I'd pick up the phone.

'Hi Rose, it's Simon at the Cancer Research Campaign shop. I'm doing the roster for next week. Do you think you might be able to come in?'

'Oh, I can come in for half an hour next Wednesday lunchtime.'

'Lunchtime, Wednesday, half an hour. OK, that's a popular slot. I'll see what I can do.'

Midday on a Wednesday was when our main bundle of donations arrived from the charity distribution centre. Some volunteers wanted to come in around that time so they could have first dibs on the best clothes. I had to help manage a team, many of them fragile souls, and all for a really good cause. It helped with my self-esteem, as well as giving me advanced training in diplomacy. I stayed for six months or so while schlepping from one job centre to another in a hunt for work and applying for full-time jobs. But I was discovering that when you leave school with no qualifications, no connections and no real idea of what you want to do there's not a lot of help out there.

Everyone told me that any job would be a start, so I went for anything available: porter, janitor, sweeping the floors in the shopping centre. I applied for at least two dozen driving jobs before I finally had a call from the job centre for an interview to drive a small van delivering parcels for a firm on Wembley Stadium Trading Estate. The pay was terrible, but I honestly thought it was a job that was made for me. The sullen owner turned me down straight.

'You're the only one who's applied.' He had the keys in his hand. 'But I'm still not giving you the van.'

I was gutted. I didn't even need to ask him why. The question was written across my face.

He folded his arms across his chest and wagged his head from side to side. 'I don't have to give you a reason. I'm just not giving you the job.'

I still have no idea why he turned me down and took such malicious delight in telling me to my face. Maybe the job centre had forced him to give me an interview. I had run out of money for my bus fare, and it was a long walk home.

Finally, I managed to get a full-time job with H. Samuel the jeweller's in Oxford Circus. I gave up my part-time job in the supermarket and arrived keen and expectant to start selling watches and earrings. On my first day the manager told me there was one unbreakable, unbendable rule: never, ever, take the keys to the safe home. After a long day I was on the Central Line home to Acton when I found the full bunch in my pocket. It was surely the shortest retail career ever. I went back in the morning and the astonished manager sacked me on the spot. He said it had never happened before, and either I couldn't be trusted or didn't listen but neither was good enough.

Still, I was feeling better than I had in years. I began to think anything was possible. When I wasn't in the charity shop or a job centre, I was in Westminster library looking through magazines and newspapers trying to find a job. I must have read something that sparked an interest in spying, probably Peter Wright's infamous book *Spycatcher*, because I suddenly decided I quite liked the idea of working for MI6. I actually turned up at the then secret headquarters of MI6 in Century House, in Vauxhall, an anonymous office building next to the Tube.

Imagine the scene: a teenager in scruffy jeans and a cheap leather jacket wanders into the global headquarters of the Secret Intelligence Service. The receptionist did a double-take from behind a thick Plexiglas window. Standing in the background beyond her was a police guard cradling a sub-machine gun. His expression spoke for him. *What the hell do you want?*

'Hi,' I said to the receptionist. 'Erm, I've just come in to see if I can apply for a job.'

'I'm sorry?'

'I just wondered if I could apply for a job. Working for, y'know ...' and then I actually leaned forward and lowered my voice, 'M-I-6.'

She stared at me with her mouth slightly open, trying to decide if I was for real. Then she started shaking her head. 'No,' she said, ever so slowly. 'No, no; that's really not how things work. You would need to contact the Foreign Office.'

'Oh, OK,' I said brightly with a glance at the guard. 'I'll go and have a chat with them, then.'

It makes me cringe now. But I also have a sneaking admiration for myself at that moment. Just a few months before I'd been on a bridge about to kill myself. I was all over the place. One month I was in a state of desperate depression, and the next I was walking into MI6 in some vague hope of becoming a spook.

After that my approach was completely scattergun. I did actually get a job working as a clerical assistant for the Ministry of Defence, albeit by replying to a conventional advert in the job centre rather than ambling into the MoD in Whitehall or stopping an admiral in the street for a chat. I was so nervous when I started the job that I vomited most of the way there on my first day. They made me sign the Official Secrets Act then posted me to a top-secret department at the Empress State Building in Earls Court that handled communications between the nuclear fleet and the land-based command. It sounded important, but then they showed me into the office where I would be working. I was going to be locked into a small room with three middle-aged men with grey hair and grey skin, and my job was to photocopy documents. Thousands of them. Endlessly. Each time the photocopier whirred and clicked a second copy would be put into a locked safe. There was no natural light because of blast curtains, even though we were high in the building, and security was so tight, if we wanted to go to the loo we had to buzz through to a desk and somebody would unlock the door and escort us to the toilets. I was desperate for a proper job, but after an hour in there even I realised I would go mad within a week.

At lunchtime they unlocked the office door and escorted me to the lift so I could pop out for a sandwich. I dodged around a corner, hopped into the Tube and never went back. It caused something of a furore. I'd spent a morning photocopying secret documents and then I vanished into thin air. A day later two plain-clothes police officers showed up at my parents' house and identified themselves as Special Branch. I could hear them talking to my mum at the front door.

'Do you know where your son is, Mrs Reeve? We really need to find him.'

Mum stalled for me, muttering something about how I might be out.

'Mrs Reeve? We would really like to speak to him.'

'I'm so sorry, officers,' she said politely. 'But I don't think he wants to see you.'

I got off my bed, opened my door and called down. 'Mum,' I shouted, 'tell them I'm not coming out. And I'm not going back.'

Short of getting a warrant to search the house there was little they could do.

I sank back into a brief period of depression. I had applied for countless jobs, been ignored, rejected and sacked. After walking out of the only employment I might have been able to hold down I wondered if I would ever manage to find a proper job.

Dad came to the rescue. We'd had our huge, pathetic and violent differences but I knew he wanted the best for me and wanted to see me make something of my life. He didn't pull a few strings, call an old school chum to get me a job, or ring his wealthy friends, because he didn't have any. Instead he helped me find my way in life by spotting an advert in the back of *The Sunday Times*. The newspaper wanted a small team of post-boys and -girls and was holding out the possibility of some journalism training for anyone who worked hard. I thought it was a job that was completely out of my league. I hadn't gone to private school or university, let alone Oxford or Cambridge, still where so many media people are drawn from. There were thousands of over-qualified graduates jostling for any job in the media. But this ad was aimed specifically and exclusively at non-graduates, at people who weren't from traditional media backgrounds or influential families. I had a chance.

I put my all into my application. I had time on my hands and nothing to lose. I turned my CV into my own newspaper and sent it in with an essay I'd written on *Schindler's Ark*. An exec at the paper called me in for an interview on a busy, chaotic Friday and they seemed to like me. I had never lost interest in what was going on in the world and perhaps I was able to impress them with a little knowledge despite my nerves. I was keen, even desperate. They said I fit the bill, that I was exactly the sort of person they had in mind when they placed the ad. It turned out it was the idea of the editor, Andrew Neil. He's had his critics over the years, but I owe him my career. More than 5,000 people applied for the five positions. Two weeks later I was offered one of the jobs. I couldn't quite believe it. Old fears kicked in, of failure and making a fool of myself. This was the most prestigious newspaper in Western Europe – how on earth would a pathetic lad from Acton fit in?

I knew I had to overcome those fears, otherwise they would cripple me. I had to decide that my fear of regret if I didn't take the opportunity was greater than my fear of failure. I decided I had to be just a little bit more positive, hopeful and optimistic. I would take the job, embrace the opportunity and overcome my nerves by taking everything gently and slowly … step by step.

CHAPTER SIX

Foot in the Door

If going for an interview at the *Sunday Times* had been nerve-wracking, travelling there for my first day was horrendous. In the days before I started I suffered from regular panic attacks: dizzy spells, uncontrollable fear, shaking and then incredible nausea. To get there on my first day I had to take my mum along on the Tube for support. I was eighteen, I had been suicidal, depressed, unemployed and out of school for nearly a year. I was a bag of nerves.

The building itself was daunting, a huge old rum warehouse in Wapping split into various departments with the editor Andrew Neil's office at one end, then the picture desk, news-room, foreign department and investigations, and the post room next to the photocopiers and toilets in the middle. Business, sport, the style section and travel were at the furthest end. The newsroom had a sense of immediacy and urgency you'd be hard pressed to find anywhere else. There was drama and activity, and it constantly felt like a war-room.

When I started most of the staff on the paper seemed to be Oxbridge or Ivy League. I was the least educated person in the room. I often still am today. Everyone on the paper seemed frighteningly clever, brilliant and ludicrously worldly. Some were legends. I'd watched films about two journalists on the *Sunday Times*. One of them was Jon Swain, a foreign correspondent for the paper who had served in the French Foreign Legion, been kidnapped in Northern Ethiopia and held for months in the desert by a group called the Tigrayan People's Liberation Front, and been immortalised in *The Killing Fields*, the Oscar-winning 1984 film set in Cambodia during the slaughter carried out by the Khmer Rouge, which I and millions of others had watched in numbed horror. The other was Peter Hounam, the chief investigative reporter at the paper. I'd seen a TV movie dramatising an investigation he conducted which revealed the existence of Israel's secret nuclear weapons programme. It was a global scoop. Mossad, the Israeli secret service, had kidnapped his source Mordechai Vanunu and smuggled him back to the Middle East. I was going to work near these people. I was supposed to be sorting their mail. Walking in there on day one left me feeling completely awed. My knees quaked.

My nerves and fears lasted for the first few weeks. I shouldn't have worried, but I did. Then I would start feeling nauseous. To avoid being sick I'd skip meals. Yet slowly I realised that I didn't need to be dominated by fear. I was a lowly post-boy, but I felt welcome and useful right from the start. It was a ferociously busy place full of hard-bitten, ambitious hacks, but I posed no threat and from the beginning almost everyone was welcoming and friendly. They made me feel as if I was part of a team, and we were all on a mission. For all my trepidation and churning stomach, the office felt exciting. Even I could sense something tantalising: possibility.

Initially little was expected of me except to be there, often early, and make sure I did what was asked. The four other non-grads who joined at the same time were all at least a few years older. We would either work an early shift starting at 7 a.m., or a later one starting at 10. The early shift collected the first post delivery of between ten and twenty sacks of mail from the loading bay, shifted them into the central *Sunday Times* post room in a trolley or over shoulders, and then sorted them by hand. It was a mountain of mail that took hours to clear and I worked at it day after day. I had no pretensions about who I was or what I should be. Never for a second did I think that sorting mail or running errands was beneath me. Quite the opposite. I was bloody grateful for a job and I threw myself into it with gusto.

The end wall of our post room was lined with around a hundred pigeon-holes, which we would sort mail into and then empty every few hours and deliver the contents to people at their desks. It was mundane but perfect for me. I wasn't ready for anything more challenging, and sorting the post gave me an insight into who everyone was and what they did. Most people on the paper were chained to their desks, but I walked miles every day around that old warehouse delivering mail and packages. I knew every inch of the place. I couldn't have asked for a better grounding. It put me in the perfect position to take advantage of the situation.

Right from day one, I realised this was the biggest opportunity of my life. I had a foot in the door. I set about trying to make myself useful, initially just by learning how to use the fax machine and the photocopiers. Long before everything went digital, proof copies of the newspaper pages were made on huge A1/A2 photocopiers and passed to the senior executives for their checks and corrections. The copiers were ancient and forever breaking down. I learned how to fix them and kept them running. In a paper that completely depended on the copier churning out the page proofs it was a critical skill. Being the only one who could keep them alive made me unsackable.

Back then I had nothing going on in my life except that job.

I lived at home. I didn't have a girlfriend or see many friends. I would work a full shift sorting the post, then hang around talking to people, volunteering help and slowly, little by little, step by step, picking up confidence and contacts until people were asking me to do small gofer chores for them. Perhaps picking up a package from the couriers, collecting newspaper articles from the cuttings library or getting them tea and a sandwich when they were on a deadline. Then I would offer more help. Cuttings had to be returned at the end of the day, so did they want me to photocopy them? All of them? I'd copy cuttings not just as a bodged job, but carefully and thoughtfully, placing them on the machines so they could actually be read. I remember taking time over those smallest tasks. And never moaning or complaining or getting above myself. I was enjoying everything. I would have worked there for free. And that showed. It made a difference.

After a few months the arts editor David Mills, who was always seen in a three-piece suit, usually tweed, and a homburg hat, asked me to go through the cuttings and find the worst reviews of West End shows to put into a small article. It was a laborious job. I found a few to show him and to check I was getting it right.

'That works, that one doesn't, that one does,' he said, mainly to himself, as he glanced through them.

I could have just nodded and checked my watch to see what time I could leave. Instead I said simply: 'Why?'

He was rushed off his feet. He didn't need to explain himself to me. But he flicked back through the articles and pointed out what he was looking for. He was happy with what I'd already found, but I stayed there until after midnight in the airless, windowless cuttings library deep in the bowels of 'Fortress Wapping' and went through hundreds of articles and reviews looking for more juicy or malicious quotes, wrote them out, and then presented them to him the next morning. I actually found a few that made him laugh. So instead of just working them into an article he put them into a marked-out box on a page in the arts section and added my name underneath. It was my first ever byline, a tiny 'compiled by Simon Reeve'. Well, I could hardly have been prouder if I had written the splash on the front page. My grandma cut it out and framed it.

Funny how even just a morsel of success can make a person hungry for more. A few key people started to pick up on my enthusiasm. Looking back now, I think I became a bit of a project for some of the older hacks who had entered the profession with ideals and were delighted that some youngsters had been brought into the paper from different and mostly ordinary backgrounds.

One afternoon Peter Hounam, the chief investigative reporter, came to get his mail while I was sorting the post. Peter was big, bearded, kindly, and something of a hangover from the past. A union man through and through, he conducted old-school long-term investigations into corruption, arms dealing and organised crime by doggedly pursuing leads and sources. We started chatting and I mentioned I'd love to help him in my spare time.

It was nothing major at first, just photocopying more cuttings, but it quickly developed. Every success I had led on to something else. Soon I was searching phone directories for him and tracing people he wanted to find who had been involved in dodgy deals, or going out to public record offices and libraries hunting through the electoral roll.

I had only been at the paper for four months when I had my

big break. John Witherow, the foreign editor, came marching through to the post room and called me over.

'You've been doing lots of research for Hounam and other people, haven't you, Simon?' he said. I was amazed he even knew my name. 'We've got a lead on something. Might be a story. Not sure. Might need you to go to Boston.'

Boston! I stared at him. *I'd never even been on a plane.*

He said it as casually as if he was asking me to pop to the canteen and get him a prawn sandwich.

'You're free at the moment, aren't you?'

I nodded nervously.

'I've just got to go into [the editors'] conference now. I'll give you more details in a minute. Just get ready.'

He marched off. I wondered whether I should just follow him and tell him I wasn't even sure I had a passport.

I took some post down to the news desk and told the secretaries where I might be going, trying to impress them. I told some friends on the picture desk. They were excited for me. Then I told the researcher on features, the deputy managing editor, the production department and the secretary from the arts section. It's possible I also told one or two of the journalists in home news.

I trotted over to see Peter. I had a pile of cuttings for him. He could see I was flushed with excitement.

'Are you OK?' he asked.

'You won't believe this,' I hissed, nodding towards the foreign desk, 'but Witherow wants me to go to Boston. Boston!'

Peter cocked a quizzical eyebrow.

'I don't know if I have a passport. I mean, I must have a passport but I have no idea where it is . . .' I rambled on.

Peter cut in.

'Simon, um . . . he means Boston in Lincolnshire. Sorry. They were talking about it after conference.'

I felt like a bit of a plum, but also slightly relieved.

Witherow called me to a side office for a quick briefing.

'We've had a tip that two South African neo-Nazi terrorists who are on the run might actually be here in the UK.'

'Neo-Nazis?' I queried, stopping him in mid-flow. 'Terrorists?' I remember saying the words very slowly, taking it all in.

'Yes.' He looked sideways at me, perhaps wondering whether I was ready for this. I tried to look more confident. As if this was normal.

'They blew up queues of people waiting for taxis in the townships. Some say they were given weapons by a rogue South African intelligence unit that's trying to undermine the peace process. The South African police are after them. But we think they left the country overland on false passports and have since flown here. One of them has family in Lincolnshire. We've been given a number,' he said, producing a hastily written scrap of paper. 'We know it's in Boston, but nobody is answering. I've just tried it again. It's probably a dud lead but why don't you head up there? We'll try to find an address for the number and then you could pop round and knock on their door. Oh, and you could keep trying that number for us,' he said, almost as an afterthought.

My mind was spinning.

'If you speak to them tell them you're from the *Sunday Times*. We think they want to talk to us. After that it's up to you. Use your judgement and if you think they'll talk to us and they have something interesting to say, phone me.'

He gave me the slip of paper, the foreign desk manager gave me some petty cash and I grabbed my bag and jumped in a taxi to the station. I was breathing heavily, almost hyperventilating. But not just with nerves. With excitement as well. I was a post-room boy on a mission. I felt a real sense of purpose. As I'd been leaving another reporter on the paper told me the men were on the run from the South African secret service, and they were probably being hunted by an armed ANC unit. It was possible MI6 knew they were in the UK or had even let them into the country and was encouraging them to talk to us.

At King's Cross I found a quiet payphone and rang the number Witherow had given me. I expected it to ring off the hook. It was answered almost immediately, but only with silence.

I felt the hairs on the back of my neck stand up. 'Hello?' I said nervously. 'Hello?'

Silence.

'Hello?' I tried again.

'Who is this?' said an accusing voice with an Afrikaans accent, guttural in my ear.

Inwardly I gasped, then tried to speak. For a second nothing came out. And then everything just clicked into place.

'My name is Simon Reeve. I'm calling from the *Sunday Times* newspaper in London. I gather you might want to share your story with us,' I paused for effect. 'I'm on my way to Lincolnshire. I hope we can meet up, face-to-face.'

My confidence surprised me. I was speaking completely differently, replacing my laddish West London accent with a deeper tone. But I had heard Peter and other investigators talking in this direct, almost commanding way and milking the name of the paper for all of the authority it carried.

There was silence, and the sound of clicks on the line. *My God, was somebody else listening?* 'Where shall we meet?' I said, a little less certainly.

'Where do you suggest?' said the voice.

It was working. Bloody hell. I had to think quickly. I looked around for inspiration.

'Let's meet on the station platform?'

'In Boston?'

'Yes. I can be there in three hours.'

'How will we know you?' The voice was rasping.

It came to me quickly: 'I'll be carrying a copy of *The Times* under my left arm. You do the same.' There was a grunt of agreement down the line. By the time I hung up the phone I was shaking.

I took the main line north and then switched onto a branch line to Boston. The train was full of farmers, country gents and schoolchildren. And then there was me, en route to meet two South African terrorists. I must have looked faintly ridiculous, a wide-eyed eighteeen-year-old just a couple of years older than the schoolkids, wearing a leather jacket bought from Shepherd's Bush market and a tie my mum had bought me from the Makro cash and carry. But I felt a surge of pride, and a strange feeling I had rarely experienced before: a sense of purpose and meaning. I was on a mission, and it mattered.

I was late to meet them. I had arrived early but walked into the small market town, not to check if I was being followed or anything professional, but to send a postcard to my mum, telling her I was out of London. When I realised the time I fairly scuttled back to the station with my newspaper tucked firmly under my arm. Boston station is not a large place. There were no trains and no other passengers, save for me on one platform, and two neo-Nazis on the other. It was a surreal moment.

We met halfway across the track and agreed to go to a nearby pub to talk. I had never met anyone like these men. They had committed acts of pure evil. But instead of fearing them, I could see they were pathetic. One was a weaselly-looking thin guy with darting eyes. The other was a much bigger Neanderthal with hairy hands and terrible body odour. They didn't impress me. I wasn't in awe of them and I didn't feel fear. I was a pathetic and nervous lad, but even I could see they were just two thugs full of hate and venom. These two men had been identified as a powerful destabilising force in South Africa, yet to me they seemed amateurish.

Between them they carried two heavy holdalls. One bag contained clothes and weapons. They opened it to reveal hand-guns, more to show off than as a threat. The other contained documents they said could prove they had been funded, not by a rogue element within the South African secret service, but officially by something called the Civil Cooperation Bureau, an organisation run by the South African Defence Force, which had been involved in the murder and attempted murder of anti-apartheid activists.

They said they had carried out the taxi-rank bombing on the orders of the CCB man who recruited them. They claimed a 'third force' was at work in South Africa, trying to pit rival black parties against each other in an attempt to preserve white rule. They told me, and we later confirmed, that before they escaped they had been moved into a hospital from maximum-security prison after they started a hunger strike.

They also said they could prove that South Africa was chan-nelling arms to a guerrilla army in neighbouring Mozambique to destabilise the government there, and the South African Defence Force had given thousands of rifles to the Zulu rivals of Mandela's ANC in the hope of igniting war between the groups. They showed me documents and mentioned specific names of officials and officers.

We sat in a corner in the quiet pub, a few regulars glancing occasionally in our direction, while they talked in hushed tones about their involvement with military intelligence contacts, a 'Mr Sting', sanctions-busting arms deals, the white-supremacist Church of the Creator, and the extremist Order of the Boer Nation. They spoke calmly about what they had done, as if they were merely business transactions. Not once did they question why a teenager had been sent to meet them.

I should probably have walked out. Run out. Called my mum. Panicked. But I didn't. I actually felt that in this dark world I had found my calling. I listened carefully. I made notes. They sounded like the real thing, genuinely awful, and said they would talk to the paper, so I called the *Sunday Times*, spoke to the foreign desk, and told them I would bring the pair to London. Hotels were arranged, tickets immediately purchased.

I suspect all this couldn't happen today. In a time of risk assessments and corporate health and safety, I doubt a newspaper could send an untrained kid to find, debrief and deliver a couple of terrorists. But this was a different time, when risk was more acceptable, and it meant I was able to be involved in investigations that would normally take a degree, training and a decade of experience.

I persuaded them to drop their weapons back at their safe house, and then I took the South Africans, including the nervous wife and daughter of the weasel, who appeared from a car hidden around the corner, back to London. If it had been strange coming on the branch line on the way there, it was ten times more bizarre heading back on the train again with the farmers and the schoolchildren, and two nutjob terrorists.

In London I remember their shock when a police car, driven by a black officer, pulled alongside our taxi. Weasel nudged Neanderthal and then said to me: 'Well, that's not good, is it, Simon?'

I ignored him and looked out of the window. We were nearly back in Wapping. One of the senior journalists met us and took over the babysitting a large article appeared in the paper that weekend. I was just pleased to have been involved. I hadn't fouled things up. Quite the opposite. Everyone was delighted with what I'd done. Critically, I realised that terrorists, who I had always imagined as horned devils, could be worryingly human.

I mentioned it to Peter, and he told me about the philosopher Hannah Arendt, who wrote a seminal work on the war crimes trial of Adolph Eichmann, the Nazi responsible for organising the transportation of millions of Jews to concentration camps during the Final Solution. Arendt described Eichmann as 'terrifyingly normal'. She coined a phrase: 'the banality of evil'. It applied perfectly to the South Africans. They were pathetic, but they had still managed to threaten the peace process. Terrorism became something I would study intently. But first, that evening when I got back from Boston, I went straight back in to sort the mail.

My first mission led to many more, often for Peter or the elite Insight team on the *Sunday Times* which also ran long-term investigations. But I was still a post-boy, so I had to juggle two ludicrously different roles. One moment I would be collecting the mail or a bundle of designer clothes for a photoshoot from the courier drop-off point at 'Gate Six' at the far end of the Wapping plant, and the next I'd be asked to work on an investigation into drug smuggling or the IRA. With hindsight, it was absurd.

But the newspaper was a meritocratic sort of place. One of the most brilliant writers on the paper had started there on two weeks of work experience, but he kept his security pass when he was supposed to have left, sat in a corner and waited until he was asked to help on a story. People there were interested in results, not where I had come from, what my background was, how old I was, or whether there were two sacks of mail needing sorting. I found myself involved in investigations into ever more dodgy subjects, including arms dealing and smuggling. The Soviet Union was collapsing and imploding. The world was awash with weapons. One of the investigators took me to a meeting with an intelligence contact.

'Who's this?' said the contact with a smile, shaking me by the hand.

'This is Simon. He might be me in the future,' said my colleague with a laugh.

I was stunned. It was an enormous vote of confidence.

'Fair enough,' said the intelligence officer. That was good enough for him.

The contact was chatty, garrulous and charismatic. Each meeting I had with him was memorable. It was always on an understanding that we would share gossip and briefings but check and double-check anything we put into print. It might sound like a cosy relationship between the state and the media, but I came to see it as another check and balance on the power of both. He talked to us because we questioned but respected his work. He was ideological and driven by a desire for the world to be a better place. He could have been an aid worker or a campaigner, and we were a safety valve for information he thought should be shared and disseminated. Over the years he opened more doors and guided me into other areas of darkness. But then, he was talking about nuclear weapons.

In the early 1990s the intelligence world was racing to monitor the Soviet nuclear stockpile and prevent it falling into the hands of rogue regimes or terrorist groups. Secret reports suggested Russian scientists had created a strange and exotic substance called 'red mercury', that enabled the creation of briefcase-sized nuclear bombs that could be easily smuggled and yet utterly devastating. It was the stuff of a Tom Clancy novel, and years later red mercury became the focus of Hollywood movies. But in the early 1990s, in my late teens and early twenties, I was researching and investigating both its existence and the shadow world in which it was supposedly being smuggled.

Contacts told us their sources in Russia were adamant red mercury could be used to create a pure fusion bomb the size of a football, possibly even a hand grenade, that it was invisible to all available detection measures, and that if used it could wipe out life in a mile or half-mile radius. Documents later claimed to show Boris Yeltsin had issued a licence to a mysterious Russian firm to export red mercury, presumably to rogue regimes. People were talking about multi-billion-pound deals, that red mercury was a substance that could provide clean energy as well as fuel weapons, that it was worth ten times more per gram than gold, then a thousand times more than diamonds. Arms dealers who were thought to be brokering deals were found dead, shot in the head or with plastic bags over their heads. Then a British executive with a South African chemical company was found chopped into small pieces in the trunk of his luxury car in Soweto near Johannesburg in November 1991. His body was covered in a strange black gunk. Intelligence reports suggested he might have tried to sell red mercury to buyers from the Middle East. It was appalling, dark and tangled.

I was sent to Newcastle to speak to his family. I remember the way they looked – ghost-like – as they tried to come to terms with the horror of what had happened. I saw autopsy photos of his remains. They were the most graphic and appalling images I had ever seen. I was nineteen years old. There was no training. My flight to Newcastle was the first time I had ever been on a plane. I didn't know how to put on the lap-belt. I didn't eat the snacks I was offered because I thought you had to pay for them. I was such a kid. I was still sorting the post, for goodness' sake. But I was pitched into ghastly and fascinating investigations.

Peter Hounam became my unofficial mentor, and the newspaper became the education I had missed. It was my college and university. I learned how to investigate difficult and demanding subjects. How to dig, flatter and flirt for information; how to read, understand and mirror people; I learned how to move from chatting with a gang in East London or talking on the phone with a shady business in Dubai, to meeting with an MP in Parliament.

My principal weapon was a telephone, which I would have glued to my ears for hours. The name and authority of the paper helped secure access and kept people on the line. Peter taught me silence is a great way of encouraging others to speak.

Then we had computers linked to public records and, even before the advent of the internet and the World Wide Web, early databases of articles that were a powerful resource, giving an experienced user access to stories and information from around the world. The system we used gave me as much intelligence-gathering capability as that of a small country. Researching the killing in South Africa, for example, I could guarantee that local newspapers in the area would have fresh and different leads from their own contacts that we could also chase up and follow. But the database also had scientific journals, press releases, texts from obscure conferences and government tenders.

Another tool was Companies House in London, where detailed records for all UK limited companies were kept. The elite and the dodgy might be able to hire PR teams and lawyers and hide much of what they were doing, but every firm had to file annual returns and – crucially – list their directors with their home addresses. It was a goldmine. I spent hours going through microfiches looking for people we were investigating, until flicking through the documents on film would give me dizzying motion sickness.

I never hacked phones. But I certainly used tactics that would come into a grey zone of legality. My defence would have been simple. I felt then, and believe still now, as pompous as it might sound, that I was working on investigations that were in the public good. I wasn't involved in any activity my own moral code deemed unacceptable, although I was certainly underhand. I learned to obtain information by pretty much any means possible. I spent days on surveillance jobs sitting in the back of vans watching target addresses, eating cold pizzas and peeing in bottles.

The investigators on the paper were dogged, thoughtful and caring. I thought and still think the work they were doing was a vital check on power, and essential for a healthy democracy. Watching them and learning from them was an education no university could offer.

CHAPTER SEVEN

Walkie-talkies and Binoculars

It was a tip from a whistle-blower that sent me undercover into the BBC's dirty laundry. One week I had a call from an engineer who worked at the iconic Television Centre in White City. He was worried about fire safety in the passages and corridors down in the bowels underneath the building.

'The whole place is a death trap,' he told me. 'It could go up at any moment! I've complained over and over again and nobody is listening to me.'

We met and talked and agreed I needed to see the issues with my own eyes. The plan was for me to play squash with him at the BBC's internal sports club, then hide until the club closed. When we finished a couple of games he thought the area would be empty, but several people were still working around the club, so I had to hide for an hour in a large wheeled basket underneath dirty towels from the sports club. They stank of stale male sweat, like socks that hadn't been washed for weeks. It was one of the least pleasant experiences of my working life. But when everyone else left for the evening the engineer returned and I was able to hop out.

I had a covert body-worn camera, which I had bought from a spy shop for a previous investigation, to capture images of what the whistle-blower said were extreme breaches of fire safety. But I was carrying just a racquet and still wearing my gym kit, on the grounds we could say I was heading back to the club if discovered, so I had nowhere I could hide the camera. My sports T-shirt was too tight for unsightly camera bulges, so I had to strap the camera around my waist inside my shorts.

We came to an area deep under TV Centre where one fire door seemed to be missing and another was propped open by jerry cans of chemicals. Wood stanchions, posts and rolls of paper were stacked together further along the corridor almost as if they were ready for a bonfire.

'Look, look!' he said, getting very agitated. 'Go on, take a photo.'

Then I had to pull my shorts down at the front and take a photograph, before quickly hiding everything away before anyone came wandering past.

The whole thing was, of course, ridiculous, and the images I took were too dark for any fire safety expert to verify as a problem.

But I was game, and the newspaper decided to send me on a course in Portsmouth where they taught me shorthand and how to write without libelling people. I shuttled to and from London, still trying to work on projects. I don't know when I ate and I can't recall where I slept, because I was pretty much running on empty. I remember driving back from Portsmouth so tired that a voice in my head said *I'll just close my eyes until I get to the bridge ahead.* The next thing I knew was the wheels rumbling over the cat's eyes. I had tried to take a nap while driving. I'm not sure what Darwin would make of that.

Before long, Peter and other journalists were suggesting I should be writing my own stories. I started by drafting articles for the hacks. They gained by having someone collate thoughts and quotes, but they also had to work through and then rewrite the ramblings of a school-leaver. My first piece was on arms smuggling. Seriously. I sent it over to Peter's computer and sat next to him as he read it. He finished it, sat back in his chair, linked his hands over his stomach and looked at me kindly.

'Always remember there's a thousand ways of writing a piece like this,' he said.

It was a brilliant way of telling me it was a pile of manure, without bruising my fragile ego. I watched closely how he wrote the real article, and what he looked for and used from his notes. He picked a few phrases from my words and worked them into his own, which helped my confidence. I learned quickly. I've heard people say that if you start at the bottom in the media the first thing you need to do is kiss it. Very crude. I never had to grovel or suck up to anyone at the *Sunday Times*. There were privileged and brilliant young graduates at the paper. One was a peer, another was the daughter of Michael Heseltine. Several became friends. They all treated me with respect and kindness. But it probably helped that I was open-minded and eager. I watched, I volunteered, I always said yes to a request, even if I was supposed to be heading home, and I was prepared to go an extra mile to do the job well. I tried to give people what they wanted, but equally I tried to show initiative by being proactive and pushing ideas and suggestions.

Pretty quickly I learned that being flexible was also key, and that I couldn't expect everyone to accept me on my terms; I had to be able to adapt to different circumstances and situations. I stopped talking to older people at the paper in the same way I would talk to my mates in Acton. I learned to fit in. Perhaps if I had been less of a blank canvas that would have been more challenging. I think my ordinary background and absence of education actually helped.

Almost every day something would crop up and I would be off investigating or even tailing people, trying to find out where they lived or where they were going. I was part of a small pool of youngsters on the paper with no training, no risk assessment and no thought for health and safety. I didn't care, my confidence was growing every week and I loved the job. It was all very *Boys' Own*.

On one occasion I was part of a small team, armed with walkie-talkies and binoculars, that had to follow an arms dealer from Gatwick Airport into the heart of London. We had received a tip-off he was travelling on a scheduled flight, hiding in plain sight. It was thrilling, even when we realised another surveillance team was on his tail.

Another time I had to drive around London in a hired convertible Mercedes for a weekend while a black investigator drove another identical car to test who would be stopped by the police. I went off script that weekend. At one point I had six friends in the car while we drove to a party with the roof down. I clearly remember thinking that even if I lost my job it was worth it. I was not stopped once. My colleague was stopped within half an hour, and several times afterwards.

I was learning every day and the hours were ludicrous. I was at the paper six or seven days a week. Often I wouldn't make it home at all and would crash on a sofa at a colleague or friend's house and buy a clean shirt in Asda on the way back to work in the morning. Others would leave in the small hours, then come back in early, put their coat on the back of their chair and switch their computers on to make it look as if they were working, and then go back to their car or sit on the toilet for a couple of hours and have a nap. There was a general expectation that you would come in early and leave very late. Every day off I had I slept for twelve hours. Every week of holiday I had I was ill, as if my body knew that finally it was able to give up.

But it was a fascinating place to work. Every day was interesting. Every week had at least a little bit of an adventure alongside the post sorting, whether it was researching, investigating, surveillance, or being sent out to football matches or riots. In the early 1990s the IRA was still very active on the UK mainland. In 1991 three mortars were fired at Downing Street. A couple of weeks after that a bomb exploded at Paddington Station. Later in the year there were explosions on Oxford Street, the National Gallery and at Clapham Junction. Even as a post-boy researcher I would be among a group sent to the scene scouring for information.

I was helping out on the news desk one busy Friday night, just a day after the general election which re-elected John Major as Prime Minister, when the IRA detonated a massive truck bomb at the Baltic Exchange building in the City of London. The *Sunday Times* offices were a few miles away but we heard the blast clearly. For a second everyone froze. Then a few people went outside to see if they could see smoke. Andrew Neil, the editor, emerged from his office and came striding towards us.

'OK, everyone, let's focus,' he said, clapping his hands to get attention. 'You, you and you,' he said, pointing to some of the reporters. 'Get on the phones and find out what's happened.' He turned to a handful of others that included me. 'You four – go there now and see how close you can get.'

A couple of us raced to our cars. Someone else jumped on their motorbike, another into a taxi and we headed to the scene in an attempt to glean as much information as we could. Whether we were going to a bombing, a riot or a football match, often it was about seeing with our own eyes what had happened so we could give a visual account for the newspaper, or in this case talking to others who had been close to the blast or were even walking wounded. The Baltic Exchange bombing killed three people, including a fifteen-year-old girl, and injured ninety-one. It was believed to be the biggest bomb detonated on the mainland since the Second World War. Then just a few hours later another large bomb went off at Staples Corner in North-West London, also causing mayhem.

Being at the scene of a riot, or the aftermath of a bombing, can be frightening and upsetting. But I confess it can also be exciting. You feel challenged, on edge, and alive. I managed to slip through the police cordon around the Baltic Exchange and see the damage for myself. There was devastation. I wrote up my notes and sent them on to feature writers who included my copy in their final article.

I can't say I ever actually learned how to write. Eventually I learned how to put words in roughly the right order. I watched how others wrote, sitting quietly next to them for hours and weeks until I could predict what words they would use. I arrived at the paper without preconceptions or skill and I was able to train with some of the best writers in the industry. But I never studied or understood the basic rules. I still cannot define a noun, let alone a definite or indefinite article, or an objective personal pronoun. I rely on spell-check to guide my use of 'to' or 'too'. Does it matter? Colleagues said to me: 'If you want to write, just get on and write. Don't wait for a qualification.'

Peter asked me to work on an investigation into a dam project under construction in Malaysia. He had finished and published the main investigation and he was about to pen a follow-up article a couple of weeks later when he looked across the desk at me.

'Why don't you write this up instead?' he said. Then he gave me a final piece of superb advice: 'Just make every sentence count.'

I stayed late into the night with rain rattling hard on the corrugated plastic roof. I worked in every nuance and detail of the investigation, then remembered Peter's advice and stripped it back to the key essentials. I topped it with a drop-intro and tailed it with a pay-off conclusion. It was all I had learned about the style of the newspaper.

The piece went into the system with a few changes, but never made it to print. Yet I was delighted. It was a massive boost to my self-esteem. I wrote a few more short pieces that were tucked on the inside pages and within a short space of time I was writing articles that went into the paper pretty much unchanged. Then the news desk editors began asking me to glance over other copy and 'give it a quick tweak'. I would take an article in the news desk holding queue and doctor it a little. The way the system worked meant that writers could see where their articles were in the sausage machine that led to the editor's system, sub-editors and then 'the stone', where type was set into a final layout for inclusion and printing, in the old days using a stone slab. By checking the computer, you could tell exactly where your article was in the line and whether someone had it open on their computer. It didn't take long before experienced journos realised an article they had been slaving over for days was being edited by the twenty-something post-boy. Initially a couple stormed over and asked to know what I was doing. I had to explain that the news editor wanted me to take a look at it, and I was trying to help get it into the paper. Egos were involved, but publication was the ultimate aim for everyone, and most people accepted that if the news editor wanted the post-boy to tweak it then he was the boss.

After a year or so of tweaking articles I became one of the news department's main re-writers. Several of the expert correspondents were specialists from their particular fields rather than trained journalists, and I would sometimes be given their articles to rework into the *Sunday Times* style. I had been promoted out of the post room into the newsroom but people from other sections would still ask me to fetch their cuttings or take a package to the post room. More than once I had to explain I wasn't really working in the post room any more, and I had a front-page article to copy-edit.

The original *Sunday Times* articles about the Malaysian dam scandal caused something of a stir. Relations between the UK and the Malays soured, legal letters flew back and forth. It became a major diplomatic incident.

The article had helped to reveal that a sale of British weapons to Malaysia had been linked to the provision of hundreds of millions of pounds in UK aid for the Pergau hydro-electric dam scheme in northern Malaysia, a project deemed hopelessly uneconomic by officials in Britain and Malaysia. It remains one of Britain's biggest aid scandals. In response to the newspaper revelations, the Malaysian Prime Minister, Mahathir Mohamad, imposed a sweeping trade ban with the UK, freezing negotiations for Malaysian government contracts worth billions.

Around the same time a group of British soldiers went missing in Malaysian Borneo and a veteran reporter from the *Sunday Times* was sent out to cover the search. The following Saturday we were working to get the paper out when a phone rang in the newsroom. I picked it up. 'Newsroom,' I said.

I could hear shouting, the sound of banging, then a voice

came down the line, strained, desperate; panic in the tone. 'Who is that?' it said.

'It's Simon,' I said blankly.

'Reeve?!' I recognised the voice of my colleague.

'Yes. What's going on? Are you all right?'

'No, no, they're taking me. I'm being taken.'

I shouted over to alert the news desk and put the call on speakerphone.

'They're taking me away. Get someone from the Embassy.'

We heard more shouting, then another voice came closer to the phone screaming abuse in what we presumed was Malay.

The line went dead. It had to be some sort of retribution for our articles about the Pergau dam. The news editor ran into the editor's office. He emerged in seconds and told me to get on the phone to the Foreign Office while someone else called the British ambassador in Kuala Lumpur. The deputy news editor began preparing an article for Reuters, the global news wire. I was on the phone to the Foreign Office as my colleague was tapping away at his keyboard: *A senior Sunday Times correspondent has been arrested in Malaysian Borneo . . .*

An article for Reuters meant the news would spread world-wide in a matter of minutes. I spoke to a senior official at the Foreign Office and asked them to inform the Foreign Secretary and flash an alert to the Ambassador in Malaysia. There was a degree of panic at the other end of the line:

'What are we supposed to do? It's Borneo, for heaven's sake. It's the middle of the night over there. We've only got an honorary consul anywhere near there and he's four hours away.'

'Phone him,' I said. 'Wake him up and get him over there. The editor is demanding you take this seriously.'

Twenty minutes or so later they called back to say the consul had jumped in a car and was already driving through the jungle. By now the article was ready to go to Reuters, but before it was sent the news editor suggested that maybe we should try to call a stringer in Borneo, a freelance journalist who had worked on a couple of articles for us in the past. He, in turn, managed to speak to a highly indignant local chief of police. Far from being carted off as retribution over the dam articles, our *ST* man had been embroiled in a heated argument in a restaurant over the price of a lobster. He had strong words with the owner, and then became involved in an unfortunate altercation with a man he thought was a waiter. In reality he was the brother of the owner, and he was also the local chief of police.

We had called the emergency line to the duty officer at the Foreign Office and sent the honorary consul halfway across Borneo. Very embarrassing. When our correspondent was released in the morning and slunk home a few days later, he found a blow-up plastic lobster on his desk. He also found one under his desk and another in his filing cabinet. It should have taught me the importance of checking and double-checking facts before you put them into print.

After I had been on the newspaper for a few years a senior colleague called Maurice Chittenden, a charismatic and witty reporter, wrote a slightly sneering article about a group called 'The Lesbian Avengers'. The following Saturday afternoon there was a kerfuffle at the door and a bunch of young women burst into the newsroom carrying massive water pistols and shouting slogans. The first person they confronted was Maurice, who stood there in semi-shock as they demanded to know where *Maurice Chittenden* was. He recovered quickly.

'Maurice Chittenden?' he said innocently. 'Oh yes, Maurice

Chittenden, I think he's in the library, I'll just go and fetch him.'

He took off leaving the rest of us to deal with the group, who were chanting slogans as they handcuffed themselves to our computers and filing cabinets, and started soaking everyone with their water pistols. Pretty soon the entire ageing computer system was in danger of exploding.

'If we're still here at 5 p.m. can we watch *Brookside*?' one of the protestors said to me, just as an entire regiment of white South African security guards stormed into the building. They had a tendency to direct all of the black members of staff to the car park furthest from the office yet had failed to stop the invasion. Their punishment was to stand in front of the computers while the women sprayed them up and down, before van-loads of police arrived, cut the women loose using bolt-cutters and took them away.

THE EDITOR

60 COPPERS

8 LESBIANS

(AND 4 PAIRS OF HANDCUFFS!)

read the banner headline in the *News of the World*, which ran a full-page article the next day on the 'mayhem' and quoted an aggrieved policeman who said: 'I was playing football. I can't believe they called so many of us out. There are seven police vans here.'

Most of us had a chuckle. But some of the senior executives were outraged by the attack. In a misguided attempt at retaliation one hatched a plan for the newspaper to infiltrate the Avengers. They asked several female journalists on the paper to go undercover in the group, but they pointedly refused. One of

the secretaries also turned them down. Then they asked one of
the new youngsters in the post room. The most obvious issue
was that he was male. When they summoned him to the office
to discuss the job they closed the door. That guaranteed they
were serious. When he emerged he was pale. The poor lad
couldn't believe it. 'They want me to wax my legs and put on
make-up,' he said. 'It's crazy. But if I don't do it I'll be out.'

It was a ludicrous idea, followed by other idiotic schemes. A
star-chart reward and punishment system was introduced as if
we were at pre-school. Then I was asked to work on an ill-fated
drugs investigation which was proving especially tricky because
some of the targets were threatening and powerful. One of our
team had his legs broken during a mugging attack that appeared
to have been organised by the drug gang.

It was my job to look after a whistle-blower, and it genuinely
appeared his life could be in danger. He was a sexually aggressive
and odious man who couldn't keep his mouth shut. We were
driving from one hotel to another in leafy Surrey and he leapt
right across me to lean out of my window and shout at a young
woman riding a bicycle in the opposite direction. When I
wouldn't turn the car around to pursue her, he turned on me,
screaming abuse. We had to keep moving him from hotel to
hotel because within an hour of checking in he'd be drinking in
the bar and trying to impress the staff with tales of what we were
doing. He was a total liability. I began to feel the support and
back-up from the London office was inadequate. One senior
exec just laughed when I said we had been forced to jump out
of a first-floor hotel window and flee in the night when someone tried to get into our rooms. They tried to get a
work-experience kid at the paper to take over babysitting him,
followed by a young female journalist, even though I said I

thought she would be in physical danger if placed alone with him. She had to barricade herself into a room as protection.

One of the final straws for me came when a friend of mine at the paper, a secretary who several colleagues thought looked like supermodel Cindy Crawford, was asked to travel to Kent to interview Alan Clark, the notoriously lecherous Tory Member of Parliament. Clark, who was once described as 'the most politically incorrect, outspoken, iconoclastic and reckless politician of our times', had been cited in a divorce case in South Africa, in which it was claimed he had affairs with the wife of a judge, and both her daughters. It was a media sensation, a tale of politics, sex and a dysfunctional family. The interview was scheduled to be at Clark's home. Everyone knew his reputation. I thought she would be a lamb for a wolf. Many of us felt it was outrageous.

CHAPTER EIGHT

The Towers

On 26 February 1993, a huge bomb exploded underneath the World Trade Center in New York. Six people were killed, hundreds were injured, and America was rudely awoken to the realities of international terrorism. The explosion rocked the towers like an earthquake – tourists one mile away on Liberty and Ellis Islands in New York harbour felt the ground shudder, all power in the towers was severed and the entire building was plunged into darkness. Commuters on the subway below were buried in concrete and twisted metal as the roof above them collapsed. America was stunned.

I was at the *Sunday Times* working on an investigation involving the IRA when news reports first came in from New York. Within an hour I had switched focus and began collating information on the WTC attack.

It took hundreds of firefighters two hours to extinguish the blazes and more than five hours for them to evacuate both towers. Gasping for breath, their faces blackened by soot and muck, thousands of workers and visitors staggered out onto the street and collapsed into the snow, many of them hacking up blood from their lungs. It was a devastating attack. The bombing created more hospital casualties than any other event in domestic American history outside of the Civil War. The New York City Fire Department sent a total of 750 vehicles to the explosion and did not leave the scene for the next month.

For two weeks I researched the attack for the newspaper. Events moved quickly in New York and I kept coming across details and snippets of information about the attack I found extraordinary. Within days investigators had found the vehicle identification number of the truck that had carried the device. A few calls and checks established that it had been rented from a Ryder hire firm in nearby Jersey City by a man whose name appeared on an FBI militant watch list. Staff at the leasing agency told FBI agents the man had actually returned to the office since the bombing to claim a refund on his $400 deposit for the van, which he said had been stolen the night before the explosion. Staff had told him to get an incident number from the police, and he was due back in a few days. The FBI staked out the hire firm and quickly caught three of the men behind the bombing. Within a few more days a man called Ramzi Yousef was identified as the mastermind of the attack. He had fled the US just after the bombing. A global manhunt began. The FBI even extended their famous list of ten most wanted fugitives to eleven to include their new quarry.

We published a comprehensive account of what had happened on the first Sunday and a follow-up piece the next week. But then other terrible things were happening in the world and the newspaper lost interest. I didn't. I became fascinated and then obsessed by the attack. A British intelligence contact told me explosives experts on our side of the Atlantic had been asked to provide assistance, because the device used to bomb the World Trade Center was so rare that the FBI's explosives laboratory believed it had only been used once before in more than 73,000 separate recorded explosions. It was almost unique. In the mainstream media the bombers were portrayed as a small, isolated group of lunatics. But I was being given snippets of information by contacts that suggested there was a much bigger story behind the attack.

Week after week I kept returning to the bombing and the aftermath, discovering more leads and angles. But nobody on the newspaper was interested in taking another story on the attack or approving more research. Peter Hounam had left the paper, along with several other friends and colleagues, and the whole atmosphere there was changing.

The kind of investigations I had previously been involved with were expensive and time-consuming. I was told pockets were no longer as deep as they had been. Gradually there wasn't enough money to fund investigations properly, and I was being moved from deep research on to stories that were more regular news. I found it hard to summon the same levels of enthusiasm.

A prime example was one of my last jobs. I was supposed to drive to a house in Northolt, I think, where a third-rate politician involved in yet another scandal was going to hold a press conference and confess his sins. It was all very last minute. I was late and I wasn't especially bothered about the story. I was sitting patiently in a traffic jam idly wondering whether I would get there on time, when a souped-up BMW came streaking along next to me, driving on the wrong side of the road at high speed. At first I thought it was the police. Then as it whizzed past my line of traffic I caught a glimpse of the driver, who had his window open and was barking into a mobile phone the size of a brick while steering with one hand. I recognised him immediately as a reporter from a rival paper. I knew him vaguely from Friday-night drinks in the pubs around Wapping. And I knew instantly that not only was he going to the same dead-end scandal press conference, but he was infinitely keener to get there, and in that second I realised I never wanted to care so much about filing copy on a grubby politician that I'd weave through traffic risking my neck and the lives of any schoolkids who might step out into the road.

By the time I got to Northolt the press conference was already over. The BMW driver was there, still on his mobile phone talking loudly to the office. I remember smiling to myself. I knew the job was no longer for me. I didn't have the drive or desire. I wasn't actually very good at the job of reporting and finding completely different stories every week. It was research and investigations that I loved, and the writing. I was a fan of what the veteran managing editor at the *Sunday Times* called 'a scoop of analysis'.

I was a staff writer by then, apparently the youngest in the venerable history of Times Newspapers, and I was working on the news desk most weeks writing and rewriting copy and as the deputy night news editor on a Saturday. It was an enormous responsibility for someone as young as me, but I revelled in it. The newspaper was my life, not only professionally, but personally as well. I had grown up there. I socialised with colleagues, moved in with friends I met at work and had a couple of relationships at the paper. I wanted to spend more time investigating subjects I was passionate about, but I hadn't seriously planned to leave. Until, that was, the wrong rugby score was printed on the front page of the paper while I was on the news desk. It was a huge mistake, only spotted in the final edition, which meant hundreds of thousands of copies were printed and scattered around the country. I have a horrible feeling the mistake reversed the result, but I have largely blocked out the memory due to the trauma of the aftermath. It was like the Spanish Inquisition the following week. Several people were culpable, but I was one of those supposed to be in charge, so part of the blame stuck to me. The whole atmosphere there had soured.

I felt it was time to leave, and I came up with a crazy plan to write a book about the World Trade Center bombing and the aftermath. I wrote more than a dozen letters to London literary agents in the hope someone would represent me, then went to see a couple before settling on a lovely chap called Robert Kirby, who I am still with to this day. He had the warm and friendly air of a social worker, and a relaxed confidence that put me at ease. Crucially he was also intrigued by my proposal and by my claim the WTC attack represented a new type of terrorist strike, by a new type of terrorist. I wanted to write a book that would tell the story of the attack and follow the huge investigation and aftermath. Robert thought we had a decent chance of getting it published. That was good enough for me. I negotiated a small redundancy payoff, and I left the *Sunday Times*.

It was 1994/5 and I was barely into my twenties. In a few short years I had gone from being the boy on the bridge to somebody who had the confidence to quit my job with a plan to write a book. I ploughed on with the research and Robert started to look for a publisher prepared to back the project.

At the same time life outside work was taking off as well. I had studied for an A-level at night school, so at least I have one to my name, and with my book still in research mode, I started to wonder about further education. Despite all my chippy comments and views about elite universities I went for an inter-view at an Oxford college, arranged on the basis that as the youngest staff writer on a newspaper I might qualify as an excep-tional candidate. I thought not going to university might be something I always regretted. Sitting in the waiting room with twenty boys, all of them dressed in public-school ties and tweed jackets, and at most two girls, I knew immediately it was too late. I had made a mistake. Arrogantly perhaps, I felt that after all I'd seen and done there was no way I could go back to full-time study. These kids still had spots, for goodness' sake. I was so certain that I stood up, apologised to the gracious staff and left. I was becoming an expert at walking out. They had given me the powerful gift of a second chance, but at least I had confirmed it wasn't for me. I never had another serious regret about my lack of education.

My girlfriend Anna was waiting outside the college. She had been hugely supportive of my idea of going to university, and she was a pillar when I changed my mind. Anna was my first serious girlfriend. Certainly the first woman I tried to move in with. Glamorous, charismatic and fascinating, Anna had fallen in love with Russia and Russian literature, and so of course she went to live in Moscow, sang in jazz clubs and learned to speak the language fluently, with a heavy Georgian accent that to other Russian speakers marked her out as a gangster. She lived in a sunny flat in Hampstead and drove a convertible. We met at work and she started writing a column for *The Times*, partly about my attempts to inveigle myself into her life.

Anna's father was a well-known British journalist and war correspondent. He died, tragically young, after being shot by a sniper while he was covering a civil war in Central America, and she was at university. She had suffered a huge trauma, and she taught me much about grief and life. I'm not sure what I gave back. I think I was a charity case. I remember I kept flooding her bathroom. Then I blew it all by being too jealous and she dumped me.

After her my love life was a series of short and often disastrous relationships. There was one girl from Sicily, gorgeous, vivacious; although a bit vague as to why she was in London. It took a while to get at the truth.

'O-K,' she finally said in her thick Sicilian accent. 'I know you want to know so I'll tell you. My family had a leetle bit of a problem and they decided London was safer for me. The truth is, three of my uncles, they are in prison for twenty-five years for being Mafiosi.'

Twenty-five years apiece wasn't minor theft. When I tried to end our relationship – fairly soon after she revealed who my in-laws would be, actually – I'd come home and find messages on my machine left in her distinctive accent.

'Si-mon, Si-mon, where are you?' she'd sing-song. 'Why don't you answer my calls? Dar-ling, we have to go on holiday to Sicily. My family really wants to meet you.'

I went on a series of holidays, but with my friends, travelling and training across Europe. In a rammed hostel in Paris a mate of mine fell off his bed, landed on top of me and cracked my rib, but I laughed hysterically through the pain. In another hostel dorm we stayed with a Dutch netball team. They made a big impression. Then a group of us were due to go on a lads' week-end to Barcelona. We were all looking forward to some sunshine after dreary weather in London, but at the last moment the tickets were changed to Copenhagen. Still thinking we were going to a beach, half of us showed up at the airport without coats, and three were in shorts and flip-flops.

Copenhagen was freezing. We had no guide book, no idea where we were going and our first port of call became an army surplus store for winter coats. We were all pretty grumpy about the cold and the change of plan, but we dealt with it in the only way possible, by getting hideously drunk. Then we went to Christiania, the self-proclaimed anarchist district of Copenhagen, accidentally ate some spiked cakes, and everything went a little blurry. I vaguely remember walking into a pub in Christiania and feeling like I had walked into an off-world bar from Star *Wars*. I thought there was a polar bear in the corner. Everything was very trippy and psychedelic.

For some reason one of our group then called an ex-girlfriend who lived in the city. She was a construction engineer, and she took it upon herself to take us to the Oresund tunnel and bridge that was being built to link Denmark with Sweden. This was an extremely foolish decision. There were ten of us, and we were drunk and tripping. I can only assume it was her professional enthusiasm. She fitted us out with hard hats and took us down into the huge tunnel. We were stumbling and staggering around, and then several of us were completely spooked by space ships flying down the tunnel towards us, which I now suspect were dumper trucks. A few of us fled through a door in the tunnel wall in a panic and that led to one or two alarms going off, the entire site being put on lockdown and security being called to extract us. Apparently I was hiding under a tarpaulin with a friend and we were hugging each other and babbling when we were rescued.

Fortunately the Danes were very forgiving. Someone explained we were English, and the site manager decided not to press charges. We left and found refuge in yet another bar. We were too well-mannered to be obnoxious, but few countries like wandering drunks. Yet as we staggered around Copenhagen all we encountered was kindness, tolerance and mild amusement. People helped us, advised us, took us to bars, and bought us more drinks.

By the time we went home I couldn't walk, and the others had to push me in a shopping trolley to the train that would take us to the airport. I was half-carried to the plane, and I'm frankly amazed the cabin crew let me on board. For a full week after, I had alcohol poisoning and my poor flatmates graciously cared for me.

At the time I was living with Julie and Elspeth, a couple of friends I knew from working at the *Sunday Times*. We had moved into a cheap flat, with an interior that resembled a shoddy alpine chalet, just around the corner from my ex Anna in Hampstead. Our flat was an awful 1970s block, but we looked out at some of the most beautiful and expensive properties in London. Poor Anna. I bumped into her on the High Street one day and the look on her face didn't need translation – *You've moved around the corner from me? Really?*

Life with Elspeth and Julie was fun and social, like a series of *Friends* set in North London. We had wonderful parties where the flat was full of scores of burning candles and a total mix of characters and pungent smoke. Elspeth was a witty delight who had me in stitches with pithy one-liners and Julie was a bundle of energy and joy who spread love wherever she went. When we entertained, which was often, the floor in the living room would bow with the weight of people dancing. One night after a long party we decided to walk onto Hampstead Heath to watch the sun rise. Twenty of us set off and it was only when we were making our way up Parliament Hill that someone pointed out it was already completely light and people were out jogging and walking to work. We were so far gone none of us had noticed.

Morning recoveries were painful, but then I would start work researching and writing, wearing a dressing gown, of course, like any recently liberated writer. There I was, just into my twenties, trying to live like a Woodstock boho while at the same time researching a book about what was then one of the worst terrorist attacks in US history. I remember one afternoon sitting in my dressing gown on the phone to the Joint Terrorism Task Force in New York, so hungover I was struggling to focus.

I would spend the afternoon researching, the night being social, and then the early hours trying to write to a soundtrack of Ibizan dance and urban jungle broadcast on pirate radio stations run from tower blocks by friends from school in Acton. None of this was a good idea. Inevitably after spending most of the morning sleeping I would have to unpick and rewrite the incoherent stream from the night before. This was not conducive to productivity.

I was following and researching the investigation into the World Trade Center bombing by phone from London. But then my agent Robert managed to secure a UK publishing deal for my book on the attack, followed by a small contract for the US, and I worked myself into a rhythm and a focus, and started to take the whole project much more seriously. The book I ultimately spent five years researching and writing became the single most involving and exhausting project of my life.

My research had two tracks. There was the 'Tradebom' investigation into the World Trade Center attack, which was being run by a Joint Terrorist Task Force (JTTF) out of New York, directly comprising perhaps seventy agents drawn from the FBI, NYPD, the US Secret Service, the US Marshals Service, the Bureau of Alcohol, Tobacco, and Firearms, and others. There was also a more secret global intelligence operation studying the wider terror group and emerging connections behind the attack. By phone I was already working my way along a chain of contacts ever closer to the JTTF unit, and soon meetings in

London with contacts in MI6 helped my entry into the intelligence world.

On the investigative side my initial approach was to call the media departments of both the NYPD and the FBI and ask to speak to their investigators. It took persuasion, discussion and time, but essentially it was as simple as that. They connected me to agents and detectives who were peripherally connected to the investigation, and I spent hours on the phone milking them for everything they would tell me, going through it all in minute detail. I had a book to fill, after all. Then, after winning their trust and exhausting their patience, I would simply ask if they could pass me on to colleagues working more closely on the investigation for another angle, saying I wanted to accurately capture their professionalism and skill. One phone call led to another and I was passed from person to person until I had a network of contacts.

With the help of the tiny funds from the US edition of my book, which almost covered my international phone bills, my sources ultimately expanded to include the FBI Supervisory Special Agent running the Joint Terrorism Task Force, who was exceptionally generous with his time, and officials from the Directorate for Special Operations and Low-Intensity Conflict at the Pentagon. In London I met contacts from MI6 individually in pubs in Vauxhall and Soho. They passed me on to more contacts in their own world, including in Pakistani intelligence and the CIA. Sometimes it was farcically informal. I still have a pub coaster somewhere with the scribbled telephone number for a former head of Pakistani intelligence.

Why were they meeting me, talking to me and sharing information? It's something I've thought about since. I think there were many reasons. Trust was important. I did not pose a threat.

I wasn't going to burn their cover or reveal a source. I was also unassuming, perhaps a bit disarming, and – crucially – I was interested. Many of those involved in this world felt they were operating in something of a vacuum and that nobody was listening to their concerns and warnings. The prevailing feeling internationally in the 1990s was that the Cold War had been won, the West was unassailable and nothing really posed a threat. Many in the intelligence world disagreed with that idea. They felt the WTC attack was different from anything that had gone on before. So when I popped up on the phone asking questions, people were happy to help. They felt it was their duty. Plus I think everybody wants to feel appreciated. Everyone wants to feel that their work is important, it's human nature. The main reason people answered questions from a wide-eyed, twenty-something Brit, was simply because I asked.

My sources made it clear the scope of the WTC investigation was unprecedented. Every one of the fifty-nine FBI field divisions in the US and every one of the sixty-three global FBI Legal Attachés, known as LEGATs, and each effectively an investigative field office, was involved. The volume of information generated about the attack and the group behind it was enormous. Even just the number of telephone numbers thrown up during the investigation was huge. Three or four agents worked full-time uploading numbers onto computers and identifying suspects. The FBI developed databases based on the names and numbers that were used by investigators for years.

The mastermind of the 1993 World Trade Center attack, Ramzi Yousef, fled the US shortly after the explosion. He could have slipped quietly away and lived out the rest of his life in a friendly dictatorship. But he was determined to launch more attacks. Just months later the detonator of a bomb he was placing to target Benazir Bhutto, the secular candidate for Prime Minister in the October 1993 Pakistani elections, exploded in his face. His right eye was injured but after treatment in two Karachi hospitals, where he told staff a butane gas canister had exploded, his facial injuries healed and he disappeared.

Yousef next appeared on a Philippines Airlines flight bound for Tokyo from Manila in December 1994. He placed a bomb under his seat and left the flight at Cebu, 350 miles from Manila. Two hours later an explosion killed a Japanese man and injured a dozen people sitting nearby. The other passengers on the flight were lucky their plane was not blown out of the sky. The bombing, and an earlier explosion in a Manila cinema, were practice runs for a horrific scheme called the 'Bojinka Plot', a plan for simultaneous attacks on twelve airliners. Terrorists would have boarded American-bound flights in the Far East and slipped miniature bombs designed around Casio wristwatches under seats. Undetectable liquid nitroglycerine hidden in contact-lens solution bottles would have been connected to a Casio timer by detonator parts hidden in shoes. Yousef had assembled the parts for his own bomb in the toilet during the flight to Cebu. And then he vanished.

Less than a month later in Manila, police saw smoke rising from an apartment block, raided a flat, and arrested one of Yousef's co-conspirators. It was a crucial breakthrough. A map was discovered tracing the route Pope John Paul II was to take during a visit the next week, as well as a priest's robe, a fragmentation grenade and a timer constructed from the shell of a normal digital watch: all ready for a suicide attack on the Pontiff. Yousef's Toshiba laptop computer was also discovered. But again Yousef himself evaded the authorities, escaped from the country and returned to Pakistan. He became the target of a huge global manhunt.

Yousef, who was probably born in Kuwait to a Palestinian mother and Pakistani father, specialised in inventing bombs that can escape airport searches. He would convert a digital watch into a timing switch and use light-bulb filament to ignite cotton soaked in nitroglycerine explosive. An explosives genius who studied A-levels at the Oxford College of Further Education, he then moved to South Wales to study for a degree in computer-aided electronic engineering at what was then the West Glamorgan Institute of Higher Education, or 'Wiggy'. When the police raided his flat in Manila they discovered a chemistry textbook from Swansea Library with passages on the manufacture of explosives highlighted.

Everything about the attack and investigation was astonishing. I had some money I'd saved from when I left the *Sunday Times* so I flew to the US. I met senior investigators and FBI 'brick agents', a term the FBI uses for the guys doing the legwork; tough, experienced people that are out on the streets literally pounding the 'bricks'. They took me into bars and mosques in Brooklyn and Jersey City, meeting neighbours of the bombers and people who had prayed with them, and were pious and sometimes militant. I spent hours deep inside the Twin Towers, wandering around with guides so I could understand the layout of the area where the bomb had been placed. I sourced court reports and interview transcripts, and I met officials and agents from the Central Intelligence Agency, the Defense Intelligence Agency and the even more secret National Security Agency. I sat down with nervous, uptight spooks and never discovered their real names, let alone which ultra-secret agencies they really worked for. But on repeat trips to the States I also made contacts working on covert operations who were friendly and worldly, would happily hang out and share their time and a beer, and talk about their childhood growing up around the world with parents who were in the US military.

I was taken to gatherings in a bar near Washington DC that was like a second base of operations for intelligence specialists from different agencies who were studying the wider militant group that emerged at the time of the Tradebom investigation and had connections to the WTC attackers. We know it now, of course, as al Qaeda. They even told me they had a fax machine installed in the bar. I was vouched for by a respected analyst, but not everyone seemed to be aware I was writing a book. On more than one occasion I was mistaken for some sort of junior agent seconded from MI6.

'This is all just between us, isn't it, Simon?' said my guy, looking meaningfully at me and tapping his nose.

I have never really talked about this period before, but I was moving in shadowy circles. Those at the sharp end felt they were encountering an emerging threat to global security. They were talking to me because they believed nobody in power in the US or Europe was taking the threat seriously.

It was Benazir Bhutto, the former Prime Minister of Pakistan, who first mentioned the name Osama bin Laden to me. We were having breakfast together in the restaurant of a small hotel in Kensington, just around the corner from the Royal Albert Hall. There were a pair of Italian honeymooners at the table opposite, some American tourists directly behind us, and Benazir was talking loudly. She said there were links between the 1993 WTC bombing and bin Laden, and she was adamant that bin Laden posed a huge threat to Pakistan, the West and the world.

We were sitting at a small table, just the two of us. She kept stressing, and was one of the first to point out internationally, that Muslims were the first victims of terrorism. Then she moved on to tell me how Ramzi Yousef had tried to kill her with a bomb, and then later with a rifle. I was having trouble focusing on what she was saying, because Benazir had a huge blob of strawberry jam stuck to her upper lip. I tried to motion to her, but she was in full flow. I nodded towards and looked at her mouth, but she ignored me. I passed her a napkin. Finally she paused and flicked it into the cloth with a practised flourish. It was all very bizarre.

Bhutto told me that within two months of the 1993 explosion outside her home, Yousef developed a plan to assassinate her with a sniper's rifle. 'I was supposed to be addressing a public meeting in Karachi, and I got a report from one of my party people that according to police sources there was going to be an assassination attempt on me that night,' she told me.

Bhutto still went along to the meeting, but by the time she arrived it was 'complete chaos'. 'There were people everywhere and armed men on the stage. In the midst of all this my mother also arrived. So I decided to go up, but the police were not coming to clear the stage. So I had a choice of leaving or taking the risk. So we took the risk and went up there, and it was absolute bedlam. I don't know how I spoke on that stage, or how I got out unscathed, but I did.' Only later did Bhutto learn the details of the botched assassination plan. 'He was supposed to have shot me. He had gone and done a recce of the place and with his associates he had got on top of the building.'

However, a rifle that was supposed to be delivered to Yousef never arrived in time. 'So in other words Ramzi Yousef would have shot me if he had got the weapon in time,' said Bhutto. 'As you can imagine, I was quite shocked by this.'

I met Bhutto several times to discuss the emerging threat from al Qaeda. Her second government had been abruptly dismissed by the Pakistani President amid allegations of widespread corruption and economic incompetence. She was travelling with courtiers and a retinue, like a monarch on the move, but we met alone at the same mid-range hotel where she stayed during frequent visits to London. She had a powerful, intimidating gaze. I thought of her as a cross between Margaret Thatcher and Princess Diana.

I had been introduced to Bhutto by the former head of the Pakistani equivalent of the FBI, who was one of her close aides and was also out of office and in exile. I met him successively in a cheap hotel in Swiss Cottage, in a curry restaurant on King Street in Hammersmith, and near his offices on the North Circular Road, where he said he was involved in the petroleum industry. I had been passed on to him by contacts in MI6, and he proved to be a mine of information, sharing extraordinary documents that detailed the scale and spread of the terrorist group we now know as al Qaeda. They included intelligence reports and Pakistani interrogation transcripts. The reports had been transcribed verbatim and could be tough even just to read. There would be a section of speech which would say something like:

[Interrogator] 'Tell me the name of your handler.'
Silence.
'The name of your handler.'
Silence.
Screams.

'Your handler.'

More screams.

'Tell me the name of your handler.'

I had an endless series of frightening and strange experiences, encounters and adventures working on that book. I was followed by the agents of at least two countries and almost certainly had my phone tapped. During my previous investigations I had been part of a team with the back-up of the *Sunday Times*. Writing the book, I was on my own and there was no one to call should things go pear-shaped.

On one occasion I needed to watch the house of a shady Lebanese businessman allegedly involved in supplying weapons to militants. I was getting a little carried away with the investigation, so I disguised myself as a vagrant and staked out the building. I even peed on my clothes in a misguided attempt to dissuade anyone from taking too much interest in what I was doing. It only encouraged the police to move me on.

Another time I decided I needed to attend a party in a country house outside London that a contact told me various dodgy spies and arms dealers would attend. He wangled me an invite, and for some reason a media friend said that to help me with my cover story they would put me on a list to have access to a convertible Aston Martin DB7 the company was lending out to writers. Then I borrowed an Ozwald Boateng suit from a friend of the fashion designer and set off for the party, feeling bizarrely confident I could pull off my act. I only made it a few streets from the flat. Every time I went around a corner the Aston Martin would lose power and then stall, the power steering would die, and I narrowly avoided crashing into several vehicles. I drove it slowly back home, worried I had damaged an extremely expensive car. An engineer from Aston Martin arrived the next afternoon wearing a suit and carrying a laptop, lifted up a panel in the door sill, plugged in the computer, and ran a diagnostic check. It turned out the person who had the car before me was a motoring correspondent, and he had been driving it at ferocious speeds on tight tracks.

'It has a learning computer that adapts to the driving style,' said the engineer. 'The guy before you was taking corners at 50 mph, so the computer adjusted the power to account for that. It should have been reset before you got the car. Very sorry.'

I drove over to see my mum and dad and took them out for a joyride. They were thrilled. But I never made it to the spies' party.

I had some other near-disasters. I spent all of my savings, earnings and my advance researching the book. I found myself canoeing down a river in South-East Asia, looking for a supposed terror training camp. It seems crazy now. A twenty-something author with no back-up and no one to call, in a wooden canoe with a guide I did not know, trying to locate a terrorist training camp. Talk about overcoming my teenage fears. I was foolhardy, or at the very least naïve, and I had no concerns about where the research might lead or what dangers I might encounter. I never found the camp, but in several dark dreams I've since wondered what would have happened if I had. Can you imagine my canoe bumping up to the shore and some guy with a Kalashnikov springing from the shadows?

'Oh hello, so sorry to bother you. My name's Simon. I was really hoping we could have a long talk.'

At the time I really thought I would find them and that they would talk to me. I remember a deep feeling of failure when we finally had to turn the boat around.

Perhaps my most frightening experience at that time came when contacts in Pakistani intelligence put me in touch with a group of bin Laden's supporters in northern Italy. Eventually they agreed to a clandestine meeting.

I travelled on my own. I still didn't understand how dangerous al Qaeda really was, and anyway the money for my book barely covered phone calls, let alone security.

At an Islamic cultural centre I was ushered into a room with six men. I knew from my Pakistani contacts they were 'Afghan Arabs' – men who'd travelled from around the world to Afghanistan to fight the Soviets during the 1980s. When the war ended many went home quietly. The men I was with in Italy had gone to the Balkans, fighting the Serbs. They were warriors, and as tough as old boots. We drank coffee and talked through my interpreter, and everything was going fine. I asked them what they believed and what they were trying to achieve. They were radical, for sure, but they weren't hostile.

Then two other men arrived. They had particularly bushy beards and a more hardcore air. The men in the room seemed surprised to see the new arrivals, and they were very surprised to see me, and immediately angry.

I had stepped into a very dangerous world. The mood in the room changed from being slightly threatening to something much darker. I knew that Egyptian and Italian intelligence, and to a lesser extent the CIA, was investigating the Afghan Arabs. They saw me as a threat. I was sitting down, along the back wall away from the door. A few others were sitting, but the two who arrived were among those standing above me, shouting at the others and pointing at me. I felt incredibly threatened. Even my interpreter, who was one of them, looked pale. I knew a few words of Arabic and could tell that not only were they furious about the fact I was there, but they were arguing about whether I should leave alive.

An American source and friend had only just been telling me a few weeks before about a time when he was briefly captured in Somalia and had to fight his way out with fists and bullets. 'If you're ever in real trouble, Simon, you'll know it,' he told me. 'Then whatever you do, don't do nothing.'

A thousand things were going through my mind: could I get to the door? Could I leap out of the window? What the hell was I doing there? I was the most scared I had ever been. One of the men was so angry his spittle was flying everywhere. I suddenly felt very stupid and very small. I was playing a dangerous game with very serious men.

I tensed in case I had to rush for the window, while the arguing continued. It lasted for a few minutes but somehow I kept my cool, then things calmed down, my translator found his voice and hospitality prevailed over militancy. The bearded two left with half the group. I tried to sip coffee and appear normal, but my body was shaking. My interpreter was also shaking and we just wanted to get out. I knew I had come face-to-face with the most radical of zealots. It chilled me. I flew home and had nightmares for weeks.

Ramzi Yousef was finally captured in Islamabad in February 1995. Pakistani special forces and the FBI caught him preparing another atrocity: several remote-controlled toy cars packed with explosives. On his flight to New York the next day he told JTTF agents he had wanted to topple one of the Twin Towers into the other, and had deliberately built the bomb to try and shear the support columns holding up the towers. He had also considered a poison-gas attack on the complex, but claimed he had ruled it out because it would have been 'too expensive'.

In American eyes at the time, Yousef had a legitimate claim to the title of most dangerous man in the world. He was sentenced to 240 years in jail and imprisoned as if he was a virus. He is still the most secure prisoner on the most secure wing of Supermax in Colorado, the most secure prison in the world.

Yousef and bin Laden became the focus of my book, titled *The New Jackals: Ramzi Yousef, Osama bin Laden and the Future of Terrorism*, which came out several years before the attacks of 9/11. It has the dubious distinction of being the first book in the world on bin Laden and al Qaeda. My conclusion was that Yousef and bin Laden were a new breed of terrorist, men who had no moral restrictions on mass killing.

I quoted a former director of the FBI's Investigations Division, who said: 'In the past, we were fighting terrorists with an organisational structure and some attainable goal like land or the release of political prisoners. But the new breed are more difficult and hazardous. They want nothing less than the overthrow of the West, and since that's not going to happen, they just want to punish – the more casualties the better.'

It was a debatable comment: by the time the book came out bin Laden had revealed some of his goals, saying publicly he was attacking the West because the US and Europe supported regimes in the Middle East. But my overall point was that we were entering a new age of apocalyptic terrorism. That was my conclusion.

I had worked on the book for years, risked my life and put my all into writing it. You can imagine how disappointed I was when I felt it sank like a stone.

CHAPTER NINE

Grief

The New Jackals came out in 1998 and hardly anyone read it. My parents went around bookshops moving it from the dusty shelves at the back of stores and placing it at the front. Not only had I said Ramzi Yousef was the first of a new breed of terrorist, but I'd added that many more were being prepared in terrorist training schools dotted around Afghanistan and Pakistan. Nobody was interested.

There was a review of the book in the *Sunday Times*, my old paper, which said I'd clearly had ample access to Western intelligence sources, but that I was scaremongering, and that my 'apocalyptic vision' was wrong. It was written by an older expert on the Middle East, who in my view had no idea of how the world had changed, but it was published in my old newspaper, and I felt a sense of betrayal. Even now I remember where I was when my friend Maurice called to warn me and read the review to me.

What could I do? Step by step. I carried on.

While I had been researching *The New Jackals*, I had also been working on other projects to make sure I could pay my rent. I conducted an investigation for *Time* magazine into how the Swiss put Jews into labour camps during the Second World War. That caused a stink, and Swiss newspapers paid an infamous private investigator to steal the contents of my bins in an attempt to find some dirt on me. I also worked with my old mentor Peter Hounam at a new investigative publishing company he founded, writing, editing or rewriting a handful of books on such light-hearted topics as biological warfare, organised crime and nuclear smuggling. Peter secured a leaked copy of the Chancellor of the Exchequer's budget speech, some details of which were published in the press, and he won the *What the Papers Say* Scoop of the Year. I was only peripherally involved, but I was questioned by a senior officer from Scotland Yard. To get me to reveal the source of the leak the officer tried to use the fact I had signed the Official Secrets Act years previously when I worked for the government for less than one day. I suggested in somewhat impolite terms that I would love to see him try.

More importantly during those years I was reconciled with James, my younger brother, who had moved into my rented flat after my friends Julie and Elspeth moved out to live with partners. James and I had a sometimes tricky relationship after I left school, and I had seen little of him. Helping him to move boxes into the flat, then cooking meals together and sharing tales and a space, was completely wonderful. He's two years younger than me and I have always adored and admired him more than he realises. There was nobody I wanted to have closer. His first job had been whitewashing the infinity board in the local photographic studio and he was building a career as a photographer after starting at the bottom just like me. He didn't get a degree in photography or media studies; he just threw himself in at the deep end and learned on the job. Enthusiasm and ability meant he began to climb the ladder, and he went on to work as an assistant to some of the world's greatest photographers, and later became an award-winning photographer in his own right. Living together felt like we were placing pieces back into our own emotional jigsaw, rebuilding the people we would have been without the traumas of our childhood. Or at least that's what we decided together after we'd had a couple of drinks.

At the end of the 1990s both of us were also reconciled with our dad, despite all that had gone on between us. He had retired from teaching and become calmer and less combative. He no longer treated us like irritating kids. He talked to us like adults, and we became friends. We all spent time together, went for day trips together and on holidays. I remember James and I taking him to see *Saving Private Ryan* at a cinema on the King's Road in Chelsea. I drove us all there but then couldn't find anywhere to park. I offered to drop them off.

'No, let's stick together,' said Dad, smiling. He was savouring a moment with his sons.

We had to park half a mile away, and the film was about to start. We all ran together through the streets, jokingly encouraging each other onwards. We arrived, glowing with sweat. Dad was just beaming with joy and pure delight. At that point, at that moment, more than ever, we felt bonded, and together.

And then after a brief period of illness he was diagnosed with cancer. He became mortal, in all our eyes. It was heart-wrenching, of course, but like so many others we found that illness brought us even closer together as a family and encouraged final forgiveness on all sides. James and I went with Dad and Mum for his diagnosis at Hammersmith Hospital. We held hands together. We cried. James and I were often able to go with him for the interminable rounds of chemo that followed. He seemed to be improving.

I had been working on another book, about the 1972 Munich Olympic massacre of Israeli athletes and officials. Called *One Day in September*, the book was researched and written in parallel with a documentary feature movie of the same title which went on to win an Oscar for best feature documentary. My book, subtitled *The Full Story of the 1972 Munich Olympics Massacre and Israeli Revenge Operation 'Wrath of God'*, was published in 2000. Shortly afterwards Dad's sickness worsened. I had been on a book tour of the US, flitting from city to city with my then girlfriend, who was effectively my fiancée. We had planned to go south to Florida for a few days in the sun. I called home from JFK Airport in New York and spoke to Dad.

'It's not good news, I'm afraid, son,' he said, trying to sound calm. 'The cancer is back, and it seems to be really aggressive.'

It was a hammer blow. I put down the phone, changed our tickets right there and caught the first flight home. I moved my office into a tiny room at our family home so I could be around him as much as possible and help Mum to take care of him. We did everything we could, garnered second opinions and tried all manner of treatments and a few quack ideas but nothing had any effect.

He kept telling James and me how proud he was of us. I reminded Dad how he had spotted the advert in the newspaper that kick-started my little journey. I made sure he knew that without his encouragement I would probably never have made anything of my life. I knew and I know he always loved me.

By the spring of 2001 he was largely bedridden. Soon he could no longer make it up the stairs and we had to set up his bed in the lounge. My dad was a strong man, but towards the end he sank fast. It was devastating to watch.

I wrote the following in haste the day he died. It is perhaps the most deeply personal moment of life I can share, but we are too private about both the tragedy and beauty of death.

On the morning of 28th June I arrived at Mum and Dad's just after 11 a.m., made a few phone calls, did a little tidying, and woke up James, who was asleep upstairs in his old bedroom, trying to stay close to Dad. We knew the end was coming. I was on the phone to a funeral director when Mum shouted we should come quickly because Dad was going.

I ran into the lounge, and it was obvious Dad was on his last legs. He was sitting up slightly in the bed, resting against my large blue cushion, with Mum sitting by his legs and James sitting on the other side of the bed. The whites of his eyes were turning yellow, and he was breathing slowly and with obvious difficulty.

We sat with him, holding him, telling him loudly that we loved him, and surrounding him with family love. He kept his eyes focused ahead, looking at a photo of Mum, James and me that was stuck on the ceiling directly in front and above him.

We asked him how he was, and he replied with just one word. 'Wonderful.'

It was the last word he ever said. We kept up a barrage of love, telling him he had been a great Dad and we would miss him forever, and then I said to him:

'It's OK. You can go now. It's all right. Don't fight it.'

Dad winced twice, as if he had a bad taste in his mouth, and then he exhaled deeply. His life flowed out of his body.

We cried, we hugged, and then I went out into the garden, cut some roses, and put them between his hands, which I folded across his chest. James rang 123 to get the right time, and we sobbed some more.

Two hours later, we started to wash Dad, and dressed him in his best pants, vest, shirt, suit and tie. James buffed his shoes with polish and we carefully dressed his body. By the time we had finished our washing and dressing, he looked serene and peaceful.

If a father has to die, it could not be more perfect than Dad's passing. He looked beautiful, restful and content.

I still think about him all the time. I just sobbed for an age when I found the note I wrote about his death buried in my computer. Grief is difficult. It *should* be difficult. Anna, my first serious girlfriend, taught me something vital. Her father died without warning, shot by a sniper. People would say to her things like: 'Don't worry, you will get over it. One day you'll wake up and feel better, and you'll face the world again.' They were trying to be caring.

'No, I won't bloody get over it!' she would say. 'And no, I won't wake up one morning and think, "Oh, everything is OK and it's fine." I don't want to! My dad is dead!'

She was adamant, and she was right, that all we can do is try to carry on. To accept. To incorporate death, grief and memory into our lives. People we love never leave us. They *should* never leave us.

Losing my father was desperately traumatic. I miss him still. I have travelled the world and experienced countless cultures but nobody has since managed to change my view that while life can certainly be beautiful and memorable, it is also tragic and desperately, desperately unfair. Why is my father no longer around to see my extraordinary son? Why is there an empty hole in my family? I know he would love Anya my wife and adore my son Jake, his grandson. But knowing it is not enough. I miss him.

We held his funeral at Acton Hill Church. The same church I had grown up in. Then we buried him in the cemetery. Two weeks later my then fiancée left the flat we shared near Ladbroke Grove in West London one morning and went off to work. I never saw her again. I called her that evening when she didn't come home. At first, she didn't pick up my call. When she finally answered, we talked briefly on the phone. She told me she had fallen in love with her boss. She mentioned the money he earned. She was sorry, but she was leaving me.

I was devastated. We communicated by text and arranged for me to be out when she went back to the flat to collect her life. But that was it. We ended.

It had been a difficult relationship, but it was another massive blow. I moped about the flat drinking heavily. Alcohol has never been my addiction, but I turned to it then, and I felt a deep trough opening in front of me.

After losing my dad and my partner, that summer in 2001 was the closest I came to slipping back to where I was as a teenager, teetering on the edge of a bridge. My highs can be very high, but my lows are often still very low. I have never forgotten the feeling of the railings under my hands. The cold metal, the rush of traffic, the lorry horn. It is always within me. Always part of me. I was a slip away from tragedy. I know I am still.

There have been many times since I was a desperate teenager when I have started to feel there was no hope, and no way out. But as I have aged, my experiences and, I think, adventures, have helped me to find comfort and solutions. As a tool for dealing with the lows I stick to my mantra. I put one foot in front of the other and take a step. I do something – anything.

For many years in my early twenties, when I was in a hurry to make my life a success, thinking achievement would keep the dogs of depression from nipping at my heels, I had 'MAFA' written on a note pinned to my desk. It stood for 'mistaking activity for achievement' and was supposed to focus my mind on being productive rather than faffing. But then I realised, in moments of darkness, when I am staring into an abyss while going through the end of relationships and depression, for me at least, activity *is* achievement. Activity or movement, any movement, rewards me, lifting me up out of the rabbit hole.

As I have aged, acceptance has also helped. Depressive thoughts will probably always be with me. The negative voices can be hushed, ignored, sometimes even laughed at. But doubtless they will always be at least an occasional background whisper. Like grief, my answer is to face them and take them with me. So many of us are taught to think of everything as black or white, happy or sad, depression or normality, high or low. Life has taught me so often that instead everything is just shades of grey. Every life and every journey shares tragedy with happiness and light with shade. Even a simple moment of joy. Because, like life, even a moment ends.

That summer of 2001 I was older and just a tiny bit wiser. I had a breadth of experience to draw on. I stopped drinking after a couple of months, started going to the gym, and reassured myself that one day I *would* find my partner for life. In the meantime, I refused to stand still. I remembered what I'd done after saving myself on the bridge and recalled the still serenity when I stood on that summit in Glencoe. I climbed out of the trough.

Looking back now, my fiancée leaving wasn't the worst thing that could have happened. The relationship was rocky. Marriage would almost certainly have ended in divorce. We wanted different lives. On our first date we met in a bar and she turned up wearing a fake fur coat and next to nothing underneath. Exciting, perhaps. But not exactly a guarantee of a stable relationship.

But that summer was still exceptionally hard. My father had

just died in my arms. My fiancée had walked out on me. My beloved grandma was also ill. In a few months she would sicken, and then she would die. I would race to West Middlesex Hospital on the edge of Brentford, driving on the wrong side of the road with my hazard lights flashing and jumping red lights, because I was so desperate to get there before she passed. But I didn't make it. In a blink of a life my brother James, mother and I lost a vital part of our tiny family. We were devastated. I felt completely bereft.

And then 9/11 happened. And I had written the only book in the world about the group behind the devastating attack.

CHAPTER TEN

9/11

My phone rang. It was James. He sounded breathless, and disbelieving.

'Si, have you got the TV on?'

'No, why? What's up?'

'Turn on the TV, quickly.'

'Why?'

'Just turn on the TV.'

I switched on. The first tower had been hit. The screen was full of smoke billowing above the New York city skyline.

There was a mention of a plane. I knew immediately who was responsible. I felt instantly sickened to the pit of my stomach. I watched for a moment, then dropped the phone, ran to the bathroom and was physically sick.

Everyone remembers what they were doing when those two planes hit the Twin Towers. What Ramzi Yousef had tried to do in 1993 bin Laden had finally accomplished. Everything I had feared had come true. My mind was racing. Sources, contacts, and meetings all flashed through my head.

Like many others I was struck by the obscenity of the scene. By the clear blue sky, and the dart of a plane cruising almost casually into the side of the building. As tragedy but also as horrific drama, it was epic and unparalleled. Although I had no relatives in the buildings or on the planes it was a devastating shock. It was what I had researched and written about. I had warned it was only a matter of time but nobody had taken any notice.

My phone began ringing off the hook before the second tower had been hit. It did not stop ringing for a year and a half.

Initially I did not answer. I realised I had written the only book on al Qaeda and I knew every news desk in the world would be clamouring for someone, *anyone*, who could talk about what had happened. But this wasn't a news event for me, it was personal. I knew people who worked in those towers, I had spoken to them after the first attack. I pictured the inside of the towers. I had spent hours walking around them, and many hours more talking with people who would have been inside when the planes hit. How many were dead? How many were stuck in the fire with no way to get free?

Finally I answered the phone and was pitched into a media feeding frenzy. I couldn't blame them; everyone was desperate to know what had happened, why it had happened, and who was responsible. Within an hour TV news crews found my supposedly secret address and were waiting outside my flat. By the end of the day a Brazilian and a Russian TV crew had each turned up at an apartment where I used to live. Meanwhile I was being shuttled between the studios of US news shows in London. Other people started calling me too, people who should have had their own experts to rely on. I answered one call to find Downing Street on the line requesting a meeting. I didn't see Tony Blair, but I did put words into his mouth.

I spoke to the government and security agencies. I said the same sort of thing to all of them. I didn't have a redacted spiel for the media and a secret one for those in power. I was a writer, and I had laid out what I knew in a book. It was all public.

Then I went to the States, where it was one studio after another, for interviews, comment and discussion. And to talk to the bosses of some of the same spooks and operators I had been following around Washington just a few years earlier. I met senior people from the White House, and had meetings, a lunch and a dinner with people who were portrayed in *The West Wing*. I advised them to go after the culprits hard but pursue terrorists as criminals wherever possible like the British had successfully in Northern Ireland, ultimately helping to bring peace to the Province. I also stressed how important it was to resolve the underlying issues that were driving people into the arms of militants, including the Arab-Israeli conflict and Western support for corrupt regimes in the Middle East. People nodded, and seemed to listen, but those seemed like intractable issues.

One of the great tragedies of the post-9/11 world is actually that the US President didn't use all of the power the crisis gave him. He could have said that not only was the US going to pursue the perpetrators to the ends of the earth, but that the attacks had also shown that the US and the Western world were too dependent on oil from the Middle East, that money from the sale of the oil was partly being used to fund terror, and that there *must* be a peace settlement in the Middle East.

Sadly they didn't listen. I remember having lunch with a close aide to President Bush in the iconic Old Ebbitt Grill restaurant, a fixture on the Washington scene since the 1850s, just steps from the White House. He was focused not on the need to resolve motivating issues, but on a plan to hunt down and kill everyone involved in the attack. I said I could understand that desire, but that if too much force was used, inevitably mistakes would be made, innocents would be killed, and more recruits would rally to al Qaeda. 'We have no choice,' he said. 'They came to us. They attacked us here. It was an act of war. We have to hunt them down. We have to kill them. We have to put their heads on sticks.'

I was twenty-nine, and I was sitting down and arguing with officials guiding and advising the leaders of the free world. Why did they want to talk to me? Few others had looked at the issue from multiple angles as I had. Few others, it turned out, had talked to militants, Pakistani experts, Western investigators and intelligence agencies. I was in an unusual position. There were certainly individual analysts who knew chapter and verse about specific issues, but very few had been required to join up the dots the way I needed to do for my investigation and book. Plus in the aftermath of 9/11 the leadership simply did not trust their own experts.

It all became very weird very quickly. Post-9/11 America was a strange and deeply wounded country. Quite frankly – understandably – people went a little crazy. More than once people became completely awed when they saw me.

'You're the guy,' said one man, 'the guy who knew, and we didn't listen.'

Two young women started crying in a restaurant. They literally just wanted to touch my arm. Another woman saw me, paled and backed away, as if I was the incarnation of her loss. The entire country was shocked, wounded and on edge. Some thought I was a prophet of some kind and that I had been able to foretell this tragedy. Others seemed to suspect I might have somehow been involved with the actual event. Profiles appeared in the press asking how this guy from Britain could have known

what was going to happen that day in New York. I didn't know
it was going to happen, but my research had led me to believe
they would attack massive targets. Past experience showed that
when the group failed once, they would try again. Nobody
should have been hugely surprised that after the 1993 bombing
the WTC became a target again. Some of the victims' groups
were asking – if I had known – why had the authorities not
done anything about it? I had several upsetting encounters with
desperately sad people who had lost loved ones in the towers
and were trying to make sense of their nightmare. As time passed
other books came out claiming I must have been an MI6 agent
because of the access I had secured in the States and the intelligence information I had been passed. I can categorically say I
was not. I had certainly been asked to work for intelligence
agencies, but that was inevitable in the world I was in.

Nobody really read my book before the attacks. Then after
the attacks it became a bestseller, one of the biggest-selling non-
fiction books in America after 2001. I made money from it, but
never a fortune. I have no island. I took only small fees from
media interviews to pay my expenses, when I could have asked
for six-figure sums. My motivation wasn't financial and it never
has been.

I kept feeling that I should have done things differently, and I
still wonder today whether if I had shouted louder, banged my
drum with more passion or intelligence, perhaps someone would
have heard me who could have done something, anything, to
prevent the tragedy. I felt deeply, intrinsically involved. I had
written a book about al Qaeda and bin Laden and it occurred
to me that because I had – other people hadn't. Maybe there was
someone out there who would have got the message across
better than I did. Were any seasoned writers unable to cut a deal

with a publisher because *The New Jackals* had already been written? What if there was someone desperate to write a book who could have made more noise than me?

Heaping further weirdness into my life, suddenly the actor and producer Kevin Spacey was in contact, wanting me to front a TV show. This was many years before he was accused of being a predator. Spacey had seen me chatting on *Good Morning America*, one of the flagship US shows. He had his own company producing movies and shows for television. It was the first time anyone had suggested I present a TV show, and I was intrigued.

Initially I went with my friend Claudia to the premiere of one of his movies in London. At the after-party we were ushered through the velvet rope into the VIP section where champagne was flowing, and then from there into the VVIP section, where a group of Hollywood A-listers were sitting more sedately and drinking cups of tea and coffee. For them this was less of a party and more of a professional requirement. Spacey welcomed me like an old friend. We hit it off. He was political and interested, angry and upset about the world. We chatted, partied, argued and debated for hours. Claudia and I were buzzing by the end of the night.

I was in the back of a cab driving to a party in Notting Hill a few weeks later with friends. Robbie Williams' song 'I Will Talk and Hollywood Will Listen' was on the radio. Robbie was singing: 'I wouldn't be so alone, If they knew my name in every home, Kevin Spacey would call on the phone', and then thirty seconds later Spacey called me on my mobile. We were all a bit freaked by that. My friend Jason said it was such a coincidence it might make him religious.

I met Spacey a couple more times before he invited me to the Century Club, a private members' club on Shaftesbury Avenue in Soho, London, to meet 'his team'. Arranged in a line were the head of his production company, his lawyer, his female publicity agent, his manager, all of them deeply tanned, dressed entirely in black, and looking fabulously wealthy and successful. They were the epitome of Hollywood power. Spacey, it turned out, wanted me to front a television talk show, an alternative to the *Charlie Rose* show, which had been a fixture on US TV for decades, and consisted of the eponymous host interviewing all manner of entertainers, writers, politicians, athletes, scientists and sports stars. Anyone remarkable, basically.

'Sounds interesting,' I said.

I signed a deal, became friends with Spacey, and when he was in London or I was in New York he would invite me along to a party, a meal or a premiere. Ultimately nothing ever came of the talk show, obviously, otherwise I would probably be on my island by now, but I still met some incredible people through him. He was friends with Hollywood royalty, the Clintons, models, sports stars. I remember after one party sitting with Chelsea Clinton and another friend outside a simple restaurant near Southwark tube station. It was dark and distinctly unglamorous, because our table was lit by the light from the back of a bus shelter.

Chelsea was a real delight; friendly, witty and relaxed, with no visible security. Even when some late-night revellers spotted her and asked for a photo, and then came back ten minutes later and jokingly but physically tried to drag her to a party, she was just bemused and amused. No Secret Service appeared. We talked about life and the world, as you do after a few too many drinks, and for some reason started chatting seriously and I mentioned a powerful article I'd read about a women's health project in the Horn of Africa. I started to explain the issue in simple terms. I had completely forgotten who I was talking to.

'Yep, there are huge health challenges in that area,' she said, deadpan. 'I've been there a few times.' She wasn't cutting me off, just tactfully reminding me of her life.

'With her mum. On Air Force One,' said her friend with a slight giggle.

'Sorry,' I said.

I met some extraordinary people through Kevin and had a string of short and superficial relationships. I swapped drunken dating tips with George Clooney, went to Naomi Campbell's birthday bash, flew in private planes to parties, misbehaved and drank far too much champagne. Attendance at those celeb events was supposed to be the pinnacle of social success, what many seem to fantasise about while flicking through glossy mags. They were fun, but also forced and hollow. When I eventually started my TV journeys I found them infinitely more memorable and thrilling than a Hollywood party.

Spacey existed in an A-list world and people flocked to him. I was walking along Piccadilly with him and a few other friends one evening and he was talking about how much he loved London because he didn't get hassled like he did in Los Angeles. At that exact moment someone leapt in front of him like a jack-in-the-box.

'It's you!' they shouted. 'It's him!' again, to no one in particular. They had a complete celebrity meltdown.

'Keep moving,' Spacey said to me. 'It's when we stop that it can get chaotic.'

But within seconds people had turned and spotted him. It was as if a veil had fallen, revealing him to them, and people began to swarm around him. We all had to jog through a department store to get away.

Obviously this was many years before Spacey was publicly

accused of inappropriate behaviour. He never behaved in an unacceptable physical way towards me or in my presence. One time a group of us had been partying and we went back to his private apartment next to the Athenaeum Hotel in Mayfair, which Spacey would book into under an assumed name so the paparazzi couldn't find him. The others left and I was alone with Spacey. We had all been drinking, and I suddenly felt that he might be working up the courage to make a pass at me, so I just laughed and left. Reading the reports now of how he groped young men has been a terrible shock. When I knew him I could tell he was attracted to women and men, but I never saw him behave like a predator. I liked him and thought of him as a friend. I only stopped seeing him much later after I started dating my future wife Anya, and felt the partying and shallower social side of life needed to end so I could focus on my relationship.

That was in the future, though. When I first met Spacey in the early 2000s I was writing, but no longer about terrorism. In the aftermath of 9/11 I was approached by a former Colombian judge who had personally investigated and waged war against Pablo Escobar, at one time the world's biggest drugs trafficker and 'narco-terrorist'. She had been the target of multiple, extraordinary assassination attempts by an army of hitmen. A surface-to-surface missile had been fired at her home inside an army base. She had helped to defeat the Medellin Cartel, but then had to flee to the United States, where a huge chunk of the federal budget for protecting foreign dignitaries was spent on keeping her alive. She remains one of the bravest, most selfless people I have ever met. I thought she had an extraordinary story that I was sure would make an exceptional and important book. I worked on it for six months. I spent a small fortune researching the story. But nobody was interested. South America was a dead zone, publishers said. They wanted me to write another book on terrorism.

I tried to turn it into a movie. A top female producer came aboard. Then the actress Selma Hayek took out an 'option' on the story, basically paying a small sum to secure the rights, and would have been perfect for the main role. But she became pregnant and the whole thing withered away.

I talked with publishers about books, and production companies about TV projects, but nothing really inspired me. One idea that came through was that I should infiltrate al Qaeda for a BBC TV series. I'd had some crazy experiences by that point, but even I thought that was a mad idea.

Then one sunny Saturday afternoon I was playing football in Kensington Gardens with a group of friends, including Danny and Tony, who I was living with in a flat near Ladbroke Grove. We sat around on the grass afterwards, sharing beers and chatting. I was saying I needed a project, something of substance, something really involving.

'Mate, you need to try something new,' said Tony, laughing. 'You need to find yourself a whole new adventure.'

I'm not the sort of person who deliberately seeks out an opportunity. I haven't plotted and planned a career. But I have been open to change and chances. From when I was at the *Sunday Times*, I've volunteered, and when people have asked me to try something new I've generally said yes.

As luck would have it a friend of a friend had been playing football and was now sitting with us listening. He was a producer-director at the BBC and we got talking, and he invited me in to the Beeb for a chat. I didn't know it then, but the BBC had already been doing some research on me. By the time I showed up at the White City complex near TV Centre, they had already decided I had potential as some kind of presenter. They had reviewed shows I'd been on, interviews conducted with me, and some of my writing.

I met up with Karen O'Connor, the head of the BBC's international documentary strands, then called *Correspondent* and *This World*. She was a producer and a commissioner. That meant she had the ability to create or pick ideas and had access to the funds to get them made. She was an impressive character, tougher than some of the FBI agents I'd met while investigating bin Laden.

We sat in her small office, surrounded by mountains of tapes, photocopying paper, maps, files, folders and chaos. The whole place looked like a fire hazard. I thought I was there to have early and probably fruitless discussions about presenting some TV shows, but gradually I realised she had already made up her mind to get me involved.

I didn't really have to do anything. There was no interview. I didn't have to take a screen test. We just talked around a few ideas, the most appealing of which was to go on a journey through Central Asia, the countries to the north of Afghanistan, a forgotten corner of the planet that fascinated both of us, and then turn it into a TV series. Karen and I looked at an atlas together. We decided there was no area of comparable size about which so little is known in the West.

We talked about the possible style of the series. We wanted it to be a journey and a real adventure, and we wanted to incorporate both the joy and the darkness of the countries I was visiting, what I called the light and the shade.

'Normally there are travel shows, and then we have current affairs documentaries focusing on specific issues,' she said. 'What we're talking about is a slightly different kind of TV programme. Something that blends elements from both.'

I loved the idea. It sounded completely different and thrilling. I remember Karen turning to me and saying with a terse smile: 'What do you think, Simon? Are you interested? It won't be easy.'

'All right,' I said, perhaps a little too casually. 'Sounds exciting. Let's do it.'

CHAPTER ELEVEN

Anthrax and Caviar

I never set out to be on TV. I didn't chase down production companies and bombard them with my show reel. I just worked on books and projects that fascinated me. And eventually, to my surprise, TV came calling.

It might be the pinnacle of popular culture, but television can also be shallow. I was an author, which gave me some credibility, but at least part of the reason I found myself with a BBC series was because I was a thirty-year-old with my own hair and teeth.

Karen had already decided I was going to travel with Will Daws, a former stand-up comedian turned producer-director with a strong reputation. He had the unenviable task of creating and shooting the programmes. We would be joined by a relative youngster called Dimitri Collingridge, an assistant producer who spoke fluent Russian and had an exotic family background that included an auntie who was a Russian baroness and possibly also a Russian spy, and a cousin called Nick Clegg who was an MEP and the future Deputy Prime Minister.

That was it. Three of us. So much for the days when a camel train of people would leave the BBC and head off on shoots carrying hampers. We were supposed to travel light, filming on small cameras in tricky countries and difficult situations.

The three of us would visit Kazakhstan, Kyrgyzstan, Uzbekistan and Tajikistan in a series that Will had wittily titled *Meet the Stans*, which would be broadcast late at night on BBC Two. It was meant to be a one-off, and even while I was helping to research our route and plans I was thinking about what I would do when I returned.

Before we left I was told I would need to complete a couple of health-and-safety courses. I raised my eyes. I had followed arms dealers and terrorists. But the BBC insisted.

'Don't worry. It's not exactly sitting in a classroom,' said Karen with a smile.

The first course was chemical weapons training, deemed necessary partly because of the developing conflict in Iraq, the ongoing fighting in Afghanistan, and some of our filming plans for Central Asia. I met Dimitri for the first time when I picked him up from home and we drove down to an army barracks south of London. We got lost three times on the way, which I thought boded badly for the epic adventure we were about to undertake. But then we were locked in a chamber wearing respirators and full nuclear, biological and chemical suits while tear gas was pumped in through openings, and I had other things to worry about.

After release I was told I had to complete something called a 'Hostile Environment Course', which was apparently mandatory for anyone from the BBC heading to countries deemed excessively tricky. The course was a six-day residential at Easthampstead Park in Berkshire, a council-run conference centre in a grand, sprawling Victorian mansion.

The joining instructions were all very military. 'This is not a hotel. Report by 0800 hours. We have attempted to identify representative tasks for operational deployments to Hostile Environments,' said a flurry of emails. 'You will need to be able to run 100m in body armour and helmet without stopping, drag a similar size/weight casualty 30m ...'

On arrival we were drilled by ex-special forces soldiers who taught us how to find hard cover if bullets started flying.

'Don't believe the rubbish you see in films,' said one officer. 'A car door is like a paper bag to a Kalashnikov bullet. You need to get behind the engine block, a tree trunk, a thick wall, or solid ground.' They explained how to identify small-arms fire and large-calibre weapons. They showed us what to do if we found ourselves in a live minefield, were kidnapped, or if we were caught up in a demonstration that turned into a riot.

We were a mixed group. A few of those on the course were working on children's TV shows or an internet project and were going somewhere risky only briefly. Others were veterans of wars and riots, stationed in the Middle East or sub-Saharan Africa, and had only returned to the UK briefly for the course. It turned out that completing the course only provided certification for travel to tricky places for three years. Some people had done the course several times. I've since earned stripes by doing it five times.

Other groups were using the conference centre at the same time. On the second day we were told to walk across the manicured lawn at the back of the mansion and react appropriately to anything we discovered. As we strolled across the grass, certain something awful was going to happen, a gunman in camouflage and a balaclava ran out from among the trees ahead of us carrying a Kalashnikov. He paused, lifted the assault rifle to his waist, opened fire on us with a full clip of blanks, and we all scattered like frightened deer.

As I was running zig-zag towards a fallen tree I glanced up at the mansion. The team from IBM's Southern England Sales

Conference were milling around the windows during their tea break. As the gunman changed magazines and opened fire again, I could see their jaws dropping at the scene of horror outside. God knows what the guests at the Berkshire Wedding Fair, which was taking place in another wing of the centre, must have thought. People have got completely carried away on the courses. One senior BBC member who did it leapt over a fallen tree, cracked two ribs and had to be taken to hospital. It was all so surreal I thought it ripe for comedy. I'm amazed nobody has turned it into a sitcom.

After we dusted ourselves down, it was on to the medical side of the course, which was gruesome but fascinating. First we would have the proverbial scared out of us with details and images of bullets travelling through human flesh. Then combat medics showed us how to treat battlefield injuries.

'Get your hands in there and get some compression on the wound,' they'd say enthusiastically. 'I want to see your fingers covered in fake blood.'

We were shown how to turn off the blood supply to the hands by pressing hard into the soft flesh of the upper inner arm, and how and where to press into the groin to halt catastrophic bleeding in a foot, either after someone has stepped on a land-mine or been in a car crash. But it also applies if you have injured yourself in the kitchen or cut the top off your finger like I did as a child. It works immediately. We practised on each other, with one person monitoring the pulse in their wrist, and then another turning off their blood supply. Why aren't such basic life skills taught in schools?

The fact we were trained by highly skilled and experienced soldiers made a huge difference. They had shocking stories but also practical suggestions. I learned you can pack bullet wounds with tampons in an emergency, and use a crisp packet and some gaffer tape to save the life of someone with a serious chest wound.

Then we had detailed paramedic lessons from Terry, a serving firefighter, who described in gory but sobering detail the road traffic accidents he had attended around Southampton. 'Every time I go to a crash I want to see a friction burn mark across the chest,' said Terry, 'because that means someone was wearing their seat belt. Even in a war zone your life is most at risk from a car crash. You must always, always wear a seat belt.' It was advice I took to heart.

We trotted outside and Terry walked us towards some old tennis courts in the woods. Smoke was rising from two cars that had been arranged as if they had been in a pile-up. A group of instructors were scattered in and around the wreckage, wearing make-up and wounds to simulate a mini-disaster. They had fake wounds hidden under their clothing which spurted blood. We had to assess the situation, triage the victims and treat them as best we could. It felt surprisingly real and the whole course was magnificently organised. If only school had been as dramatically interesting. If you get a chance, sign up for a course or pay to go on one.

The whole week culminated in our entire group being driven to an army training centre an hour away and introduced to the fake country of 'Hostalia', where countless disasters befell us. We had to talk our way past fake road blocks, and stop apparently drunk pro-government militia gunmen in camo uniforms from taking away the female members of our group. We drove along a track and there was a huge explosion off to the side. A woman dressed a little too realistically like a Balkan peasant staggered out of the bushes bleeding heavily and clutching her intestines.

We dragged her into the back of our Land Rover while she fitted and thrashed around, and then she bit into blood capsules and began bleeding from her mouth. I was quite taken aback by how lifelike it all felt. We later discovered she had been acting on *Casualty* that morning and had then raced down to the training centre, only stopping to buy a bucket of pig guts on the way.

Armed government soldiers stopped us further along the track, took the peasant away and shot her. We fled on foot through the trees and arrived in a full-size village where we found a rebel base and a moustachioed commander. He was just starting to tell us about life in Hostalia when a platoon of black-clad government soldiers mounted a full-on assault with mortars and small-arms fire.

Well, I tell you, it was all very dramatic, and not a little exciting. The day finished with an artillery strike on a United Nations compound and the resulting carnage we had to deal with: missing limbs, endless screaming and pints of fake blood.

By the time Dimitri and I drove back to London we felt bonded and ready for anything. Ten miles from the M25 we saw an accident on the other side of the road and immediately went into a response mode, remembering our training and racing to the scene. It was only when we got close that Dimitri pointed out there were two ambulance crews at the scene already and they would probably be able to handle the situation without us.

We landed at Almaty airport in Kazakhstan at three o'clock in the morning to start the journey around Central Asia. It was absolute madness. Even at that time, the arrivals hall was heaving and we had to fight our way through a scrum of people. Somehow our guide Bayan Orumbayeva was waiting to meet us airside to help us through customs and immigration. Bayan was a tiny, fragile bird of a person, with a warm heart but steel for bones. She could persuade anyone to do anything. Bayan had a way about her that people trusted. I have met hundreds of guides and 'fixers' in the years since, but Bayan remains my benchmark. She was exceptional.

Outside the airport she ushered us into a van driven by Marat, a former Soviet police captain who happened to have won the Kazakh version of *Who Wants To Be a Millionaire*, and we drove to our hotel. I had only just closed my door to catch a few hours' sleep when two prostitutes with supermodel looks tried to push their way into my room.

I politely declined their offer, wedged the door closed and allowed myself a moment to consider the journey. For weeks I had been reading books on the country, poring over maps and wading through masses of photos. Our rough plan was to travel from Almaty up to the far north-west of Kazakhstan, by the Russian border, then travel by train, helicopter, horse and four-wheel drive across the vast Kazakh steppes towards the Chinese border, then south through Kyrgyzstan and Tajikistan to the Afghan border, and west through Uzbekistan to the ancient Silk Road cities of Bukhara and Samarkand. Finally, we were on the ground. We were starting the journey. I was filled with an incredible sense of possibility and excitement.

On the flight over we had talked about how we were going to work together. This was my first outing as a presenter in front of a camera, but nobody had discussed what I should actually *do* in any detail.

'Without wishing to sound like a total novice,' I asked Will, 'how do you think I should play this?'

'You need to just be yourself,' said Will. 'We're going to be filming for weeks. Nobody could pretend to be something they're not for that length of time. So don't play it at all. Don't overthink it.'

That sounded like a good idea, but I glanced at Dimitri as if seeking confirmation. He nodded. 'Will's right. You have natural empathy. You're interested in people, and you're enthusiastic without being over the top. You've got a way of saying things that's understated and that ought to work well. Just go with the flow and don't try to be something you're not.'

I thought about the simplicity of what they were suggesting. It made sense. It's true I felt and still feel a strong sense of empathy with others. I'm interested in people. If I put myself on the couch doubtless I could trace it back to childhood, perhaps to counselling for teenage depression and even the talks I heard at church as a boy. Back then I had been listening remotely to stories from places I never imagined I would ever visit. Now it was the early 2000s and I was sitting on a plane at the beginning of what I hoped would be an incredible adventure, exploring a region that rarely featured on TV. I was delighted, elated.

If the style of my programmes was to be inspired by anyone else, I thought it had to be, of course, the great Michael Palin. Why not try to follow someone declared a national treasure? I watched *Around the World in 80 Days* when it was on the TV and it was a revelation. Michael showed respect to everyone he met along the way, treating them like fellow humans. Gone was the patronising amusement and contempt for local customs, food and traditions that TV travellers displayed before him.

On an old dhow in the Indian Ocean Michael sat with the Indian crew and shared the headphones of his Walkman. He sat down next to them. Not above them, but shoulder to shoulder, with no airs and graces, no Englishman and Johnny Foreigner. A shared seat, shared music; and then the chap next to him nodding his head to Bruce Springsteen. Michael never let anyone's situation define them. He started to break down barriers and helped a generation of viewers dismiss the stereotypes that had plagued our view of other cultures. In a smaller way, a much smaller way, I decided I would attempt to do the same.

I woke in Almaty to a city shrouded in grey. It wasn't depressing, nothing could have depressed me that morning, it was just a blanket of rain. Will put a radio microphone on me linked to his camera, I tucked it under my shirt, then we piled into the van and drove through the streets of Kazakhstan's largest city, and until 1997 the capital. All around us were chilly, grey concrete blocks. Sometimes it was hard to tell the factories apart from the flats. It all felt very Soviet. Bayan saw me staring at a grim factory and smiled.

'It will change, but slowly,' she said. 'I really hope this programme will be a pathway for future tourists.'

I nodded to her, but it was hard to be enthusiastic. The place looked bleak, and our first destination was definitely no local beauty spot.

Bayan took us to a complex of buildings surrounded by a six-foot wall with barbed wire scrolled across the top. It was an old biological weapons factory that had been converted to a research centre for the bubonic plague. Why were we going there? When the Soviet Union collapsed many military installations lost all their funding. Weapons were going missing. It was a huge issue in Central Asia and something we wanted to incorporate into the programmes.

As we drove the camera was already rolling. This was it. We were filming. I made a few general comments and said whatever came into my head, Will filmed, and it all felt very natural. We drove through the gates of the research centre and the first thing that struck me was the lack of security. There were just a couple of guards who waved us through with barely a check on our credentials; no search of the vehicle and no sniffer dogs. Beyond the gate a series of tarmac roadways and paths drifted like tributaries through patches of grass littered with leafless trees. Marat parked outside a faded pinkish building, we got out, and Will readied the camera.

At that moment it could all have gone horribly wrong. Some people who are relaxed off camera go to pieces when a camera is turned directly on them and the recording light goes red. I've seen it myself regularly when filming in the years since. Will had told me to be myself when talking to the camera, but he had no idea if I would start to speak in a staccato tone as if I were on some live link on the ten o'clock news, or whether I would just freeze like a rabbit caught in headlights.

I felt confident I wouldn't stiffen, but I stood watching Will, waiting for him to tell us what should happen next. He was the experienced director, after all. But he didn't say anything, he just turned the lens on me. I waited for him to lead us in, but he said nothing. And then it struck me, one of those moments when a switch just flips in your head. *Ah. So this is how it's going to be. I need to lead, and the camera will follow.*

I was a moment that set the pattern for the style I have tried to employ on my travelogues ever since: no script, no rehearsal, no lead-in, no real recce where a member of the production team goes out in advance and works out where I am going to stand and where the camera will sit on a tripod. From those first frames most of my programmes have been filmed in a relaxed, off-the-cuff style. I walk into situations with the camera rolling and take each moment as I find it. This might not sound fundamental, but many TV programmes are carefully plotted, planned and scripted in advance. Personally, I was never hugely keen on the more traditional TV documentary style where a camera is already set up in a room on a tripod with floodlights burning away, and the presenter walks in and looks around in surprise as if it is the first time they have seen the place. To me at least, those entrances can look just a little fake. So instead I try to make sure the camera and viewer are following me into situations, as realistically as possible.

Sometimes in the years since I have taken the idea of the camera following me to extremes. When I used a home-made zip wire to cross illegally from a remote area of India into a dangerous and virtually unknown corner of Burma while travelling around the Tropic of Cancer, on one of my most dangerous adventures, the team, completely understandably, wanted to send a camera ahead of me so they could capture me arriving on the other bank of the river inside Burma. We had the briefest of barneys about it at the time. I felt I needed to lead from the front and be the first across.

There will always be elements of creation and structuring in making a TV programme, but I was keen to make shows that are as natural as possible, and to knock on someone's door, church or caravan, meet someone on camera for the first time and capture a genuine moment of surprise, as they wipe their hands on a tea towel or something, and then launch naturally into conversation. I craved that sort of authentic moment and interaction, and I have been incredibly lucky to work with cameramen and crews who have been prepared to film in that style. It might not sound much, but actually it's a real challenge for a cameraman to follow me from daylight outside to relative darkness inside a hut or a house. As I walk through a door they usually have to flip through myriad settings so it's not too light outside or pitch-black on the film when inside. Very few cameramen are entirely happy to do that without at least checking the light inside first because of the risk that the resulting footage might look slightly less than perfect. It can be a challenge for the team, certainly, and things can go wrong, of course, but the result, I hope, is the viewer gets a sense of a natural interaction and a genuine meeting.

The simple style of most of my programmes was set from that moment outside the plague research centre in Kazakhstan. Ultimately it was Will who made it easy. He just looked out at me from behind the camera, smiled and nodded in the direction of the research centre door. 'Go on then,' he seemed to say. It was the best instruction I ever had. I looked directly down the lens, said simply, 'C'mon then, let's go,' and started walking towards the building.

We were welcomed into the plague research centre and shown around by a scientist who led us to a room where the only furnishings were a chipped parquet floor and a selection of old fridges. This was where the researchers kept their store of deadly diseases. Security was woefully inadequate, and the door to the main stock of biological nightmares was secured with a wax seal. So although they would struggle to stop intruders, at least scientists would know if stocks had been stolen after a break-in.

I could see labels on the fridges but the only one I recognised was anthrax. The rest seemed to be differing strains of the plague. The lead scientist unlocked a basic padlock securing the anthrax and took out one of four canisters. As soon as she opened the canister I went to point at it with my finger.

'No, no,' she said, batting my hand away from the vials of deadly toxin.

'Did you just try to touch the anthrax, Simon?' said Will from behind the camera.

Almost every holiday as a child was spent on beaches in Blighty. I didn't get on a plane until I started working.

Just some of what my poor brother James had to put up with.

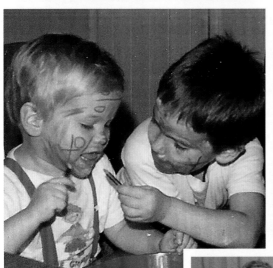

Some classic seventies looks. I'm on Dad's lap, with my Grandma Lucy on the left, Uncles Angelo and Ian on the sofa, with James on Ian's lap, and my Grandma Delsie on the right.

Early selfie!

Dad was a champion tennis player as a lad and nearly made it to Wimbledon. Even into his sixties he was beating players more than twenty years younger than him.

Happy times. Dad was a teacher in a tough comp and Mum worked part-time in a local hospital. A treat for us all was Sunday lunch at Makro Cash & Carry on a nearby industrial estate.

James and I next to the river in Wareham, Dorset, near Studland Beach, where we went year after year on holiday.

First job. Delivering what felt like half a ton of *Leader* freebie newspapers. 4 hours work for less than £2.

Where are we going? Cheap childcare in the 1970s.

Late teens. Just starting to emerge from the darkest period of my life. I had left school with no real qualifications or hope and felt like I had no chance in life. Late one night I found myself teetering on the edge of a bridge.

It's Herman Munster, but with more hair. Staying in a chintzy B&B for a family wedding.

In my twenties out with good pals Maurice, left, and Mike, centre. Many a great night, some I can remember.

I had a difficult time in my teens, but I will always be grateful that James and I were eventually reconciled with our dad.

Dad nearing the end. He passed away in our arms, surrounded by our love.

In New York researching my first book, about the attack on the World Trade Center in 1993. The Twin Towers are looming in the mist behind me.

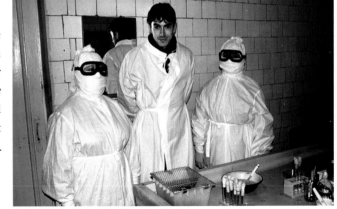

Day one of filming for the BBC, in a plague research centre in Kazakhstan for my first TV series *Meet the Stans*. It was a bizarre and eye-opening journey, right from the beginning.

With my guide Shahida Tulaganova and some Teletubbies in Uzbekistan. Dipsy wasn't entirely convincing when he said life had improved since Soviet times.

One of my favourite views from an early trip. This is the Kalon minaret in Bukhara, Uzbekistan, built in 1187. Genghis Khan spared it from destruction when he rampaged through the city, enabling later rulers to execute victims and criminals by throwing them off the top.

With a team of local guards in Mogadishu, Somalia, filming for my series *Places That Don't Exist*. The city was completely lawless, and we went to the local market and I bought a Somali diplomatic passport in my own name and with my own photo from a man called Mr Big Beard. Still one of my strangest travel souvenirs.

The brilliant Kazakh Beatles tribute band in Kazakhstan, during a beery chat late one night while filming *Meet the Stans*. The chance to meet incredible and inspiring people like the Beatles is what keeps me travelling.

With Shahida Tulaganova, Iain Overton and Will Daws, who all worked tirelessly creating the *Places That Don't Exist* series, as we won a One World Broadcasting Trust Award for 'an outstanding contribution to greater world understanding'. We all felt we could retire happy.

A few months after meeting Anya, avoiding the crowds in Prague.

I love this photo of my lad Jake and I, holding back the tide together in our tiny fort on holiday in Greece.

The scientist replaced the vial again and shook her head at me. 'We have to be careful, very, very careful.'

But then as she went to put them away she accidentally whacked the fragile glass vials. One of her colleagues gasped in fear. Everybody in the room froze. Nobody dared to breathe. For what felt like an age they rattled like a set of maracas. I thought they were going to fall and shatter on the floor. Fortunately, they settled, she put them away, and nothing was broken and no bacterium was released. But it was a minor moment of horror. If one of those vials had smashed I might have had a very short-lived television career.

Seeing the contents of the cabinets made the lack of security outside even more shocking. This was 2003. Afghanistan, where groups like al Qaeda were training terrorists, was to the south. Other militant groups were springing up in neighbouring Kyrgyzstan and Uzbekistan. It didn't take much imagination to see what kind of mayhem a determined group could create if they made a concerted effort to break inside.

Even if the facility had better security, the director of the institute was not exactly reassuring about the risk of determined terrorists obtaining biological weapons.

'If I need to get a virus, as a scientist I can infect myself, then go outside, infect other people with the virus and then I can cure myself,' he said. 'I could do this if I was paid enough.'

He assured me it wasn't something he would do, of course, but I couldn't help thinking it was an attractive exit for a militant with designs on becoming a martyr.

By the end of the first day of filming I was buzzing with everything we had seen. I knew this was exactly where I wanted to be. The journey was already shaping up to be an unbelievable experience. On day one we had been somewhere bizarre, thrilling and frightening. The journey was already a privilege and responsibility rolled into one. It felt like this was what I had been looking for all my life. It was adventure with purpose, travel with meaning.

From the start we thought that by blending issues into the adventure, mixing the light and the shade, we might encourage people to watch the shows who would normally switch off or change channels when something about Central Asia came on the TV. Turning it into a travelogue might just be a way of getting forgotten stories and little-known regions of the planet onto TV. Perhaps it was my chance to make just a bit of a difference, or at least put a gentle ripple across a pond.

We flew north-west to an oil field that seemed to hint at the future. US firms were already working there, as were companies from the UK, Canada, Russia and China. With huge reserves in the ground they had all bought leases as Kazakhstan threw off the shackles of Soviet rule. The Stans are home to some of the largest untapped energy reserves in the world, and the foreign firms were all battling for drilling rights to exploit oil reserves in a replay of the nineteenth-century 'Great Game'. Optimistic estimates suggested the reserves could rival those of the Gulf States. It was thought oil from Central Asia could reduce Western dependence on oil from the Middle East and help to change the global balance of power.

Before there was oil, there was caviar. A few hundred miles south we were shown a vast, ice-encrusted lake where fish used to swim in huge numbers, and caviar was harvested, before the Soviets over-fished the prehistoric sturgeon that produce it. When I was there the only caviar produced was farmed. Abish Beckeshev, a Kazakh caviar expert (he was once head of the department for the central scientific research institute on sturgeon) showed me the lake and then took me back to his humble flat to meet his wife, who was also one of the world's leading caviar specialists. Abish produced an enormous block from their freezer.

'This is the finest caviar in the world,' he said proudly.

He carved a chunk off the side as if it was meat loaf and spread the jet-black pearls on thick bread. The only caviar I had eaten before was cheap and definitely not cheerful. I dutifully put a slice into my mouth, and my eyes widened in shock. Now I knew what all the fuss was about. It was rich, creamy, with a tang of the sea, and completely delicious.

I gorged on slice after slice, then eventually noticed Abish was just eating bread and sipping vodka and tea.

'I have been eating caviar for decades,' he said. 'I am actually quite sick of caviar.'

There was something a little melancholic about Abish that was echoed in Bayan. It felt like a throwback to the time when Kazakhs were under the Soviet yoke, and emotion and enthusiasm could be interpreted as signs of indolence or weakness. She might have been world-weary, but Bayan was an amazing guide. A day or two later we missed our train from the tiny town of Aktobe close to the Russian border after it left an hour earlier than scheduled. The next wasn't due for days, but Bayan went to the home of the local mayor late one evening and hammered on the door. His wife answered wearing a dressing gown and nightdress, and then the mayor appeared on the stairs in his pyjamas. With a combination of guile and charm, Bayan persuaded or forced the mayor to drive to the train station with her, still wearing pyjamas under his coat, where he rang the central despatch for the region and ordered them to stop a train at the station in the morning to pick us up.

It worked. The following morning, waking to snow on the ground, we made it to the station early, and we boarded a train that did not feature on a timetable. I stowed bags then hung out of the window as we left the town behind and rolled through a flat, ice- and snow-bound landscape that stretched to the horizon in every direction like an unending blanket. We were travelling across the vast Central Asian steppe, across which the Mongols and the equally terrifying Scythians had once roared. Now for mile after mile there was nothing to see but telephone poles. It was hard not to romanticise the scale and the distance. It felt like we were on the edge of the known world; in an area so vast and remote almost anything was possible.

I moved through the carriages, where people slept on bunks and slumped in chairs on either side of compartments. The train would roll for days across the enormous interior of the former Soviet Union. We chatted to a few of our fellow travellers and discovered many were ethnic Russians on their way to visit relatives in Moscow.

I talked to one elderly lady who was resting on a bunk with a pillow. I asked how life had changed since independence and the collapse of the Soviet Union. She told me that things were all right, at least at that moment.

'Immediately after independence there was nothing. But now there is food, there are clothes, this means a lot for us,' she smiled wanly. 'Look, I survived the Second World War, now that was a difficult time.'

Two policemen on the train came to check on us and then stopped to chat. Ethnic Kazakhs, they were there to protect the country's borders from drug smugglers and illegal immigrants. Kazakhstan was by far the wealthiest of the four 'Stans' and the policemen told us everyone wanted to live there.

One of the policemen was keen to know what I thought of Central Asia. I stumbled a reply, unsure how to tell them I was already finding Central Asia wonderful and eccentric, like a lost world. So instead we swapped stories about growing up on opposite sides of the Iron Curtain.

I explained that for decades we had been told the Soviet Union was about to invade Europe, and that created a sense of fear and suspicion. They nodded in understanding and said they had felt the same on their side. Only when borders are open can reality dawn, said one of them. One of them pulled out his handgun to show it to me, I put my hands up, and we all had a little laugh. It was a brief but sweet little encounter. Clearly things were changing in Central Asia.

Outside the window the landscape never faltered. The view for hours was open, rolling plains. Kazakhstan is the size of Western Europe, with only a quarter of the population of the UK. I saw only the occasional herd of cattle and horses and an odd glimpse of the nomads who tend them. But it was a hypnotically beautiful journey.

Beyond the steppe and the train we rejoined Marat and his van and headed south-west until we found ourselves driving across a sandy desert. Not far from the border with Uzbekistan, we were actually on the bed of what had once been the Aral Sea. The further we went the more surreal the experience became. Camels wandered past the hulks of dozens of rusting ships trapped and then abandoned when the water drained away.

Spreading as far as the eye could see, the land seemed cast in a desperate beauty. I asked Marat to pull over so we could get out and take a closer look at the ghost-like shipwrecks. The Aral was once the fourth largest inland sea in the world. Back in the

1960s Soviet planners pumped chemicals into the sea and then deliberately diverted rivers to irrigate thirsty cotton fields. What resulted was nothing short of environmental disaster. The sea shrank to half its size. When I visited, it was fifty miles away. Parched, contaminated sand blew over villages and sickened unemployed fishermen.

'I remember these ships crossing and the whole thing was full of life,' said Bayan, sobbing gently at her own memory of glistening waters. She was dazed by what we found. 'The whole thing is dead . . . just like being among ghosts.'

But the damage was not limited to the landscape. People were suffering physically. Appalling dust storms were ripping through villages around the old Sea, and the chemical residues in the sand were causing eye infections, stunted growth, reduced fertility, lung and respiratory problems and worse. One investigation discovered that rates of liver cancer doubled between 1981 and 1991. Another study found that by the end of the 1990s infant mortality in the area was much higher than in the rest of Uzbekistan and more than double the rate in Russia. It felt to me like the people had been left, like the boats, just to rot.

We followed one huge camel to a worn-looking village which used to nestle right by the sea. The place looked beaten, the buildings old, flaked and rotten. Villagers who used to catch five or six hundred tons of fish a year were now breeding camels to survive in a desert.

'The people here believe that water will come back,' said Bayan. Neither of us was hopeful. We were visiting a graveyard. For me the wasteland of the Aral Sea was a dramatic example of the power of our species to alter an entire landscape.

Early on in my TV travels, in Kazakhstan and elsewhere in

Central Asia, I realised I was seeing the world at a time of incredible change, and that we are transforming our planet. Nobody should be in any doubt about that. In the years since, one of my biggest challenges has been trying to show the reality of what's happening to our world. Even today I don't think we quite understand the full extent of what we as a species are doing to the planet. For anyone who doubts the reality of climate change, consider this: how could 7 billion extraordinary humans *not* be having an impact on the climate? Since standing on that empty seabed I have been in dozens of situations around the world where remote and indigenous people have told me, unprompted, their world is changing.

In Kenya people from the Maasai community have warned me that the climate in their region is becoming more extreme, with more intense storms and longer droughts. They wondered how much longer they would be able to roam and herd.

In the mountains of Colombia I have stayed with an indigenous people called the Kogi, who live in huts and wear white robes. Men carry gourds which they stand around coating with their saliva, almost as we would twiddle our thumbs. They are a deeply spiritual people who are the most intact surviving civilisation of the Americas pre-Columbus, and are said to be the inspiration for the peaceful folk in the movie *Avatar*.

The Kogi have survived invasion by the Spanish, by missionaries, and by drug cartels. They are extremely wary of the outside world. But they agreed to let me and a small BBC team visit because they are seeing their patch of the planet changing: mountain caps are melting, rivers have stopped running, there are new diseases, fewer insects, and the climate in their mountains is more unpredictable. The Kogi are very isolated, but they think of themselves as stewards of the Earth. They believe they are 'Big Brother', we – the rest of humanity – are 'Little Brother', and they are horrified by what we are doing to the world. They told me they have tried to warn us we are destroying our home, but Little Brother isn't listening. Whether it's in Africa, Asia or the Americas, remote people who don't read the *New Scientist* know that something terrible is happening. The climate is changing, and they are frightened.

On the bed of the Aral Sea in Kazakhstan the situation was stark. We left the area feeling very solemn, a feeling accentuated when we came upon an abandoned Soviet missile testing site nearby. It looked like the set of an apocalyptic movie. There were torn-down fences, broken concrete buildings and a few villagers scavenging for scrap iron among the ruins, most of which had already been stripped away. What with that and the Aral Sea, it felt as if Kazakhstan had been invaded, pillaged and abandoned. Despite the oil reserves in the ground, I wondered what the future would bring.

We drove on, and Bayan began to open up. We passed through the remote town where she'd grown up. She told me her parents had been intellectuals banished to the wilds of Kazakhstan by Stalin, along with scientists, writers and musicians from across the Soviet Union. She had grown up surrounded by artists. As a child she'd been taught to play the piano by the aristocratic daughter of the former Russian governor. We popped into a store to buy some meat and cheese for lunch and one of the middle-aged women started flapping around trying to get some-one else from the store at the back.

'What's going on?' I asked Dimitri, who could hear what was being said.

A stunning, tall, young woman appeared at the back of the

store and strutted down the aisle as if she was on a catwalk. She was wearing a white baker's outfit. The middle-aged woman was fussing around her and talking loudly.

'Ah,' said Dimitri. 'Bit weird. They think we might be model scouts.'

Apparently the young lass was descended from aristocracy, and the middle-aged woman was telling her we might be able to rescue her from the town. She looked gutted when we said we were making a TV show and there were no spare seats in the van.

An hour or two further down the road and for the fourth time that day we suffered a puncture. We were all out of spares. It was almost dark and freezing, but we were told by passing drivers that a police checkpoint was a brisk walk ahead. It was our only hope, and we walked through the darkness until the Kazakh traffic police took pity on us and, thanks to Bayan's persuasive charm, gave us a ride onwards to the town of Kyzylorda, a sleepy provincial capital in the Kyzyl-Kum Desert.

By the time we arrived at a hotel in the town it was 2 a.m., but we had rooms and a special treat waiting up for us. Bayan had arranged for us to meet the Kazakh Beatles, a tribute band who suffered years of state harassment during Communist rule. Striking up on electric guitars and a bass, and with the percussive note of a snare drum, they seemed to know every line, chord and drumbeat of every song, and they played with raw passion.

It was extraordinary to see Western icons in a small hotel in the wilds of Kazakhstan. After they worked their way through the classics we sat in the back of the restaurant, cracked open beer and bottles of vodka, and talked late into the night with Bayan and Dimitri translating. Each of them seemed to adopt the mannerisms of the Beatle they mimicked on stage. They didn't speak much English but every now and again they would inject the conversation with a lyric from their repertoire of songs.

Formed in the darkest days of Soviet oppression, 'Paul' told me he had found an old bootleg tape of the Fab Four that had been smuggled into the country and wound its way to the middle of nowhere, having been passed from hand to hand and no doubt copied a thousand times. The music blew him away. It was like nothing he had heard before, because the only music allowed back then needed to be cleared by the authorities.

It was hard for me to imagine. I grew up with Radio One and vinyl, tape decks and then CDs. I used to record *Top of the Pops* onto a tape player held up to the TV, shushing my family when they dared to enter the room. That was all alien to the Kazakhs. When they came across that Beatles tape they were living in a cardboard box of a world where what they could watch and listen to was carefully monitored. I heard it again and again in the former Soviet Union: there had been no colour in life, no taste in the food, and the music was usually soulless and chosen by the government. For those guys discovering that old Beatles tape had totally inspired them. Long before they learned to play, the music transported them to a different reality.

That night in Kyzylorda was exhaustingly inspiring. It was a powerful demonstration to me of the wonder of travel, and the joy to be had from a strange encounter. One by one the Beatles told us how music had changed their world. They had been determined to get hold of instruments and learn the songs and perform for themselves. But they were living in the Soviet Union. For the next few years they managed to keep their love of the real Beatles both secret and alive, even when there was no outlet for their passion. They were not living in Moscow or St

Petersburg, where occasional musical dissent was allowed; they were living in a largely closed area of the Soviet Union that was so remote it was used for nuclear tests and missile launches. In Kyzylorda, local scrutiny was much more obvious and clinical than in one of the cities. Yet, somehow, those four Beatles managed to maintain their secret until the walls came tumbling down.

I was tired, but the conversation was fascinating. They told me music was how they were able to stay mentally and emotionally alive, until their world opened up and they could play the songs without fear of being discovered by the state. They poured out their hearts and shared their lives with us that night. We drank and drank and then they played us another couple of songs before we finally went to bed. I didn't find it easy to sleep, and it wasn't just me who was affected. All of us were deeply moved by their story.

A couple of months later, after we'd flown home, Will pulled every string possible and managed to persuade a Kazakh airline to fly the group to the UK so they could play two gigs at the Beatle Week Festival in Liverpool. They actually played at the Cavern, the legendary spot where the Beatles first came to the attention of an adoring public. Their proudest souvenir? They had their photo taken crossing Abbey Road.

CHAPTER TWELVE

Polo with the Corpse of a Headless Goat

We rolled out of Kyzylorda with sore heads, and trailed through one broken town after another in a Soviet-era Lada, on a dirt road and across rivers and waterways on makeshift bridges constructed from planks that appeared to have nothing but hope holding them together. On and on we travelled until finally we came to an isolated village where we found people dressed in traditional clothing and a large carpet laid on the ground outside a yurt. Bayan explained she had wanted us to see a traditional baby-naming ceremony, a very special occasion for semi-nomadic Kazakhs. The child himself looked none too pleased. He was bawling his head off.

Beyond the houses, I could see more of the traditional yurts and dozens of small horses saddled and waiting on a patch of open ground. I asked Bayan what was going on.

'It is called *kokpar*.'

'And what is *kokpar*?'

'Ha! You will find out, Simon. Just you wait.'

I was mystified, but before I could quiz her further the family of the toddler asked Bayan if I would do the honour of naming their child.

'Really?' I said. 'Are they absolutely sure?'

'Yes, yes,' said Bayan. 'I think they have had some alcohol, but they are sincere, and your role is just ceremonial, don't worry.'

It was a little absurd. They didn't know me but were affording me a huge honour. I was discovering the power of travelling with a camera crew. Even in a remote corner of Kazakhstan being filmed by the BBC makes people think I must be important. It gifts privilege and access. Alcohol was thrust into my hand, by the villagers rather than by my team, and I tried to play to the gallery by giving a short but still faintly ludicrous and theatrical speech in which I thanked the people of Kazakhstan for their welcome, hospitality, history, culture, and possibly their weather, transport system and caviar as well. There was a surprising amount of applause, perhaps because the Kazakhs were used to ordeals, and I waved a scarf around as instructed and proclaimed the name of the baby, who continued to scream through the entire experience.

Then we had a few more drinks and waited for the mysterious *kokpar* to appear, or begin, or descend – it was initially a bit unclear. Meanwhile neighbouring villages had heard we were filming, and a large crowd began to gather. They treated us like a royal visit.

Finally Bayan explained the *kokpar*. It was a contest between two teams of men on horses (like polo without the champagne) where they would fight over the headless corpse of a goat. When I first heard that last bit I was sure something had got lost in translation.

'Sorry?' I said to Bayan. 'The corpse of a headless goat?'

Bayan explained that *kokpar* is as old as Kazakhstan. Some think it was used by the Mongol hordes to train their warriors in the finer techniques of horse warfare. Goats are beheaded, disembowelled and soaked in water for a day or two to toughen them up.

I am not making this up.

Then Bayan explained there was another jolly game called

the *Kyz-Kuu*, which mercifully we would not be involved with because it was the wrong time of year. *Kyz-Kuu* is basically a violent form of kiss chase on horseback. A woman sets off on a galloping steed, and then a moment later a group of men on horseback gallop after her. The aim is to catch the girl and give her a kiss while both are still on horseback and at full gallop. A man who tries to catch and kiss her but fails can then be horse-whipped by her all the way back to where they began.

Again, I am not making this up.

Despite being a hopeless horseman, I was invited to play *kokpar*. I have had bad experiences with horses. Because I'm six feet three I am usually given huge and powerful beasts called Storm, Thunder, or Lightning, who rarely do anything I ask, and instead either stand around munching daisies, or race off through trees in an attempt to behead their rider.

Fortunately, my *kokpar* horse was the size of a tough pony. I leapt into the saddle. The other players were delighted. One of the men on the opposite team had the goat partly tucked under his leg just in front of me. The corpse had already been trampled under hooves and dragged around the field. It was in a desperate and bloodied state. But I didn't want to insult my hosts by pointing this out. So I grabbed the body of the goat and tried to take off across the field. My skittish horse seemed about as sure of me as I was of him and kept threatening to buck me off. I managed to stay in the saddle long enough for honour to be satisfied, and for Will to capture a little of the antics on camera. It was an experience that still today ranks among the most bizarre of my life.

As the sun set I was the guest of honour at the village dinner in a huge traditional Kazakh yurt. It was lit by candles inside and looked completely ethereal, like walking into an elvish kingdom in *Lord of the Rings*, or travelling back in time to a feast on the eve of a medieval battle. I wasn't comfortable, but it was nothing to do with the food or hospitality. The problem was my hands. The only way I'd been able to hold the headless goat and keep it close to my saddle was to grip it by its rancid and slippery testicles. There was nowhere to wash my hands before I ate, and the only cutlery was fingers.

I woke in the morning with a dose of food poisoning. I was sick a few times and Bayan arranged for a doctor to see me in my room at our guesthouse. I was drifting in and out of sleep and woke to find a very large woman flanked by two sizeable younger women standing at the end of my bed. None of them were smiling. I had no idea who they were or why they were there. Grabbing at the sheet, I half sat up.

'Who are you?' I squeaked.

'Doctor,' the woman poked a meaty thumb at her chest. 'Daughters,' poking at each of them. They regarded me as if I was a rat in a medical experiment.

'You sick. I make better.' Her accent was heavy and priceless.

'Really?' My tone suggested doubt. I looked from her to the two daughters. I wasn't sure why a doctor would show up with her girls in tow. Perhaps she had thought I might have marriage potential.

They started to fuss over me and tugged at the nylon sheet which was all I had to cover myself. It was my shelter and dignity. I held tight.

A wilting plant was struggling to survive in a large yellow plastic flower vase the size and shape of a bucket on the window-sill. One of the daughters took it in her hand, pulled out the potted plant inside and placed it on the ledge, then emptied the remaining water out of the window without checking what was below, and went to the bathroom and gave it what sounded like a rudimentary clean. Then they filled a kettle, let it heat a little and poured the entire contents into the vase.

I stared at them with increasing alarm.

The doctor produced a chunky sachet the size of a Cup-a-Soup and poured a fluorescent purple powder into the tepid water, then gave it a swirl before handing it to me.

'Drink,' she instructed. 'Drink it all.'

Even at the time it worried me that I did what she said without questioning her further. I just thought it better to do as I was told or she might produce a nozzle to force it down me. So I drank. Not just a sip, I had to keep drinking on and on and they made sure I did by urging and chanting at me. I gulped and guzzled till my stomach couldn't take any more. I could feel an inevitable eruption beginning and dashed to the bathroom just in time to vomit an entire bucket of purple puke into the bath. While I slumped on the floor, the doctor looked satisfied. There was a lone piece of meat amid the mess in the bath.

'There,' she said triumphantly. 'It stuck in stomach. Make sick. Now you better.'

And do you know what, she was right. Immediately I started to feel more comfortable. I talked to Bayan about it later. The doctor was a Chechen friend of hers. They were followers of the same Indian mystic called Sai Baba. Bayan looked a little sheepish when I described the scene and questioned whether her friend was an actual medical doctor with an actual medical qualification. But then Bayan reassured me the Chechen had used a remedy from Soviet times, which 'always worked'. The powder was a potassium mix used in vomit therapy. Certainly effective, but I tell you, it makes a terrible mess.

★

The following morning, Marat was driving us close to the Chinese border. Nature blesses Central Asia with spectacular scenery usually untouched by tourism or development, and nowhere is this truer than the Sharyn Canyon, a few hours east of Almaty, which we finally reached after travelling the full width of Kazakhstan.

Marat took us to the floor of the canyon in his four-wheel drive. We slid down a steep, dusty track and crawled slowly around a towering boulder the size of a block of flats and perched so precariously over the track I held my breath as we passed. The canyon is second only to the Grand Canyon in scale, grandeur and natural beauty, but I found Sharyn infinitely more impressive, partly due to the complete absence of other visitors.

We stopped on a gravel precipice and my jaw dropped as I stared into the vast, deep canyon. I was determined to savour the moment, knowing it was somewhere I was unlikely ever to visit again. The canyon seemed to go on forever, stretching miles in each direction and coloured warm rust and golden by the setting sun.

The Sharyn Canyon was a perfect metaphor for the entire region: vast, unspoilt and unknown. The Stans had been a backwater of the Soviet Union, and the Canyon's proximity to the Chinese border rendered it off limits even to Kazakhs. It did not appear on maps, and to this day many Kazakhs remain unaware it even exists. I was falling in love with Kazakhstan. We had been welcomed, embraced and entertained. Everyone had a story to tell, and the rugged scenery carried a drama all its own.

We had wanted to head south from the Canyon, but the road took us back to Almaty, and sharing a few drinks gave us a chance to bid farewell to wonderful Bayan. Late dinner was followed by a bar called Heaven, which shared the design aesthetics of a counterpart in London or New York but was empty when I arrived at 11.30 with Dimitri. The only other foreigners were a couple of young Australians in town to sell tennis nets. Together we bemoaned the $10 entry fee, a month's wage for most in Central Asia, and then went to leave, but a tank-like Soviet bouncer stopped us by closing the exit just as we approached.

'*Nyet,*' he said forcefully, which even I could understand. 'You do not want to leave.'

I thought we were about to be fleeced or roughed up. But with what passed for a smile in Kazakhstan, he added: 'Stay till after twelve.' He looked at his watch. 'It will get . . . better.'

We decided against arguing. Sure enough, the upstairs dance floor opened at midnight, and the club began to fill with a collection of the most glamorous women and men I have ever seen. By 1 a.m. there were confetti cannons firing over a dance troupe from *Moulin Rouge*, and I was doing the can-can while arm-linked with a bunch of lads who appeared to be the Gucci-wearing local mafia.

It was a long road south from Almaty the next day into Kyrgyzstan, the most obscure of the Stans, a land of gorgeous meadows and jagged peaks. Our new guide Kadyr was a twenty-two-year-old local journalist who looked even younger. He had a bright energy that made me feel old. I suddenly felt I had been through a complete transformation since I was his age. Intelligent, thoughtful and enthusiastic, he spoke English with an American accent and told us he'd spent part of his childhood in the United States. We'd found him through our research back in London and he was supremely excited Kyrgyzstan was going to be featured on the BBC.

We hired vehicles and Kadyr took us straight towards the Fergana Valley, a huge area of Central Asia nearly 200 miles long and more than 40 miles wide, which sprawls across eastern Uzbekistan, southern Kyrgyzstan and northern Tajikistan. Home to more than 10 million people, it is by far the most populated area in the region and at the time had a difficult reputation as a hotbed of discontent and developing militancy.

In the early 2000s unemployment was rampant in Central Asia. Poverty, censorship and government repression were the norm. Partly as a result, but also because of funding and encouragement from Saudi Arabia, militant Islam was on the rise. American political support for authoritarian regimes in Central Asia was further fuelling anger and hatred of the West and driving more young men into the arms of new and established groups that supported al Qaeda.

We made for Osh, a small city in the south of Kyrgyzstan where unrest was beginning to spread. We stopped on a bridge when Kadyr spotted illegal posters pasted to lamp-posts calling for the establishment of a Muslim Caliphate across Central Asia. This was long before the emergence of so-called Islamic State. Kadyr was shocked and told us that even to be caught in possession of such material would mean ten years in jail.

Kadyr and other contacts arranged for us to meet an activist in Osh from the shadowy banned militant Islamic group Hizb-ut-Tahrir, which was becoming active across the whole region. One of their stated ambitions was the destruction of Western democracy. Kadyr was nervous. We hired a small bus with curtains and blacked-out windows so we could talk to the activist discreetly without risking taking him back to our hotel. We had no way of knowing who he was, or what he was capable of doing.

Arriving at the agreed contact point, we found a heavy-set, dark-eyed and grim man waiting for us. He was keen to talk despite the fact we were Westerners and, as he kept reminding us, therefore his enemies. We drove out to the edge of the city to avoid any attention from the authorities.

He wagged his finger at me as he was speaking. 'America wants to dominate the world but it'll never happen.'

'You think that's really true?' I asked him. 'You think that's what America wants – to rule the world and crush you?'

The man answered with a sneer. 'America will die. Why? Because they're 25 million gays, more than 4 million lesbians, 17 million drug addicts and many people who live in poverty.'

He told me that, although he and other militants didn't have an atomic bomb, they had ideas, which were far more powerful. Perhaps one day, he mused, they would get their own bomb. All the talk of bombs was unnerving Kadyr, who was translating. Three times during our talk the militant said he wanted to martyr himself against the West, making Kadyr nervous he was about to blow himself up in our van.

Even as the guy left our van he was ranting. Kadyr told me that as he shook hands, he was repeating that we were his enemies. Kadyr was visibly relieved when he left. He said he had looked closely at the man's clothes to see if he could spot any sign of a suicide vest.

'I was getting ready to jump on him,' he said to me earnestly.

Despite goat testicles, militants and sickness, I was loving my time in this forgotten corner of the world. But I had and still have a nagging concern it might still be a future flashpoint for militancy and conflict. I hope I am wrong. But militancy has raised its head in Central Asia before. In the 1990s the battered neighbouring state of Tajikistan, the poorest of all the former Soviet states, endured a violent civil war between government

forces and Islamic militants in which tens of thousands of fighters and civilians died.

That night I slept fitfully. So much had happened. How would
we fit weeks of intense filming into short late-night programmes?
What on earth had we been doing with a militant in the back
of our van when this was supposed to be a travelogue? I started
to doubt how we would show the madness of *kokpar* one
moment, and then a guy who wanted to martyr himself.

But these programmes were always supposed to encompass
the extremes of life. The light and the shade. Ironically, one of
my favourite moments in Kyrgyzstan was the night after we
met the militant. A pirated version of the movie *Titanic* was
showing on the single Kyrgyz TV channel. It was shown almost
every single Saturday night for a year, despite the fact it clearly
had a banner caption running across the bottom of the screen
which stated: 'For the consideration of Academy Award voters
only'.

We were amazed. Imagine a clearly pirated movie showing
in peak-time on BBC One. Then Leonardo DiCaprio and
Kate Winslet started to speak, and we all had a bout of hysterics. The fact they were showing a bootleg film was bad enough,
but it had been dubbed into Russian with just one actor speaking all the lines in a completely emotionless, monotonal male
voice.

'Jack! Jack!' cried Rose as she ran through the ship, as her true
love answered.

'*Tchack, tchak, rows, rows,*' said the dubbed voice loudly.

Ageing posters and *Titanic* memorabilia were everywhere in
Kyrgyzstan. The Kyrgyz version of *Titanic* deserved its own
award. It was certainly more entertaining than the original.

★

Just down the road from Osh was another legacy of Soviet rule. Above the broken former mining town of Mailuu-Suu were more than twenty unstable radioactive waste dumps and pits for uranium waste tailings. Uranium had been mined in Kyrgyzstan for the Soviet nuclear weapons programme, but there was only a cursory clean-up of the sites after the Union collapsed.

There were environmental concerns about the waste dumps, of course, but some experts were also worried people could get access to the sites and be able to steal some of the material and include it in a radiological or so-called 'dirty' bomb.

It was definitely a darker side to the story of Kyrgyzstan, and something we all felt we should include in the programme. But of course you can't just *mention* something like that in a TV show; you actually have to go there, and you have to see and film it.

We drove out towards one of the dumps with a local scientist who had been trying to monitor their condition.

'My method of protecting myself from the radiation is two-fold: milk and vodka,' he told me with a fatalistic smile. 'Milk to counter some of the effects of radiation and vodka to forget about it afterwards.'

Ours, by contrast, was full nuclear, biological and chemical containment suits. They wouldn't protect us from excess radiation, but they were supposed to protect us from contaminated radioactive dust, which could lodge and linger in our lungs. The site was part of the reason I had been required to do a chemical weapons course before heading out to the Stans.

Getting dressed in those NBC suits felt surreal. We were standing by the side of a dusty track in an unknown corner of an unknown country in an unknown region of the world, and I was putting batteries into a Geiger counter, used for detecting and measuring radiation, and explaining to the camera that we were going to walk into an abandoned Soviet radioactive waste dump to check its condition and assess the security around it. I suddenly thought, *This is completely mad!*

But it was for TV, and I was learning that in front of the camera what otherwise would be absurd can rapidly become normal.

Will and I prised the shiny grey suits from sealed polythene wrappers and pulled them on as we stood by the van, then had our only row of the entire trip when we realised we had forgotten the instructions for the Geiger counter. Kadyr looked on in amazement. We insisted the local scientist wear a suit despite his protestations that he had never bothered before. He produced an ancient map outlining where the various dumps were and which were the most dangerous, and that was it. We adjusted our full-face respirators, or military gas masks, and set off up the hill towards the dumps, sealed in NBC suits and carrying the Geiger counter.

We looked like three alien beings, and within seconds of us starting to walk the sun emerged and we began to bake. Not just swelter, but steam. Within 100 metres we crested a small hill and through the fogged glass lenses of my respirator I could see a couple of locals ahead on a dip in the track trying to push-start a Lada. One glanced round and saw us, then did a double take, tapped his friend on the arm and they backed up against their car in bemused horror.

'*Zdravstvuyte* [hello],' I tried to say as we walked past in slow motion, but through the mask it might have come out as a strangled alien war cry. They gawped at us. I gave a cheery wave and we walked on, past a couple of perfunctory signs warning of radiation. There was no fence and no guards. I looked over my shoulder to see the guys with the Lada still watching. How long had they lived here? Probably decades. Perhaps since they were children, and with no protection.

I pointed back at the men and gestured to our scientist. I thought he should shoo them away, but he just shrugged, as if to say: 'What do you want me to do?'

Then I realised there was a village just across the valley, on the edge of the radioactive site, and later the scientist said people had been told the area was safe. But that wasn't what the Geiger counter indicated. It began clicking away, slowly at first, then faster. The whole area was a huge pit where the Soviets had buried radioactive waste, despite the fact the entire region was prone to earthquakes. The dump had been covered in a thin layer of earth and grass, but far from being safe, there were places where the levels of radiation were spiking to more than a thousand times what was normal. We chanced upon a hole somebody had been digging at one radioactive site. Villagers were grazing their cattle on the dump. A few years later Mailuu-Suu was found to be one of the ten most polluted sites in the world in a study published by the Blacksmith Institute.

Radiation wasn't the only hazard, though; to be locked inside one of those charcoal-lined suits for any length of time is like being shut in an oven. The sun was high in the sky, and we were bakingly hot. We all had to stop and have a rest, sitting on the ground on top of the radioactive waste dump. Unbelievable. But the alternative was collapse.

We turned back to the van where Dimitri had been tasked with making sure he got a good shot of our return. As we came over the hill we were clearly arriving much earlier than expected. Despite heat exhaustion I had a giggle as he flapped around trying to find a spare battery for the camera. Will was still filming as we walked, his arm stuck at a permanent right angle.

When he finally put the camera down, a strong stream of pure sweat poured from the cuff of his NBC suit.

We finished the last of the water in our packs as we tore off our suits, and then headed to a nearby town, where the delightful Café Rich Man resembled a small Spanish villa. Their water supply had been switched off because it had been raining hard for a few days and the river was muddy. They couldn't draw more water from the river until the sediment had settled.

'So, what should we drink then?' I asked Kadyr.

'There's only one thing for it,' he said with a smile. 'Soviet champagne!'

Such a bourgeois indulgence didn't seem to fit with the principles of Marx and Lenin. Champagne was produced and Kadyr went to pop the cork. It rocketed out of the top and the champagne erupted everywhere, leaving just a glass or two to drink.

'The champagne shows the power of the Soviet military,' said a waiter with a smile.

Relaxing after our sweaty walk, I felt a sense of exhilaration. We weren't just talking about situations from afar, we were engaged in them. Vials of anthrax, the Kazakh Beatles, the Sharyn Canyon, goat testicles. I was surprised what the BBC were prepared to let us do. We were having madcap *Boys' Own* adventures. Whatever I'd thought the job would entail, I had never imagined it would be so brilliant, frightening and sheer, bloody gob-smacking, often all at the same time. Even when it was bonkers, even when we were walking into the madness of a radioactive waste dump, it was exciting and memorable.

We drove on to Lake Issyk-Kul, the second largest and highest mountain lake after Latin America's Lake Titicaca, where a scattering of resort hotels which used to cater for Soviet leaders had plenty of spare rooms. They were, quite frankly, a bit of a dump, yet the Kyrgyz government was hoping to attract adventure tourists seeking white-water rafting and mountain trekking. We stopped at one decent guesthouse which had fresh water and power.

'Who comes here now?' I asked the manager.

'Diplomats, VIPs, and beezneez elite,' he replied.

'What exactly does business elite mean?' I asked naïvely.

'Beezneez elite ... means ... beezneez elite,' he replied with a euphemistic smile. Organised crime is certainly a problem in Central Asia, but rarely for visitors. Local criminals are more interested in the rich pickings garnered from shipping heroin from Afghanistan through Central Asia to Russia and Europe.

We were coming to the end of the first leg of our journey around the Stans, and we arrived at Bishkek, the sleepy Kyrgyz capital, from where we would fly home to rest, recover and plan the next stage of the journey. Our hotel was full of American special forces on leave from Afghanistan. While they lounged in the hotel's dayglo casino, we headed for the national museum, an eccentric celebration of the Soviet past.

The casino now happily accepts the US dollar, but murals in the museum portrayed evil Americans, one of whom bore more than a passing resemblance to George Bush, sitting astride nuclear missiles and laying waste to legions of defenceless women and children. Outside teenagers asked me in English if I liked ganja while they roller-bladed around the base of a statue of Lenin, still standing proudly in the main square.

'We're quite tolerant of Soviet history,' said Kadyr, my young guide. 'Many people think life was better under Communism.'

The main consequence of the end of the Soviet Union seemed to be economic collapse. The Stans were left reeling, and most people I met longed for a return to the financial security of the past. 'At least we knew where we were then,' said Kadyr.

CHAPTER THIRTEEN

The Slave and the Tigers

Landing back at Heathrow after finishing filming the first half of *Meet the Stans*, my first ever TV adventure, I was humming with everything I'd seen and experienced. I couldn't wait to see family and friends to regale and bore them with tales from Central Asia.

London felt strange and yet familiar. Going home to the house in Ladbroke Grove I shared with my friends Tony and Danny was particularly difficult. I spent days unpacking, washing kit, cleaning equipment and checking my notes from the journey for the script I would need to write for the programme. After a long and exciting adventure almost everything felt like an anticlimax. I wanted to get a megaphone and tell everyone what I'd seen and done. I wanted to share my tales.

It might have felt to me like I'd been away for months, but in reality it was just a few weeks, and everyone I knew had carried on quite happily with their lives while I was away. Sometimes the comedown from a trip can be instant and intense. I remember coming home after finishing my journey around the Tropic of Cancer, a fairly epic six-part journey around the northern border of the tropics, and discovering the toilets were blocked in the flat I shared with my now-wife. The first thing we had to do, even before unpacking our bags, was get some gloves and wellies on, lift up the manhole cover hidden under the floorboards in the back room, and rod out the overflowing sewers. It was such a colossal fall back down to earth. For a moment I was pretty grumpy about it, but then I smiled to myself: going off on a trip around the world, or an adventure in Central Asia, is not a normal thing to do. It's an abnormal privilege. Rodding out the sewers, washing my kit, or heading to the supermarket, is an equally wonderful normality, and it needs to be embraced and enjoyed.

Once I'd finished my unpacking and washing after my first trip to Central Asia and when everything was under control, I sat around the kitchen table with Danny and Tony and shared a beer and told them a few stories from the road. I didn't drone on for hours, I hope, even if I felt it was what I wanted to do, partly because I could tell the guys were keeping something from me. They looked a little sheepish.

'What's going on?' I said. 'What's happened? Why are you looking like that?'

Danny finally came clean.

'All right,' he said. 'You're going to find out sooner or later anyway. You remember when we moved in, we agreed that with three blokes living together under one roof we could never get a games console?'

'Yeeees,' I said slowly.

Tony held his hands up. 'I've bought one.'

He shrugged. I smiled.

'Rush of blood, out-of-body experience. Before I knew what was going on, I came home with a PlayStation.'

We laughed. We knew we were all slightly weak-willed and had banned games because we thought we'd never get any work done. Danny and I were particularly bad. We spent the next week doing nothing but drive a car around London shooting gangsters. In a funny way, though, it was cathartic. We only ever had one game for the console, and once we'd completed it, admittedly by playing all night in one matey beer-fuelled session, we felt as if we'd been through some rite of passage where we had passed from being shallower twenty-somethings to slightly more serious thirty-somethings. Thank God Tony never bought another game or I might never have made it back to the Stans.

Once we had finished the game, I had told everyone I knew about the delights of Central Asia, and had enjoyed a few nights of deep, deep sleep in my own bed, I was itching to get stuck into the preparation for the next trip.

One thing was very clear, my travel kit was completely inadequate. I had just taken my normal clothing and basic equipment bought from a camping shop down the road. As a result, I had been cold, wet, hungry and uncomfortable. So I started sourcing new kit and compiling a now legendary (at least in my family) packing list that has grown over the years to be more than twelve pages long, and is divided under simple headings like: cold, heat, medicine and – most importantly for me – food. I have had to become meticulous, with long lists of stuff I might require that I can then pick from with each new adventure. What's that old saying? Fail to prepare, then prepare to fail.

I have come a long way since I was a kid who climbed into Glencoe wearing little more than an old cagoule. Since I started these TV journeys I have had to become, I now confess, a kit obsessive. In the years since *Meet the Stans* I have sometimes spent eight out of twelve months travelling and working abroad. So I can't afford to forget anything, and my travel kit has to be just right: tough, light, dependable and functional. There is no space in my bags for anything that doesn't work or doesn't last.

Obviously the kit I need varies dramatically from trip to trip.

Travelling by road through a former Soviet Republic in the Caucasus during winter is completely different to boating through sweltering southern Colombia. But some old friends are always in the bag. I wouldn't dream of travelling anywhere without a trusty Leatherman and a small, powerful torch, because – time after time – carrying both has saved my skin.

In the capital of Transnistria, an obscure, exotic breakaway state between Moldova and Ukraine, where manhole covers had been stolen and sold for scrap metal, my torch saved me from falling into hellish, pitch-black sewers on unlit city streets. In Botswana's Kalahari Desert, obeying an urgent midnight call of nature deep in lion territory, a sweep of my torch across the bush revealed the silent approach of sets of shiny, carnivorous eyes. Thankfully I was able to scare away their hungry owners by smashing a spade into dry branches.

Travelling for *Meet the Stans*, I took one huge expedition bag that weighed as much as a tractor. In the years since, I've generally taken two bags for the road: one duffel bag, with compression straps to reduce bulk and rucksack straps that mean it can be slung comfortably on my back, and a hardened waterproof case that can withstand a truck driving over it, or the outbreak of thermonuclear war. Sleeping bag, mosquito net, clothes and boots, all go in the duffel. Anything breakable goes in the case. It's a bulky system that wouldn't work for everyone, particularly gappers and backpackers, and it's too much for a normal holiday, but even after Stans 1, I realised that on a filming trip I need to be prepared for almost anything.

Trekking into Burma, illegally and undercover, from a remote region of India, while filming *Tropic of Cancer*, was a particular challenge that required new levels of kit obsession. With my colleagues Jonathan Young and Andrew Carter I travelled to meet the Chin people, who suffer terrible human rights abuses in a remote region of Burma bristling with more than fifty Burmese military bases. We tried to prepare for everything, carrying ropes, machetes, a medical trauma kit, camouflaged hammocks, locator beacons and food. We even had survival kits strapped to our thighs just in case we encountered a Burmese army patrol and had to dump our rucksacks and make a run for it.

But careful planning and preparation encouraged confidence and ensured we were able to deal with all emergencies, major and minor. And the same applies to any trip. If you plan what you want to pack for a holiday well in advance, you won't suffer the stress caused by last-minute packing as you throw your clobber into a bag a few hours before a flight. I now try to leave myself plenty of time to pack, so I can enjoy the reassuring feeling that I have everything I want or need, so I'll be able to cope with any journey challenge, whether it's making sure I have a book for a delay at the airport, or a compass on my watch strap to help me out of the Burmese jungle at four in the morning.

I also don't feel embarrassed that my packing extends to the inclusion of a few edible home comforts. Obviously, I need to be eating the local grub, wherever I am, because that's a vital part of a trip, and a great chance to bank some memorable experiences. But from the second *Meet the Stans* trip onwards, I have taken squeezy tubes of honey, spicy sauce and Marmite to liven up boring breakfasts on the road, and a pack of tea bags for those rare and priceless moments when a hot brew can be slowly savoured. I might be abroad, in some far-flung part of our planet, but careful packing ensures that certain essential standards can be maintained.

★

While I was faffing around with my packing lists after returning from the first Stans trip, Will Daws had been busy transferring all the raw footage to the editing suite, where the unsung heroes of the television process work their magic.

I saw some of the rushes from the first two programmes and cringed. Not at the landscapes or the way it had been filmed, or the people we met, but at watching myself on camera and the way I came across.

'I'm awful,' I said to Will. 'People will hate me. My voice is annoying.'

'Everyone hates watching themselves on the TV,' Will said soothingly. 'You're OK, don't worry.'

I hated watching myself then, and I still don't like watching myself now. People ask if I sit down in front of the television when my own shows are on. No! Almost never. I'm too self-critical. But from the beginning Will and the BBC reassured me that while I might indeed be annoying, on balance I was probably slightly less annoying than many people would be if they were filmed. I took that to be a good thing.

'And anyway,' Will said, 'we'll be able to make you look better in the edit.'

He had captured a huge amount of material on film, but it had to be funnelled and shaped into a coherent telly programme. What would emerge partly depended on the skill and style of the editor, who has an enormous role in the creation of a show. For several of my early programmes, that was Ryshard Opyrchal. He patiently turned my babble into TV I was proud of, and dozens of other editors have since performed the same alchemy. Nowadays we often have 60, 80, sometimes more than 120 hours of footage from multiple cameras that needs to be wrangled and watched and linked together. Editors sit with the producer-director, often in a windowless room in a basement, and have roughly six weeks to turn it into an hour of TV, struggling and scrolling through the material, looking for moments of clarity from the presenter.

When the editor finishes a composer creates the music, then graders enhance the finished film so it looks glossy and inviting on the TV. Pound for pound nothing improves a programme faster than a skilled colourist sitting in front of a vast *Star Trek*-sized console playing with scores of dials and sliders like Jean-Michel Jarre, tweaking colours and shadows. Meanwhile back in the office there are production co-ordinators and production managers who help to plot the journeys, secure the visas and filming permits, book flights and places to stay, and generally keep an eye on the money. Series producers and executive producers run the journeys and get their hands dirty alongside assistant producers and directors with the research and planning for where we are going and what on earth we will film. Everyone is vital. Everyone does two or three jobs. Some of the newspapers might sneer at the BBC and claim there are too many tiers of management. I see none of that. I see tight, small teams and people working long hours.

On *Meet the Stans* we had a young researcher called Shahida Tulaganova, an Uzbek journalist and fluent Russian speaker living in London who helped to put together the journeys and shows, and was then due to travel out with Will, Dimitri and me on the Uzbek leg of the journey because of the challenges of finding a guide in the country.

Shahida was working with Will to iron out some visa issues, and then we would be back on a plane, heading out to Uzbekistan and Tajikistan. There was just time for me to sit down and consider what I had loved most about my first TV journey.

The landscapes had certainly been epic. Standing and looking out at the Sharyn Canyon had been one of many moments I would treasure forever. The wildlife had been magnificent. As we crossed the steppe I had been captivated by a diving eagle. The food had often been strange and occasionally spectacular. I would remember all of it. Everything.

But what had really stood out were the people. For me the strongest memories from that first trip, and from every trip since, are from my encounters with us, with our inspiring, intriguing, long-suffering, comic, clever and caring fellow humans. When we plan a journey I am always asking and thinking, who are we going to meet? Meaningful encounters with other people in a strange part of the world are the real experiences to treasure. If I'm not meeting people then I'm not on a proper journey.

In Central Asia I was lucky to spend time with locals who were warm, generous and fascinating, and in the years since I have been blessed to meet folk who have been completely inspirational.

Travelling in Kenya more recently, I crossed the great African plains and arrived at a remote Maasai homestead, and the mud-dung hut of a grandmother called Lucy. She was renovating and refreshing the hut, and I was press-ganged into slapping huge cow pats on the sides while Lucy watched and giggled so wildly she had to have a sit-down and a cup of tea.

I loved spending a day with Lucy. Not because of her mud hut, or her traditional Maasai clothing, complete with colourful shawl, bead jewellery and stretched earlobes. Lucy was a proud cattle herder, but her mind roamed so much further than the plains where she lived. As we walked and chatted, Lucy bombarded me with questions, about my travels, the world, our cameras and my life. We were walking together on a vast plain, almost completely empty of humanity, keeping an eye on Lucy's herd of cattle. I was struggling to get a word in edgeways, and then a phone rang. Lucy looked sheepish, then reached into her robes and retrieved a battered mobile. It turned out she would send a youngster fifteen miles to charge the phone each week, proving old Nokias really hold their power. On the other end of the line was her neighbour, standing outside her own hut half a mile away, squinting against the sun and wondering who on earth were those tall foreigners and where was Lucy taking them in the midday heat?

Life for Lucy's family was changing. She had just sold a cow to pay for her granddaughter to go to college 200 miles away to study travel and tourism. Perhaps one day someone reading this will stay in her hotel.

Often the cast of memorable and brilliant people I meet on my journeys are completely inspiring. In Paraguay I met a woman called Margarita Mbywangi who had one of the most extraordinary life tales I have ever heard. She was in her forties, and she emerged from a dark hut in a community of the indigenous Aché people, looking ragged and weary. I found out later she had malaria, and although it had laid her low, she still managed to drag herself out so she could speak to me. She was barefoot, wearing shorts and a singlet and standing about five feet three. Her feverish face still managed to radiate calm and a deep warmth.

Margarita was an Aché *cacique*, or chief, and one of the first female indigenous leaders in the country. Democratically elected by the community, she acted as their point of contact with the outside world. She took me on a walking tour of the village, past some young men who had slaughtered a pig in honour of our visit, while she told me her incredible story. She explained that the first real contact her people had with the outside world was in 1978. Within months trees were being felled, roads laid down and the Aché were being hunted and murdered by farmers and soldiers.

Just a generation before, tribes like the Aché weren't considered to be human by the Paraguayans. Human hunts were organised where 'big game' hunters could fly in to track people in the jungle and shoot them. I was astounded. 'Indigenous people weren't regarded as citizens until 1991,' my guide in Paraguay told me. 'Most of the hunting stopped by the end of the 1970s, but in some really remote areas it was still going on until the 1990s.'

Mercifully the killings stopped, but the misery went on. With the deforestation growing worse and worse, patches of scrubland were set aside for the Aché to live on, but their traditional hunter-gatherer way of life had already been ripped away. Instead there was casual work on farms with little pay and cheap alcohol.

When Margarita was five years old her village was attacked by Paraguayans and razed to the ground. She was found cowering in the bushes and dragged away. Kidnapped, she was sold into servitude on a farming ranch to serve the family as a slave. She was forced to work cleaning the house and looking after the children of the family. But she did manage to learn Spanish, and when the family left the farm and moved close to a city, she managed to escape. She was caught and returned to the family, but then ran away a second time and made it to the city and got work in a house as a cleaner. She found a local priest and asked him to help her locate her remote village. It took two years to work out where she had been kidnapped, but eventually the priest drove her out to meet the community. By then Margarita had forgotten the Aché language and couldn't tell them who she was. But then a man appeared who recognised Margarita. He threw his arms around her and wailed. It was her brother. He hadn't seen her for fifteen years.

I was almost in tears when I heard all this. It was fantastically moving. But Margarita's story wasn't just one of return. It was one of hope. Of promise. Margarita relearned her language. She struggled with the temptations of alcohol. But she got through it and became a nurse. Then she was made chief of the community of Kuetuvy. Later, she stood for election as a senator in Paraguay. Eventually she became the government Minister for Indigenous Affairs.

I was reeling with each turn of the tale. A slave who became a senator and then a minister. Yet I have travelled across a planet full of stirring human stories, and I have heard astonishing and inspiring stories of profound life-change almost everywhere. Surely that, more than anything, is a reason to travel.

A year after travelling in Paraguay, I went to Bangladesh, and met an extraordinary guide called Tanjil, a bearded and bespectacled slip of a man, who guided me and a crew from the BBC around his country, which, although unbelievably poor, is a place I love with a passion.

Shortly afterwards Tanjil was in London and I invited him over for dinner. He was late and when he finally arrived, he explained that he had stopped to take a call on his mobile phone.

'All because of the tigers,' he said with a tired sigh.

'Eh?' I said.

Then Tanjil started to explain that many, many years before he had been on a dangerous trip with a film crew who were looking for huge tigers that had attacked farmers in the Sundarbans region of Bangladesh, an enormous area of river forest. Tanjil and the film crew were travelling on a large wooden river-boat with cabins and kitchens, and on their way into the Sundarbans they stopped in a very poor, very remote village for a few hours. The cook on the boat went out looking for supplies, and eventually he returned to Tanjil and said: 'Boss, look, I could really do with a bit of help on this trip, and there's a boy in the village who is enslaved and in shackles.'

'Apparently,' Tanjil told me, 'he had been sold into slavery by his family to pay a debt.'

The cook told Tanjil it would only cost a few pounds to pay the debt and the boy could be released and he could help out on the boat.

'No,' said Tanjil, 'it's dangerous, we're going to look for man-eating tigers, and we don't need anyone else on the boat, certainly not a boy.'

The chef pleaded with him: 'Oh boss, please, he looks like a bright lad, and I could really do with the help. I'll train him up.'

Tanjil sighed and agreed. So they paid off the family debt, and the shackle and chain on his leg was released, and the boy went on the boat with Tanjil and the film crew, and he was given some new clothes and shoes in place of the rags he was wearing, and he helped the cook on the trip.

Tanjil was telling me this in London while sitting at my dining table. The roast chicken was getting cold.

'Well, that's a lovely story, Tanjil,' I said, 'but what's it got to do with you being late?'

Tanjil looked at me. 'That was the boy, on the telephone. He called me as I was walking up your street. He worked for me for years. I trained him. He's now a man, and he was ringing me from Nepal, where he's setting up a tiger conservation sanctuary.

He's now a leading expert on tiger conservation. He's co-authored science papers on tigers that have been published in the most prestigious science journals in the world.'

That boy had been enslaved. He would have rotted in that village. But he had talent and ability, just waiting to be discovered.

CHAPTER FOURTEEN

The Kalon Minaret

Sitting with Shahida, Will and Dimitri on the plane to Tashkent, Uzbekistan, at the start of both my second TV trip and the second leg of my journey around Central Asia, I was almost sizzling with excitement about the adventure ahead. But there was also apprehension about the country we were due to explore first.

We planned to travel west through Uzbekistan to the ancient Silk Road cities of Bukhara and Samarkand, and then south through mountainous Tajikistan to the border with Afghanistan. The first leg of the journey, through Kazakhstan and Kyrgyzstan, had been an extraordinary tour of a beautiful, bizarre and unpredictable region. Now we were flying to the most violently repressive of the Stan countries.

All the countries of Central Asia had, and still have, political problems, but at the time of my travels in the area Uzbekistan seemed the most troubled. The country was facing the real prospect of armed conflict. Many Uzbeks were angry with their authoritarian leader Islam Karimov and there was talk of revolution. In response tens of thousands of militants and activists who opposed the government were being tortured, jailed or executed. Many men were mysteriously disappearing, often into secret prison cells, but also because they were the victims of extrajudicial killings, simply for growing their beards and being pious

Muslims. Sermons at Friday prayers were required to follow government guidelines and the secret police were infiltrating mosques to check rules were obeyed.

Making a TV programme for the BBC draws far greater attention from everyone, including the authorities, than if it was just me on my own writing a book. Will and I had spent ages discussing how we could have an objective guide who would give us a fair assessment of Uzbekistan without the risk of them being picked up by the secret police and potentially tortured the minute we left the country. Shahida was the answer. Guides and fixers are critical on my journeys and Shahida was right up there with the best of them. Strong, clever and erudite, she was also opinionated, young and supremely sassy. She proved to be fantastic company and our merry travel gang of three grew happily to four.

One problem with filming in a repressive regime is that much of the repression often goes on behind closed doors. At first glance Tashkent, the Uzbek capital, appeared to be a relaxed and modern city. We hoped Shahida would be candid and outspoken, and we weren't disappointed. The morning after we arrived she spotted a series of posters depicting Islam Karimov lording it over Uzbekistan as if it were his personal fiefdom. His image was shown next to statements and slogans that echoed the oppression of the Soviet era. Shahida was contemptuous: 'It's a joke,' she said. 'There's nothing here, an imaginary world. None of what he says is true.'

She was right, of course. It was a country with wonderful scenery but a wretched economy. The only growth industry appeared to be personal protection for the new breed of post-Soviet 'beezneez elite' as everyone called them. Rich businessmen did not trust the police and so were turning to private security firms.

Shahida took me to visit one training centre where strapping young men were being taught to protect wealthy businessmen by a middle-aged woman wearing a pair of Winnie the Pooh socks. She looked cuddly, like somebody's favourite great aunt, but she was actually a former colonel in the KGB. A Russian national, she had been purged from her state job by the Uzbeks after independence. The BBC producers loved the fact I noticed her socks and mentioned them on camera. It was a minor detail that was perhaps childishly funny and charming, but as far as the Beeb was concerned it humanised both the woman and the story.

The BBC also liked the fact I was happy to front up to one of the most controversial men in the country. Having seen the bodyguards training, I suggested we try and talk to some of the new business elite. A few phone calls later, Shahida informed us we'd been invited to visit the most powerful man in the country.

'The President?' I said. 'How did you swing that?'

'Not the President,' she chided me with a smile. 'Even more powerful.'

We drove into a leafy suburb of Tashkent, where homes were built behind eight-foot metal fences, and headed to the house of a wealthy businessman involved in what was described as the soft drink and cotton trade. About five feet ten, grey-haired and solidly built, he opened the door of our van as we arrived at his opulent villa and shook my hand with a grip like a Greco-Roman wrestler. With fountains and manicured lawns, the house wouldn't have looked out of place in the Hollywood hills. There were Roman-style piazzas dotted around, as well as guesthouses and garages. We were treated to a feast, but then I started quizzing him about allegations that he was connected with organised crime. Eventually he decided not to talk to us any more, and we politely made our excuses and left. It all made good TV.

Back in Tashkent, Shahida took me for a wander around the centre of the city. A clue to the mindset of the President at the time was the way he was elevating Amir Temur to almost saint-like status. Temur was a fourteenth-century warlord who founded the Timurid Dynasty with a mission to restore the 'glory' of Genghis Khan. A few years before, the President had removed the bust of Karl Marx from what had been 'Karl Marx Square' and replaced it with a horseback bronze of the new national hero. Many Uzbeks were uncomfortable about being identified with a warlike butcher.

We wandered down what used to be Marx Street but was now Broadway. Young people were wearing T-shirts, baggy jeans, and baseball caps worn backwards. There were market stalls selling clothes, shoes and street food. We could have been anywhere in the world. Then we bumped into Dipsy the Teletubby, who responded positively but unconvincingly when asked if life was better under the Soviets or the President.

On the surface, at least in the capital, it seemed there was nothing wrong. But the economy was in a complete mess, and Shahida explained that almost everyone with an education wanted to leave, including young women whose more obvious assets were mainly physical. We popped into a marriage agency through which Uzbeks hoped to meet wealthy, and usually much older, Western men. There were literally thousands of women on the books. It was rather tragic.

I could understand why people wanted out. The longer we were in Uzbekistan the more obvious it was how limited the opportunities were. The main consequence of the collapse of the Soviet Union, just over a decade before, had been economic disaster. Central Asia was still reeling. Shahida had seen it for herself but managed to pursue a career in London. It wasn't just the lack of opportunity that was stifling; it was repression and ridiculous laws and edicts issued by the President that made many feel they lived at the whim of a medieval loon.

To illustrate the madness, that night Shahida took me to a suburb of Tashkent. We crept behind a burnt-out shop, knocked on a thick iron door at the top of a fire escape, and broke Uzbek law by entering a pool hall and picking up a cue. For no apparent reason, the Uzbek government had decided to ban snooker and pool. Rumours suggested the son of a top presidential aide had lost a huge sum on a game, and his father persuaded the President to ban the popular sport across the entire country in a fit of pique. It seemed arbitrary, but that small-minded and petty action suggested a government that was out of control and might do anything to anyone.

We left the capital in the company of Mr Amir, a human rights lawyer who was a contact of Shahida's. Together we headed out across the country to an Uzbek section of the notorious Fergana Valley, a home to millions of peaceful farmers and villagers but also various old and new radical Islamic groups. Uzbek officials and secret police shadowed us closely, ferociously paranoid anyone we met might express some form of political dissent. They almost had a fit when we went to visit the family of Juma Namangani, the former leader of the Islamic Movement of Uzbekistan, a terrorist group which fought alongside Osama bin Laden and the Taliban.

Before his apparent death during fighting in Afghanistan, Namangani was one of the most wanted men in the world. His brother, however, was running a local village sweet shop, and his sister-in-law insisted we try tubs of their finest vanilla ice-cream and refused to accept payment. We were chomping away when the secret police arrived and tried to force us to leave. Mr Amir, however, lost no time in telling the police they had no right to tail us and no right to force us out. I was squatting on the ground eating ice-cream outside a run-down sweet shop in a far-flung backwater, while Mr Amir, who was only slightly more than five foot nothing, squared up to a much taller senior policeman and hectored him, literally wagging his finger in his face, lecturing him about arcane sections of the Uzbek constitution, which apparently guaranteed our rights and protection. The policeman was utterly bamboozled.

It was a comic but worrying scene. Small, middle-aged, alone; Mr Amir went up against the might of the dictatorship with a brave but reckless disregard for his own safety. We had no idea whether his outburst would cost Mr Amir dearly after we left. He knew he was taking risks. But he was putting his welfare and possibly his life on the line to campaign for human rights, and to make Uzbekistan a better place to live in. In the years since, I have met countless other human rights workers and campaigners who risk everything to share the reality of their corner of the world. People I have met on the journeys have been harassed, arrested, and even tortured after we have left.

Travelling and filming in Africa a few years later I met a brave young campaigner called Rashid in Western Sahara. Morocco had claimed the territory of Western Sahara after the Spanish left in 1975. In the years that followed there was a bloody war between the Moroccans and a guerrilla army made up of the indigenous Saharawi people, who wanted Western Sahara to be an independent country. We had communicated in coded internet messages, but actually getting to speak to

Rashid in person late one night meant sneaking out of our hotel, avoiding secret police and spies, and following him in a vehicle to a safe house. Once inside, he introduced me to a group of other activists and felt able to chat openly, saying what the Saharawi people wanted was their independence, 'no more, and no less'.

What he said to us was actually very simple. He said there was a lot of oppression, the secret police were everywhere, there was no freedom of speech, and activists couldn't campaign openly for independence. 'We can't even raise the Saharawi flag or talk about the history of the Saharawi people,' he added. We chatted for a couple of hours and then left.

For talking to us, Rashid said he was later picked up by the secret police, questioned explicitly about what he had said to us, and severely beaten by Moroccan police. He sent photographs of the injuries he said he'd received.

Was it worth it? Rashid thought so. He knew he was likely to be detained. He had told us that he was completely willing to face a beating or worse. Dozens of activists I have met around the world have said the same. They think it is worth taking the risks and enduring the consequences. We always warn them of the possible outcome. But usually they know exactly what is likely to happen. Many of them have endured abuse before. They are brave not once, but often multiple times. And the reason they take those chances and deal with the aftermath is that they are desperate to share their story with our viewers and the outside world. It is humbling, but also profound.

In the Fergana Valley in Uzbekistan the Namangani family were careful not to express anti-government sentiment, but virtually every other family I met in the Valley raged against the government and seemed to have at least one male member in jail. The valley and the country felt tense.

We drove a few hundred miles across Uzbekistan to reach Samarkand, one of the oldest continuously inhabited cities in the world. Central Asia has long been a crossroads between the East and West; it was in Samarkand in the fourteenth century that Chinese traders are thought to have first met Spanish merchants and sparked a new era of globalisation. The centre of the city, graced by the breathtaking Registan, a three-sided square which is perhaps the finest built space in the Islamic world, was a joy. We climbed a secret passage hidden behind a carpet store into one of the famous minarets. I felt a real thrill emerging at the top of the tower to look out at a city that was once one of the centres of the world, a key stop and destination for intellectuals on the Silk Road between Europe and China.

We headed onwards to Bukhara, another ancient city 300 miles west. For years I had heard stories of the place. It sounded evocative and mysterious to me, like Zanzibar or Timbuktu. I was excited as we drew close to the city, but the motion of our four-wheel drive bumping along the road sent me to sleep. The sound of a huge wooden door creaking open finally roused me as we parked, late at night, outside a guesthouse in Bukhara. I picked myself off the floor of the van, where half my body appeared to have slumped rather unedifyingly as I slept, rubbed my bleary eyes, and peered out of the van's rear window, at one of the most powerfully evocative sights I have ever seen.

The guesthouse was next to the glowing domes of the majestic sixteenth-century Mir-i-Arab Madrassa, an Islamic college.

Light streamed from tiny windows sparkling along its colossal wall like portholes in a ship and danced over striking blue tiles.

There are very few other places in the world where I have seen such exotic beauty in the architecture. I scrambled out of the van to gasp at the medieval vision. It was a numbingly beautiful sight.

To the side of the madrassa was the chubby base of the legendary Kalon minaret, an elegant mosque tower built in 1187 to call the faithful to prayer, and for centuries lit by fires to guide camel trains travelling through the night. Although Genghis Khan destroyed Bukhara in 1220, he gazed in awe at the Kalon minaret and ordered it spared, enabling later rulers to execute victims and criminals by throwing them off the top.

An ethereal golden glow from oil lamps and elegant lights played over the brickwork as my eyes widened and traced the minaret 160 feet into the dark sky, just as the haunting sound of an Islamic prayer rehearsal drifted from the madrassa towards our guesthouse. It was one of the most intense and emotional sounds I have ever heard. The whole experience was overwhelming. Tears rolled down my cheeks. Even as I remember it now a lump rises in my throat.

The following morning I climbed the steps with a young guide who explained the glorious blue tiles I had admired were thought to derive their unique colour from a mix of human blood.

'Blood?' I said. 'Really?'

He nodded. 'In the old days people who were sentenced to death were tied up in sacks and carried up the steps.' He indicated the stone at our feet. 'When they arrived here in the minaret, they were thrown out of this window to their deaths. Their bodies smashed on the tiles and their blood seeped from the sacks to mix with the clay and stone.'

It was a good story. Perhaps even true. Then I read in a guide-book about a British adventurer in the nineteenth century who had the temerity to ride into the castle in Bukhara on horseback rather than walking, as was the custom. His story was a solid reminder about the need to understand and obey local customs. Generally, I have found foreigners very forgiving of visitors who commit even the most hideous faux pas. But in the case of the British adventurer no amount of apologising could get him out of trouble. He was thrown into a deep, hideous pit. And then beheaded.

We wandered around the buildings for a little longer, and then Shahida said she was itching to go and see a fortune teller in the city.

Shahida was a very modern Uzbek, but she said she liked the drama of sitting with a teller. 'It's like a bit of therapy, Simon,' she said. 'Come along as well. You will love it.'

Fortune telling is generally frowned upon in Islam but even in Bukhara, one of the holiest of cities, there were people prac-tising the ancient art. With a grisly tale and the wonder of the Kalon still in my mind, Shahida took me to see a famous teller in the back room of a building in another part of the city. Wearing a traditional big billowy dress in gaudy yellow and green, and with a single very thick eyebrow, the teller had a mouthful of gold teeth and was quite the character. We warmed to her instantly. She winked at us both when the camera wasn't looking, and then started to put on a good show for the viewers.

With a flourish the teller started by announcing I was clearly a sincere and genuine man with an open heart, and she said that she could see that someone had proposed to Shahida recently, but she'd refused.

'Yeah, that's true,' said Shahida.

'Wow,' I said, genuinely taken aback. Not by the fortune teller's insight, but because Shahida hadn't mentioned this on our long journey.

The fortune teller rattled on. We leaned forward, desperate for insight. But then Shahida stopped translating.

'What's she saying?' I hissed to her.

'Erm, well, you cannot take their words literally, to be honest,' she said mysteriously.

'What are you saying?' I said. 'I thought that was the whole idea. What's the point in coming to a fortune teller if you can't take their words literally?'

But Shahida wouldn't budge. She talked about how the teller was just giving her life directions. She mentioned bad angels, good angels, and how only God really knows what would happen. I still don't know what the teller told her.

Instead of receiving a revelation in Bukhara, we all went for a dinner of *shashlik*, skewered and grilled cubes of meat. It was the end of our journey in Uzbekistan, a moment when Will and Dimitri could put their cameras down, and we could all have a moment for reflection.

People often ask me how much and how often we film on a trip. A great challenge on journeys is knowing what to film, but also when not to film, because in a strange and exotic part of the world, almost everything is fascinating. When everything is filmable it can be hard to find a guiding thread for the journey while shooting everything that moves and breathes. And it becomes utterly exhausting for the team if they are lugging a heavy 14-kilogram camera around for twelve or fourteen hours a day, constantly hunting focus and tensing their body to get a stable shot. Instead we have to pick our moments and know when to switch on, even while being ready for moments of spontaneity.

So there are clear moments of down time, usually when we are eating or sleeping. But even then we keep a camera handy, because we never know what will happen. That became a bit of a rule on my programmes after an early journey where I was having dinner with a team on a shoot and a huge car bomb went off near the restaurant. We dived under tables, but had left our cameras behind at our B&B. There's a saying in TV: if it's not on film, it didn't happen. So nothing about the car-bombing or the chaotic aftermath made it into the programme.

Sitting with Will, Dimitri and Shahida that night in Bukhara, eating platefuls of delicious *shashlik*, we talked about our time with Kadyr in Kyrgyzstan, and we smiled at the memory of Bayan, the baby-naming and the *kokpar* in Kazakhstan. None of us could stop thinking about Mr Amir, the doughty human rights lawyer. He made a huge impression. He didn't have a camera and he wasn't with an organisation like the BBC. He was alone, risking his own skin to speak truth to power, and to share the reality of Uzbekistan with us. I worried what might happen to Mr Amir. We all worried what might happen to him. But he knew what he was doing, and he wanted us to carry on.

We were now three quarters of the way through the journey, and the distance we had covered was immense. As we headed for the border with Tajikistan Dimitri produced a map and we considered how far we'd actually come. From the far north-west of Kazakhstan to the Aral Sea and the village of Aktobe then all the way across the steppes to Almaty and the Sharyn Canyon. We covered unbelievable distances following the Silk Road, before we had crossed into Kyrgyzstan and then eventually travelled on to Tashkent, Samarkand and Bukhara. Now we were racing towards our final border crossing into Tajikistan. Uzbekistan and Turkmenistan were the most repressive Stan countries, while Tajikistan was wild and lawless.

There was one other country in Central Asia with a leader who could rival the Uzbek ruler for despotic control. Turkmenistan, the fifth country in Central Asia, was at the time ruled by President Saparmurat A. Niyazov, known as Turkmenbashi, perhaps the most dangerously eccentric leader in the world after the dictators of North Korea. Turkmenbashi stamped his name or face on everything from the local currency to the vodka. Cities, towns and streets were named after him. I had particularly wanted to see the gilded statue of Turkmenbashi with outstretched arms in the capital, Ashgabat, which revolves every twenty-four hours so the leader enjoys maximum sunshine. But the media were banned from Turkmenistan, the borders were closed to all visitors, and BBC requests to visit were rejected.

The country's isolation was a way of keeping out prying eyes. Anti-drugs officials in the region were adamant that senior Turkmen officials were actively involved in smuggling drugs, but the isolation of Turkmenistan meant it was hard for the international community to investigate the allegations.

I still had one more country to visit on the journey, but I could almost see the end ahead and for a moment I was filled with a sense of sadness. Everything about the journey had been magnificent. This corner of the world was absurd, crazy, sometimes dangerous, but always thrilling.

CHAPTER FIFTEEN

Vodka Terrorism

I crossed into Tajikistan, Afghanistan's small, landlocked and mountainous northern neighbour, on a donkey cart. Usually at a border there is waiting, paperwork, more waiting, more paperwork and then finally you are allowed through to shake hands with the local fixer. At the border with Tajikistan, however, there was also a great chunk of no-man's-land to navigate.

'No filming,' a surly guard told Dimitri in Russian. 'And no vehicles can cross.'

The tract of land stretched more than a mile across hills covered in wild grass and flowers. It looked stunning. But we had a mountain of gear and equipment. Initially we thought we were going to have to make multiple journeys lugging the kit along the only track. It would have taken the rest of the day.

Then we spotted a craggy old man with a donkey cart. His face lit up with glee at the sight of Western travellers and their mountain of equipment. All his remaining birthdays had come at once.

I now consider myself a rather experienced traveller, immune to the flattery and deception of merchants in souks, and attempts by swindlers and conmen to part me from my money or BBC petty cash. However, that elderly trickster with the donkey cart was a genius. He had clearly organised some sort of complicated deal with the ramshackle customs and immigration post because he had a complete monopoly on transport across the border. He counted our bags, looked us up and down, and then he completely fleeced us. A single journey with his cart would cost us the equivalent of nearly £40. We had no choice. We loaded our bags aboard as he tried to contain his smile, then he cackled to himself the entire way across no-man's-land.

But of course it was worth it. Who wants to fly into a bland international airport when you could chug across a border on a donkey cart?

'Welcome to Tajikistan!' said my new guide Noor, a jolly bear of a bloke, as we arrived on the other side.

The poorest country in Central Asia, Tajikistan's economy was still reeling after civil war in the 1990s. At least 80 per cent of the population were living in poverty and wages were as low as £3 a month. Even doctors and government officials earned a pittance. Noor drove us towards Dushanbe, the capital. Burned-out Soviet factories and dilapidated houses littered the landscape. Petrol was sold in old glass jars by the side of the road. 'Life was never this bad under the Soviets,' was a constant refrain.

Corruption was rife in Tajikistan and the country had terrible roads and infrastructure and very few hotels or even guesthouses. We had arranged to stay in the personal home of an official from the foreign ministry. He had helped to arrange our visas to visit and film in the country, and we thought he was doing us a favour. He said he often gave up his home to visiting dignitaries and we were looking forward to a restful and comfortable night after a long drive and eventful border crossing.

As we pulled up in front of the house the official was ushering his family out through the front door clutching bin bags of belongings. The children were crying.

'I'm not sure you are going to like this,' said Noor. 'Are you sure you want to stay here?'

'Yes, yes,' I said breezily. 'It's good for us to see inside a house and get a sense of how people actually live.'

The official stuck around just long enough to give us the keys and tell us that he would be back later to take our payment, then he scarpered. There was exceptionally limited internet access in Tajikistan, and no TripAdvisor, so we hadn't seen the house before we arrived. From the outside it looked pleasant enough. It was on a quiet residential street near the centre of the city, which in parts still showed the scars of conflict and poverty. Housing was still intact, but ramshackle. Trees were growing into people's homes. Patches of ground were completely over-grown, as if nature was taking back what the people no longer had the time or money to maintain.

Inside the house, things were a little unpleasant. I had a windowless room with walls encrusted in a stinking, unidentifi-able black mould. I looked closely and thought I could actually see it growing. But it was just for a couple of nights, I reminded myself. Then I tried the mattress. It was smelly, and it was sodden. I had already slept on plenty of damp mattresses in dodgy hotels and had been reminded by my packing list before this journey that I should carry a black bin bag, slit at the sides, that I used to cover the worst offenders. But no plastic sheet could have dealt with this mattress. It literally squelched as I pressed it. A small pool of liquid appeared. I had a sniff but couldn't be sure what it was. An indeterminate fluid, I said to myself, possibly bodily in origin? Hard to say. Still, never mind, I could sleep on the floor.

It might sound perverse, but I feel strangely honoured to have bedded down in dozens of guesthouses and hotels untroubled by even medieval hygiene standards. No traveller should return without at least a few tales of squalor and filth. It is part of an adventure.

I went out of the room to the shared sink, turned on the tap and was idly waiting for the water to run from dark brown to clear while I watched two enormous cockroaches either mating or fighting. Then I stepped backwards and trod on the side of an enormous rat-trap the size of a brick, baited with a piece of rancid cheese. *Sod this,* I suddenly thought.

At that moment both Will and Dimitri emerged from their rooms, which were even worse than mine. Will had been trying to clean a creamy mould off his pillow. We looked at each other. Then we all spoke at once.

'This is a bit too crap, isn't it?' said Dimitri.

'Is there definitely nowhere else?' I said.

'Let's get out of here,' said Will. 'Anything would be better.'

Most of our kit was still in Noor's van locked in an old garage. We gathered our personal bags and cameras, checked outside to see if the ministry official was lurking, and then we legged it down the road. We trotted along a few streets to the centre of town, found an old hotel and Dimitri tried to book us some rooms. The lady at reception was apologetic.

'We only have a few rooms, and they're fully booked,' she told us through Dimitri. 'I'm so sorry.'

'Is there nowhere else?'

'I don't think so. We don't have many hotels in Dushanbe. Maybe you could stay in someone's home?'

'Erm, no thanks, we've already tried that.'

We were just about to give up and head back to the mould house, when the woman happened to say, almost as a parting apology: 'I'm just sorry I can't lower the price for the rooms on the top floor?'

'Sorry?'

It turned out there was a whole suite of rooms that had just been redecorated and refitted, perhaps for visiting warlords and drug barons.

'But you wouldn't want those,' she said, smiling but certain, 'they are incredibly expensive. We are going to charge ...' and with that she leaned forward to shock us, 'fifty dollars per night for them.'

It took us a while to persuade the woman that given the circumstances we could afford them, despite tight BBC budgets. Settling into my luxury suite that night was a delight. The ceiling was painted in stripes a shade of fluorescent yellow, the walls had what looked like carpet for wallpaper, and there was a scattering of pictures in the bathroom that were moving animation waterfall scenes. It was the gaudiest, tackiest place I have ever stayed, and the competition for that title is fierce. But the bed was dry. And the room even came with a free apple and a bottle of vodka.

The next morning the beezneez elite were much in evidence on the streets of Dushanbe. Former warlords, corrupt politicians and mafia bosses were driving around in expensive Western cars. An 800-mile border with Afghanistan, the source of 90 per cent of European heroin, had made Tajikistan a major drug transit route.

The police were woefully underfunded. The main drugs agency in Dushanbe was so strapped for cash they had just one van and the head of the drug squad doubled up as the driver. We had been allowed to ride along with the drug squad as they raided an apartment and captured an unlikely dealer: a forty-five-year-old mother of six trying to sell an undercover officer a kilo and a half of heroin, worth tens of thousands of pounds after it was smuggled down a long chain through Russia to Europe. It was an almost unimaginable sum in Tajikistan. In the West a seizure like that would result in congratulations all round. In Dushanbe the police just shrugged. It was a daily occurrence, they said. Then the head of the drug squad took me back to the police station and showed me his exhibits locker, a single room with half a ton of heroin worth more than £100 million, or more than half the national budget of Tajikistan. I questioned whether they were tempted to sell it. The chief of the drug squad was indignant.

'We may be poor, but we're not criminals,' he said proudly.

Tourism was virtually non-existent in Tajikistan. The only foreigners I saw were aid workers or businessmen investing in high-risk ventures. But the country was getting back on its feet, and streets that resounded with gunfire just a few years before were now hosting outdoor cafés and promenading couples. Tajikistan had a long way to go, but personally I loved the place. The Tajiks were friendly, generous, hospitable and devoid of obvious envy, even when a couple of them debating our salaries asked us, wide-eyed, whether we earned more than $10,000 for each camera shot. Anything more than $100 was considered a fortune.

Of course, for visitors seeking an entirely different cultural experience, the isolation of Central Asia should be part of the appeal. Almaty and Tashkent, the capital of Uzbekistan, had a few Western shops, but the rest of the region had been forgotten by Western businesses. Yet we ignore Central Asia at our peril. Economic growth and jobs would be a useful bulwark against political discontent and emerging militant groups.

Geographically the Stans are closer to India and the East, to which they look for cultural leadership at least as much as they look to Mother Russia or the West. At a celebration of the end of the civil war in Dushanbe, I saw teenagers queuing to take photographs with ancient cameras next to cardboard cut-outs of Bollywood stars, not Hollywood icons.

We sat in a café in a square in Dushanbe waiting for food to arrive when I spotted an elderly woman begging from table to table. She was the spitting image of my beloved grandma, who had died just over a year before. I felt the colour drain from my face. The resemblance was uncanny. Noor saw my gaze.

'She isn't a Tajik,' he said, thinking he was reading my mind. 'She's an ethnic Russian. A lot of them got stuck here after the collapse of the Soviet Union. They still have their homes but they effectively lost their Russian citizenship, and their pensions became worthless due to hyper-inflation.'

It was a complete collapse for a society that had previously made a virtue of caring for the weakest. The woman was shuffling around, but she looked at me as she approached our table. I felt uncomfortable, terrible, like a voyeur. But it was as if I was watching the ghost of my grandma.

'There is nothing you can do, Simon,' said Noor sadly. 'There are so many like her, impoverished to the point where they are reduced to begging in the streets.'

I didn't know what to do. When she got to our table I emptied my pockets and tried to give her my money respectfully. It seemed inadequate. One of the hardest aspects of my journeys is that I turn up in a struggling part of the world and find awful suffering among people who have nothing. They are almost always delighted to share their life with us but there is very little we can do for them as individuals. The BBC isn't a charity. We are not allowed to spend licence-fee payers' money on worthy causes abroad. Yes, of course we dip into our own pockets, and our money goes a lot further abroad when given directly to somebody in need. But it is always a sticking plaster.

We left Dushanbe and drove south, guided by Noor and with a Mr Bean fan behind the wheel who told us in broken English his name was Jackie Chan. We met a twenty-two-year-old ex-Etonian called Wills who runs his Canadian father's gold mine, one of the tiny number of Westerners trying to make money in what was effectively a laid-back Wild West. Then, on a dusty, potholed highway which served as a main road across the country, we spotted one of the beezneez elite driving with bodyguards in a brand-new, top-of-the-range white Jaguar. He was a former teacher who had become the president of one of the sports federations in the country, and was a commander in the Ministry of the Interior. I met him later and he said he was hoping Jaguar would put a compartment in the car door which could hold a Kalashnikov. In Tajikistan this is all completely normal.

Noor and Jackie Chan took us up into the Pamir mountains, which dominate the country. More than half of Tajikistan is over 3,000 metres (9,842 feet) above sea level and the Pamirs were completely breathtaking, hundreds of peaks like an army of spears stretched into the distance until the planet seemed to curve. We climbed steep tracks and filmed young herders leading donkeys, goats and sheep to high pasture, travelling deep into an area where people told us they had never seen foreigners before. To the north the Pamirs joined the Tian Shan mountains along the Alay Valley of Kyrgyzstan. To the south they bordered the Hindu Kush mountains along Afghanistan's Wakhan Corridor, which in turn connected to the Himalayas. It felt like we were off the map, and on the roof of the world.

As if drugs and militants were not enough for the Central Asian states to worry about, there are also legitimate concerns about a potential environmental catastrophe. In 1911 an earthquake created a colossal dam 10,000 feet up in the remote Pamir mountains of Tajikistan, behind which now sits Lake Sarez, 50 miles long, a mile wide, and more than 1,000 feet deep. United Nations experts have said they believe an earthquake of around 7.5 on the Richter scale could dislodge the dam, and engineers from the US Marine Corps have predicted the resulting flood could be the greatest in human history. It would pass through several countries and threaten the lives and livelihoods of roughly 5 million people. Perhaps it will take a tragedy of this magnitude before the rest of the world discovers this forgotten region of the globe.

The Pamirs are stunning, but their inaccessibility makes it exceptionally hard to drain the lake to prevent a disaster. Even just patrolling the mountains is nigh impossible. Bandits and smugglers have operated in the Pamirs for centuries. Noor looked at the peaks and stroked his thick moustache thoughtfully.

'You know this terrain is just like the mountains in Afghanistan,' he said. Noor had fought in the Soviet Red Army in Afghanistan against the Western-backed Mujaheddin and men like Osama bin Laden.

'You could go over there with a small team,' he said, gesturing across the narrow, rocky valley as we chucked snowballs at each other, 'and nobody could see you. You could just watch, wait, and then start shooting.'

The Tajiks worry about drugs and militants coming from Afghanistan, so we headed south towards the border, through the spectacular landscape, to see how well it was guarded.

The border region was the real badlands. Militants, drug smugglers and the Taliban were active in the area. So first we had to stop at an army base to meet a Tajik secret police colonel who would guide us, and an armed detachment of border guards. However, there was a problem. The van that was supposed to carry our armed escort was the only one they had along a long stretch of the border, but it was ancient, and lacked a wheel and crucial parts. Young conscripts and a weary mechanic scurried around to fix it, to the embarrassment of all.

The soldiers eventually got their solitary van started and we headed towards the border, finally arriving at a tiny base with barracks that looked more like huts. The few dozen guards were a ragged group of conscript Tajiks. They made a sorry sight, living in appalling conditions, surviving on bits of bread, old potatoes and soup, and wearing ancient, threadbare Soviet uniforms. The soldiers, average age nineteen, were being paid roughly £3 a month to protect one of the most dangerous borders in the world, across which smugglers were passing kilos of heroin destined for the West. The lure of corruption was obvious.

The Colonel from the Tajik secret police strutted closer to the edge of the decrepit army base on the Afghan border and gestured for me to follow. As we shielded our eyes from the sweltering sun, he jabbed a stubby finger across the river dividing Tajikistan from northern Afghanistan, picking out fields of opium poppies and a Taliban training centre clearly visible just a few hundred metres away. It was just two years after 9/11, and across the border the so-called war on terror was raging.

'It is not us who creates these problems,' he said angrily. 'But we are the ones forced to deal with the drug smugglers and terrorists. Why doesn't the West do more to help us defeat them?'

It was a question I was asked several times during my journey through the Stans, and one I found hard to answer. Although we spend billions hunting for heroin in the West, when I was there

Tajikistan had been given just $9 million by the international community to stem the flow of drugs from Afghanistan. Even with those limited resources the Tajiks had seized heroin worth an astonishing $1.4 billion.

Around 90 per cent of heroin in Europe comes from Afghanistan, and much of that is smuggled through the north of the country via Tajikistan and Turkmenistan to Russia and the West. Because we know little about the Stans, we care little about their problems. Yet even just because of the heroin trade, and the misery and crime it causes, Central Asia is critically important to Europe. For a start, why not provide more support to the Tajiks to detect and capture heroin closer to its source?

Despite empty cupboards, the border guards arranged a minor feast for us with a tin of pilchards. We had been told to leave the border region before dark and quietly because of militants and armed Taliban sympathisers. But as the sun set and we sat around talking a prized bottle emerged. I call this vodka terrorism. It had become a common type of attack in Central Asia, involving an extreme and overwhelming display of alcoholic hospitality to a weary traveller.

Attacks could occur at any time of day, from any direction. Just as Brits would offer a cup of tea, so people in the former Soviet Union would reach into a pocket or a cupboard and produce a bottle of lethal rocket fuel. One time a BBC team and I went to film at a primary school. The school head produced vodka and insisted we drink. It was 8.30 in the morning, and the rest of the day is a complete blur. I don't mind a drink, but I am a complete lightweight, and when a bottle was opened it had to be emptied. And their vodka was strong enough to French-polish my insides.

Lacking the alcohol tolerance of a Siberian miner, I had

devised numerous strategies that I now employed with the Tajik Colonel. I used subterfuge. As bowls (bowls!) were being refilled for the umpteenth time, I put mine under the table and tipped it out over a rug. The next round I emptied into a tissue. Another went into my neighbour's glass. He looked like he could handle it. The next two toasts were given standing, so I had to swallow. I was completely hammered, slurring into the camera.

If pre-warned perhaps I could have used the tactic of a former KGB officer I once knew. He claimed he would swallow hand-fuls of lard before boozy meetings with crucial contacts, because the fat would line his stomach, prevent absorption of alcohol, and keep him sharp and focused. This is still not to be recom-mended. Without lard, over time I became more professional about my refusal to drink. Generally, I just lie. Claiming my religion or ancestors forbid drinking, or over-eating – another possible method for a hospitality attack – has been remarkably successful. People usually nod sagely and indicate they under-stand. When attackers in the former Soviet Union now tell me that in their culture an opened bottle cannot be left until fully drunk, I nod and tell them with a straight face that in my culture the bottle must be left half-full so I can take it to greet new friends. I say it with conviction and pride, and it really does work.

However, back then on the Tajik border I was a relative amateur. I had run out of places to tip the bowls of vodka. Then I had a brilliant wheeze. I started tipping it into my boots.

It was after midnight and pitch-black when we finally left the base. The Tajik Colonel had told us that even in daytime we needed to be discreet while travelling in the area and as quiet as possible. But he was the one who produced the vodka. Taliban positions were just to the south. I was competely drunk and we drove back along the border with the lights on in our van, all the windows open, with Noor and I singing football songs. Goodness knows what the Talibs thought.

I didn't want to go home. I wanted to carry on to the east of Tajikistan, to Turkmenistan, to a thousand more sights and places in Central Asia. I was completely addicted to the journey, and I loved working and travelling with the team. They had put up with difficult locations, often appalling accommodation, truculent officials and long days with humour and forbearance. Will, Dimitri, Shahida and all our guides and fixers were exceptional, and the finest travel companions imaginable. We had shared an experience, a quest, and a sense of common purpose. It had been a completely epic adventure. Was this what making TV was like? I was a convert.

For me, it was a time of transformation. I had already travelled the world for fun, love and work. But I had rarely strayed from the beaten track. My trips had been holidays. There were laughs, and they gifted me memories. But they didn't change me. Yet on that first television adventure, to forgotten corners of Central Asia, were sights and experiences that made my head swim and sing.

Until that trip I was relatively happy with the often lonely life of an author. I had written more than half a dozen books. But then TV came knocking at my door. From the start the idea was to blend travel with issues. To go on an adventure, a real adventure, but also to learn about the places I was visiting. From the first day of the first trip, I realised travelling with your eyes open, and looking for the dark, as well as the light, is a guaranteed way of having an experience that lingers in your soul.

Before I started *Meet the Stans* I told the BBC it would be a one-off. I had a series of books I wanted to write. My author slippers were calling. We flew home after finishing filming on the Tajik border and I was on a high for weeks. My mind was full of the experiences, the images, the smells, the food and the incredible characters I'd met. I was desperate for more. I wrote to the BBC, said I'd loved the experience, and asked if I could change my mind about never doing it again. I suggested a few more ideas. Every trip since then has been extraordinary, every moment a privilege. Travel has gifted me some of the greatest memories of my life.

CHAPTER SIXTEEN

Hostile Environments

Meet the Stans was an awakening for me. Of all the experiences I'd had in my life, it was among the most profound and intensely memorable. An adventure somewhere remote and uneasy where the joy of discovery had been mixed with real issues – it was an experience and a challenge, and I had to explain those countries both to myself and the viewers.

Back in London after finishing filming I felt more alive than ever before. I was happier, more confident. My friends could see that something had changed. So could my family. Will and Ryshard started putting the shows together and I saw different cuts or versions and sent them endless editing notes and unhelpful comments. Eventually we all agreed on the content of the programmes and I started writing scripts for the commentary that were far too long, far too complicated, and would have involved talking over people on screen. Karen, the boss, gave me a brilliant piece of advice: 'Just write to the pictures,' she said. Simple. Obvious. But very helpful.

I don't write the best scripts, by a long stretch, but I try to fill them with information. Directors and editors have pulled their hair out with me in the years since as I cram another fact or statistic and another line of commentary into documentaries that are already packed. 'Can't we keep a bit of space there?' they plead. 'Can't we let the pictures breathe?' We discuss, debate and argue. There are small battles, but no wars. Sometimes I lose, sometimes they lose. Eventually a script and a programme emerges, usually with final changes made on the spot while I am recording the voiceover. It certainly keeps all of us on our toes.

Meet the Stans aired in 2003 on BBC Four and then on BBC Two in a late-night slot and the response was fantastic. Viewers said lovely things about the shows, the BBC were delighted with them, and even the newspapers were generous with praise. The *Guardian* said the shows were 'a thrilling postcard from the edge', the *Observer* said it was 'a spectacular journey'. More importantly, Roly Keating, who was the head of BBC Two, said the programmes were electrifying. 'Everyone seems pleased!' said Will in an email. 'They might even let us make some more!'

After *Meet the Stans* the BBC and others put me back on the TV presenting a series of programmes. I investigated the Kennedy, Disney and Bacardi clans, the causes of the Iraq War, and the death of Roberto Calvi, dubbed 'God's Banker' because of his close links to the Vatican, who was found hanging under Blackfriars Bridge in London. I even went on a long and eye-opening journey around Saudi Arabia for a TV programme, travelling from the cities of Riyadh and Jeddah down to the troubled border with Yemen and on into the isolation of the Empty Quarter desert.

It was a strange and often bizarre country to visit. I met scores of Saudis, from the most senior princes to desert Bedouin, from Osama bin Laden's former best friend and extremist supporters of al Qaeda to a brave human rights worker and trendy young women. On the streets the fiery bearded Mutawa'een, religious police from the Committee for the Propagation of Virtue and the Prevention of Vice, were enforcing their vision of morality. But an army of youngsters was desperate for change and freedom. Driving along a busy public highway on the outskirts of Riyadh one morning I found hundreds of teenagers and young men crowded by the pavement on the other side of the road watching a high-speed skidding competition.

My Saudi driver had to swerve to prevent one car, driven by a boy aged about fourteen, from crashing into our van. He turned to me, apologetic and slightly embarrassed. 'Boys,' he said, with a casual shrug of explanation. 'They need to let off steam.'

There were still few outlets for youthful rebellion in the Kingdom of Saudi Arabia. I was amazed to see youngsters, many weaned on foreign TV shows, scribbling their name and mobile numbers on pieces of paper and then throwing them at someone they fancied when the religious police weren't looking.

We travelled into the remote interior of the Empty Quarter desert and stayed in a Bedouin desert camp. The heat was astonishing. At one point it registered more than 50 degrees Centigrade (more than 120 Fahrenheit), but it was an exceptionally dry heat, and somehow tolerable if you drank litres of water during the day. In the evening a flustered female member of our team came back in a hurry from a chat with local women in their tent and started rooting through her belongings for a pricey gift. Turned out she had idly told one of the Bedouin women her solitary solid-gold ring was beautiful, and the woman had immediately slipped it off and gifted it to her. I suspect the return gift of an iPod didn't quite cut it in her nomadic community.

I was in the Empty Quarter for just a few days with no phone reception. But meanwhile my brother James was in an inaccessible area of Afghanistan, also out of range and out of contact. Our poor mum was obviously worried sick. James was working on a personal project he had devised, photographing activities that were previously banned by the Taliban, including weather forecasting, bird keeping, kite flying and the education and employment of women. When he had first told me he wanted to go to Afghanistan I tried to dissuade him. Initially he wasn't entirely sure what he was going to do there. I thought it would cost him a fortune and he would never get out of a secure compound. Fortunately he didn't listen to a word I said. He took photographs that were breathtakingly beautiful, captured the sense of a changing country, and was recognised by or won multiple awards, including the Observer Hodge Award, the National Portrait Gallery Portrait Prize, and separately, the Professional Travel Photographer of the Year award.

While he was in Afghanistan working on the project and finding a mobile phone signal, I was re-establishing contact with home from Saudi, where I was on a journey that took me to the heart of power. I became one of the few Westerners ever to attend a *Majlis*, an audience with royalty, held under huge crystal chandeliers in a luxurious hall the size of a small football pitch, where Crown Prince Abdullah, the leader of Saudi Arabia in place of his ailing brother King Fahd, would hear the polite complaints and appeals of his male subjects. Unfortunately for me, the Crown Prince was late, I had been drinking several pints of ultra-strong Saudi coffee, and by the time he appeared I was shaking with the effects of caffeine. As I moved through a crowd of tribal leaders to speak to the Crown Prince, I felt like I was drugged. I could see a couple of his guards watching me with alarm, their fingers moving for their triggers.

'Crown Prince, Crown Prince,' I said, pushing past a bodyguard with an assault rifle. 'Simon Reeve from the BBC, please could we have a word?'

He turned and looked at me patiently. 'I'm so sorry,' he said. 'I have the King of Jordan in the other room, and I cannot keep him waiting.'

As excuses go, it was strong.

Still, my journey gave me a vivid insight into the kingdom. I finished my travels down near the border with Yemen. One night in the Empty Quarter desert, in an ancient corner of the world and under stars so bright I could read by their light, my otherwise silent bodyguard suddenly started tapping away on a hand-drum and sang a haunting song to the moon. It was completely spellbinding.

These programmes were all interesting to film, but I was itch-ing for more travelogues like *Meet the Stans* that blended the light and the shade. Safely back in London, I put together proposals and plotted more adventures.

Then one summer night I went with my friends Ben and Antoine to a publishing party held to celebrate the launch of *The Coma*, a book by Alex Garland, author of *The Beach*. I was out most nights at the time when I was in London, socialising, going to parties and generally living the life of a single lad. I drove friends like Mike, Maurice and Dimitri mad with some infuriating rules which meant that if I walked into a bar or a party and there was no one I or they thought was interesting I would often turn around and try to persuade everyone to go somewhere else. Arriving at the packed publishing party, Ben turned to me and said: 'At least let's have a drink.'

I was just inside the door when I saw her. Towards the back of the party, at least 15 metres away, was a tall, elegant, laughing woman with tumbling blonde hair who stood out in the crowd so instantly it was as if she was lit by a spotlight. She was talking to a couple of men in a way that suggested they were both trying to flirt with her. She looked bright, open, interesting, and she was gorgeous.

Another of my dating rules was no 'cold-calling' at a party. I wouldn't just wander over to someone and start chatting them up without at least a tiny indication of interest. It was partly tactical, partly about not hassling lone women, and largely about ego. If there was a second glance then all risks were dramatically reduced. I haven't even mentioned my rules about no Scandinavians, no only children, and no cats.

I moved through the crowd to get a drink, casually keeping my eyes on her, and then as I went to pass in front of her I willed her to look in my direction. It worked. Anya glanced up, our eyes locked, and I smiled. Everything slowed. She held my glance for a wonderful second longer than was merely polite, something fizzed, and I Knew.

Life is always built on tiny moments of chance and circumstance. If her back had been turned, if . . . I got a drink and stood with the lads. 'So you're staying then?' said Ben and nudged me in the ribs.

I can't say it was love at first sight. I wasn't a teenager. I thought she was stunning, but looks aren't everything. The Japanese have a word for the feeling that suddenly erupts when you meet someone and know you are destined to fall in love. That was close to what I felt in that moment. I felt excited and confident, but bided my time. Anya was engrossed in conversation with her friend Leanne.

A couple of drinks later and Ben and Antoine were getting impatient.

'Go on,' urged Ben. 'She won't stay here all night. Go and talk to her.' Then he gave me a gentle shove in the right direction.

One of our first dates was lunch in the restaurant inside the

British Museum. Anya had been living in Denmark for the past few years. She was half-Danish, spoke fluent Danish, had a degree, worked as a model and had been a camerawoman on wildlife documentaries. She was opinionated, thoughtful and funny, telling tales about a horrific shoot she abandoned when a producer started gluing stick insects to a branch in a garage in Croydon. When we met she was working for her friend, a chess grandmaster from Bolton who used to captain the British chess team, developing links between universities and industry. As we left the restaurant I walked us out past the Rosetta Stone, an ancient slab of rock inscribed with three versions of the same boring decree – one in Egyptian hieroglyphics, another in Egyptian script, and the third in Ancient Greek. It was found by Napoleon's forces, I told her casually, trying to impress her, and used in the nineteenth century to finally decipher Egyptian hieroglyphics and much about the Ancient Egyptian world.

Anya was listening to me thoughtfully.

'Yeeees,' she said slowly, straining her eyes to see the top of the rock. 'It says ...'

And then she began reading the Ancient Greek on the stone aloud. I was completely bowled over. Some tourists standing next to her turned and gaped.

'How ...?' I stuttered.

'Oh, erm, I'm fluent in Greek,' Anya said, all very matter-of-factly. 'And I can read it. I lived there for a while.'

'But ...?' I stuttered again.

'It's Ancient Greek, but still Greek,' she shrugged. 'Amazing, isn't it, that the language still has enough similarities after more than two thousand years?'

'Anything else you haven't told me?' I said.

'Well, I speak a bit of Arabic,' she said brightly.

And then she realised people around us were staring. She blushed just a little and started to move away. Well, reader, I have to say, I was completely smitten.

One night a couple of weeks later I was in a pub with a few friends having a drink after a game of football under the Westway in West London, just near Grenfell Tower. One of them worked as a shipping agent. He was telling a story about sending some equipment via a place called Somaliland. I cut in.

'Sorry, where? Somaliland?' I said. 'Where on earth is Somaliland?'

'It's in the horn of Africa. It's not a recognised country, but I'm trying to send a container there.'

An unrecognised country, I'd never heard of such a thing. How could a place like that exist? Something sparked inside me. I grabbed a pen, scribbled the word 'Somaliland' on a scrap of paper and stuffed it into my pocket. Then I had a couple more drinks. Of course, I forgot it was there. I wandered home, woke up in the morning, discovered the note and wondered what on earth it was. Then I remembered the conversation, sat down at my computer and discovered it wasn't the only unrecognised state. There were scores of them. All places that technically did not exist.

Although there are almost 200 official countries in the world there are also dozens more unrecognised states like Somaliland which are determined to be separate and independent. These countries are home to millions of people, they have their own rulers, armies, police forces, and issue passports and even postage stamps, but they are not officially recognised as proper countries by the rest of the world. So they can't send a team to the World Cup, have a seat at the United Nations, or even send a singer to Eurovision.

I was fascinated. The more I looked online the more I found. There was a whole stack of unrecognised states with defined borders, governments and infrastructure that weren't officially recognised as nations. When I put them all together I realised there were more than 250 million people who lived in unrecognised countries or considered themselves unrepresented people. Within half an hour I knew this could be a new series. It was an entirely new subject area that nobody knew much about.

Soon I was engrossed in research, and Anya was a massive help.

Together we read up about unrecognised countries and unrepresented people. Both of us thought they were completely fascinating. Each place that we found sounded exotic and unknown: Abkhazia, Assyria, Batwa, Crimean Tatars, East Turkestan, Hmong, Iranian Kurdistan, Khmer-Krom and Ogaden. How can anyone even read the names without booking a flight to learn more? What about Oromo, South Moluccas, Talysh, West Balochistan, West Papua or Western Togoland? Then we discovered a group called the Unrepresented Nations and Peoples Organization (UNPO), which formed some sort of umbrella group for countries that couldn't get into the United Nations. While the UN had a grand headquarters next to the East River in Manhattan, the UNPO had an office in The Hague. But they had an annual conference coming up in a few weeks. Anya and I looked at each other. We had to go.

I booked tickets, Anya packed her camera gear and we found somewhere to stay. My friend Jo lived in The Hague and said we could use her flat. We arrived to find His & Hers toothbrushes in the bathroom ready for us and rose petals scattered across our bed.

As a quirky destination for a romantic break, the conference in The Hague was simply brilliant. I had never been to a more obscure gathering. Representatives of the most exotic and often persecuted people in the world marched through The Hague and then took their places at a huge circular table that looked like something out of Camelot. Anya and I had a long chat with people from British Cameroon and Nagaland. Then the Crimean Tatars played the Hmong at football.

Talking to the different country reps it was clear to me this was a huge, forgotten story. Almost all of the unrecognised countries were at the centre of past or present conflicts, or were likely to be caught up in an armed struggle in the future if nothing was done to resolve their status. These were people fighting for independence and identity with a voice no one was hearing, even though every tale was strong and emotional, every speaker erudite and committed. There was little interest from the mainstream media. There was no TV coverage of the conference. Anya filmed it for our research and there were a couple of students doing something similar, but that was it. The UNPO was largely unknown. It was a hidden story about our planet.

Back in London we collated all the information we had and put together a list of the unrecognised places around the world that best represented the issues we had heard. Our plan was for me to go on a series of journeys to some of the most obscure places and shine a light on their stories. We turned it into a TV proposal and sent it off to the BBC. Before we knew it, I was back at TV Centre. My second series of travelogues had been commissioned. It was to be called *Places That Don't Exist*, and against stiff competition it remains one of my absolute favourite and most memorable adventures.

★

There is a certain excitement to arriving somewhere without a clue where to stay or what to do. If you travel spontaneously you often put more thought and consideration into the journey on arrival because you are not following some predetermined tourist trail. You know memories will not be served on a plate, and you have to find them yourself. Spontaneity also means you can wander around a city or a resort area and decide where you want to stay based on reality rather than an enhanced photo on the internet.

Early in our relationship Anya and I booked tickets at the airport and headed to Sharm el-Sheikh, the Egyptian resort town on the Red Sea, for a last-minute break. We walked along the promenade and lazed on the beach for a couple of days, then got bored and took off into the desert. We bought meat from Bedouin, slept out under the stars and then took a daft turn in our little hire car on a complete whim and sank into deep sand in the middle of the desert. It was my fault. I hopped out of the car, looked around for a few moments and realised we were miles from help, then heard a worrying sound coming from the other side of the car. Anya was already down on her knees digging out the wheels and letting the tyres down so we could escape.

'Come on,' she said. 'Let's get on with it.'

Even today our strongest memories of that holiday are the hours we spent digging out the car together. That bonding experience became part of the glue for our relationship. If you want to have a spontaneous adventure, it's always worth remembering that some of the most memorable times can happen when things go a bit wrong. But I still try to follow simple rules: I don't arrive anywhere late in the evening because I want some time to have a look around before finding a bed. I travel light, put cash in my sock, don't get too hung up on review sites, and I try to avoid following the crowd, so I can have my own experiences. Plus I say yes to almost everything.

You can start locally. Upturn a glass on a map and centre it on your home. Then draw a ring around the rim and explore that circle so you know it like the back of your hand. All travel gifts memories, and spontaneity has a place. On my TV programmes we don't write a script in advance and we don't usually have a recce. I don't take a list of questions with me and I am not fed things to say through an earpiece. Spontaneity is encouraged. Much of the time when we are filming we have to make it up as we go along, which can be exciting but also nerve-wracking. If we are set to film a monument in the centre of a city and then spot a demo nearby we will always make the more exciting choice. Hopefully the programmes feel more real as a result.

However, we still need to plan a TV adventure before we go to ensure we reap the full benefits of a trip. We spend at least a few months preparing where we might be able to go and what we might be able to see and do for each shoot or series. Arriving somewhere without a clue about what we are going to do would be profligate. Careful planning and preparation guarantees powerful experiences.

Every journey is different and every production team works differently, but generally an assistant producer or researcher will start drawing up a list of possible stories and adventures two or three months before a shoot actually starts. They use the internet, guide books, newspaper articles and long, long conversations with guides and experts in the countries we are heading towards. Meanwhile we will have meetings, drink tea, look at maps and debate the merits of locations, routes, stories and people we could meet. There are no hard rules for what makes it onto the final list of what we film, but we aim for extremes, whether extremely beautiful, thrilling, shocking or inspiring. I also try to use a technique that has worked well for me in relationships: if someone believes really strongly that we should do something, whether it's the assistant producer or the executive in charge, we generally do it. Enthusiasm trumps apathy. In my relationship at home we sometimes rank things out of ten. Don't laugh. One of us might idly suggest going to see something, and the other isn't entirely keen. The proposer admits they only want to do it 'level five', which means they really aren't that bothered, whereas the opposer says they really, really don't want to do it, 'level eight'. It generally works. You have to be honest and you can't keep dropping level nines or tens, because you just sound mad. Give it a try. Even my long-suffering television colleagues have occasionally played along.

While discussing and debating the ideas for TV shows, the potential shooting team are contacted to check availability, then visas are organised, equipment hired, arms are jabbed with vaccinations, and risk assessments are completed. Eventually we get on a plane.

At the start of *Places That Don't Exist* my first destination was the largely unknown breakaway state of Somaliland, the inspiration for the entire project. A series of trips would also take me to Transnistria (between Moldova and Ukraine), Taiwan, Nagorno-Karabakh, also known as Artsakh, a landlocked region in the South Caucasus, and three regions of Georgia which broke away after the collapse of the Soviet Union. It was a chance to visit some of the most obscure and forgotten parts of the world.

All of the unrecognised nations on my list declared independence after bloody conflicts with a neighbouring state, which

I also wanted to visit. In the case of Somaliland, that's Somalia, one of the poorest countries in the world and at the time perhaps the most dangerous.

I went in with a small team. Just Shahida, my colleague and guide in Uzbekistan, and a producer-director called Iain Overton, a Cambridge graduate who had just been in Iraq film-ing a frontline fly-on-the-wall documentary about the Argyll and Sutherland Highlanders in Basra. He was ideal for the job, but we didn't actually meet until we were at Heathrow.

Shahida had become a feisty friend, brilliant travelling com-panion, and assistant producer. She was perfect because she was brave, had a no-nonsense approach to officialdom, and was pre-pared to take the calculated risks required to go somewhere tricky so we could share the experience with the viewers. There are very few jobs I can think of where you meet one of the people you'll be travelling with into a volcano just as you step off the rim. But that's how it felt on that shoot. I knew Shahida well, but Iain and I hadn't been bloodied together.

That probably sounds dramatic, but flying into somewhere dangerous you need to know what your team can cope with, how they will react in tricky situations, and whether you can trust them to have your back should things go badly wrong. You need to know whether they will carry you, and whether they will literally give you their blood.

We were heading to Somaliland but first we needed to visit neighbouring Somalia and its capital, Mogadishu. According to reports, it was in a state of near chaos with gun-toting young men on the streets. For years there had been conflict and civil war and the country was in a state of collapse. Kidnap and murder were serious risks. Warlords were feuding over disputed territory. We would need to hire a team of local mercenaries to protect us. As one of the most volatile places in the world the BBC classed it as a 'category one hostile environment', and a place of 'exceptionally high risk where battlefield conditions prevail'. Going there would be the most dangerous journey I had undertaken.

The difference between this adventure and *Meet the Stans* was that this had been my idea from the start, whereas my previous travelogue had been the product of discussion and debate. It wasn't to be a single long journey, it was a series of smaller trips, but still through often tough terrain. We would be off the map, quite literally, and first we had to get through Somalia.

A scheduled flight, with drinks, food and cabin staff, took us as far as Kenya. Then we hopped north before climbing aboard a dodgy propeller cargo aircraft flown by a couple of Ukrainians for the journey across the border into Mogadishu. We were the only passengers on the final flight and just before we started moving I looked forwards to the flight deck. The door was open and I could see the pilot and co-pilot toasting each other with glasses of vodka. In the context of where we were going, this felt completely normal.

Iain and I finally had a chance to chat through our plans on the flight, then we checked the ceramic plates in our flak jackets, adjusted the straps on our ballistic helmets, and Iain cooked up a bean curry on a bench. There was no cabin service.

CHAPTER SEVENTEEN

Mr Big Beard

The wings of the plane slapped from side to side as we made our final approach, then we smacked into the ground and bounced along a dust-blown airstrip just outside Mogadishu.

From the moment we landed we were thrust into the chaos. Another plane nearby was unloading bundles of *khat*, the local stimulant drug of choice in Somalia. Our local fixer Ajoos, a friendly, smiley man I instantly warmed to, met us at the bottom of the plane steps. Suddenly there was gunfire a few hundred metres away. We ducked, but Ajoos glanced around and told us not to worry.

'They are not shooting at us,' he said reassuringly.

We had contacted Ajoos through a guesthouse in Mogadishu that was able to provide us with more than a dozen heavily armed local mercenaries. He introduced us to the men who would be our guards. They were a ragtag group of skinny young men wearing battered clothing, random bits of military gear, flip-flops and faraway gazes. They carried Kalashnikovs and a couple of tripod-mounted machine guns. Several were slung with bandoliers or belts of bullets. They showed us our vehicles. We would be driving around in flatbed pickup trucks with whopping anti-aircraft guns mounted on the back which fired bullets the size of small bottles. The trucks were known as 'technicals'.

'Like a poor man's tank,' said Ajoos with a faint smile.

We were in a situation where everything around us felt potentially dangerous, even life-threatening, like we were barefoot toddlers in a Dickensian glass factory. We had no real idea whether we could trust Ajoos, let alone our guards. We were in a place where we could be shot at any moment or kidnapped for ransom.

Then our plane turned and flew out, and we were on our own.

We loaded our bags into the trucks and I climbed into the back of one with Iain. There was some joking and joshing with the guards as I tried to fit alongside them, and their gun barrels accidentally slapped into my leg. They laughed, I laughed, and after that we got along just fine. We kept that moment in the programme, just to show they were human, and even in a bonkers situation like Mogadishu there was humour, and light in the shade.

We drove into the city. I was quite calm. To my astonishment, I was about to enter a conflict zone with no real back-up and yet I wasn't scared; I was filled with a sense of anticipation and adventure. But the entire time I was there I couldn't get a book out of my mind that I read as a kid. It was a science-fiction story called *The Stainless Steel Rat*, about a space traveller who arrived on an alien world where everything was ferociously dangerous and everything was out to get him. The plants had evolved to eat people, the insects were deadly. That's what being in Mogadishu felt like.

I just had to roll with the situation and behave like an amiable Brit. It helped that I didn't look threatening, and I was with a couple of people who looked equally harmless. All of us were careful to strip out any old military gear from our kit before we flew. A few years earlier some French travellers wearing army surplus clothing in remote North Africa had been shot as spies. Mogadishu was no place to start looking like foreign special forces.

The city was like nowhere I had ever been. It had been destroyed by years of fighting. In some areas almost every building was partially destroyed or at least pock-marked with bullets. Masonry was hanging over streets strewn with debris. It looked like the aftermath of the Battle of Stalingrad, or Grozny. On the streets traffic was light, but there were trucks and other technicals carrying more gangs of young fighters. Ajoos told me corpses were left in the streets for days and locals survived in a state of utter chaos. We passed colonial-era Italian classical buildings, while people scuttled along looking fearful, but also staring at us.

'This is a city of a million people,' said Ajoos, 'and we think you are the only white people here at the moment.'

Even with all that Ajoos was telling us, I cannot say I was particularly worried. I felt alert and alive. It was a shocking and horrific place to be. But it felt like we were somewhere important, where stories needed to be told. We had a chance to broadcast the suffering of a place and a people who had been forgotten.

Our first stop was near the main market. Our guards leapt off the back of our vehicles and fanned out around us to form a secure perimeter. I grabbed our 'trauma kit', a shoulder bag full of battlefield wound dressings, and we set off along the street towards the site of a disaster that helped to shape world history.

In October 1993, in an operation immortalised in the movie *Black Hawk Down*, more than 100 elite US special forces and soldiers abseiled out of helicopters into Mogadishu to hunt for two senior warlords fomenting chaos.

The reasons the US got involved had nothing to do with capturing and securing vital oil supplies. They were in Somalia largely from a misguided belief that military power alone could be used to stabilise chaotic regions of the world.

The mission was supposed to take roughly an hour, but everything went wrong when one of the American Black Hawk helicopters was hit by the blast from a simple shoulder-launched rocket-propelled grenade (RPG) fired from the ground. With its tail-rotor severed, it spun in the air and plummeted into a neighbourhood 500 metres north-east of the target zone. Then another Black Hawk was downed. By the next morning, when the group was finally rescued after a ferocious battle, eighteen American soldiers had been killed and more than seventy wounded. At least 500 Somali fighters and civilians were dead and 1,000 injured. It was the longest sustained firefight involving American forces since the Vietnam War.

With Ajoos leading, we passed down streets and narrow alleys where young children peered from behind chipped and broken doors. Then he stopped.

'Here it is,' said Ajoos. We had reached what I thought was a pile of rubbish, cactus plants and razor wire next to a group of bullet-ridden buildings. 'This is one of the American helicopters.'

I felt my whole body chill. The day after the battle in Mogadishu, the corpses of American soldiers were dragged through the streets and paraded in front of television cameras. President Clinton began pulling US forces out of the country and the captured henchmen of warlords were quickly released. The debacle shaped American foreign policy for the rest of the 1990s, making Clinton extremely reluctant to commit US troops to peacekeeping operations and, I was told adamantly while researching my book, to covert operations against bin Laden and al Qaeda. Just one week after the battle in Mogadishu, Clinton ordered US Navy ships to turn back from a peacekeeping mission to Haiti for fear they would be attacked. Within eighteen months the United Nations had packed up and left Somalia. The country was abandoned and left to rot. If those helicopters had not been downed the whole world might have been a different place. Perhaps, even, 9/11 would never have happened. Perhaps Afghanistan, and Iraq, would never have been invaded.

There was still no real government in Somalia, and instead warlords controlled their own territory. Despite the chaos and violence, it was recognised as a functioning country and it had a seat at the United Nations. The suffering of Somalia was horrifying, but the real focus of my journey was Somaliland, to the north, which had split from Somalia. Somaliland was supposed to be relatively stable and secure, but no other nation in the world recognised Somaliland as a proper country.

To illustrate the anarchic situation in Somalia we plunged deeper into the main market. Ajoos led from the front, and Iain and I scurried to keep up. As gunmen from other gangs eyed us with bemusement or suspicion, I tried to play the jolly Brit abroad; no threat, no hidden agenda. Ajoos took us down narrow alleys at the side of the market, past ramshackle stalls and shacks, and our group and guards began to spread out. I started to wonder where on earth we were going, and for a moment my trust in Ajoos wavered. Then we arrived at a small building, our guards took up positions outside and Ajoos ushered me inside and introduced me to a man called Mr Big Beard, who had passports to sell.

'So you've decided to become a Somalian,' Mr Big Beard, who had dyed his hair rusty orange, said with a laugh.

There was no government here; no paperwork; no rules other

than those of the street and the gun. But the country was still recognised globally and people still travelled abroad. Instead of a government ministry, anyone with money who needed a passport would go to see men like Mr Big Beard. He had liberated a stack of passports and stamps from the official passport office during the chaos of war. He charged me about £50 and in fifteen minutes I had a genuine Somali diplomatic passport, bearing my own name and photograph. No checks, no birth certificate, of course. I still have the passport, and it remains one of my strangest travel souvenirs.

That night we took shelter in a guesthouse compound that was guarded around the clock by our gunmen. It had its own armoury and was built around a central courtyard. Rooms that backed onto the surrounding streets had furniture piled at one end as rudimentary protection against RPG attacks.

But even in the rooms we weren't safe. I pulled a plug out of a ruined socket and accidentally touched the wires. The electrocution blew me backwards across the room. I felt like my arm had been put into a tight vice, and the grip extended round and stopped just before my heart. I felt shaky and nauseous, and my arm was sore for several days. I had a sleepless night, wondering what on earth I was doing in this place, where even a simple plug tries to kill you.

The next morning our gunmen took us to buy their drugs. Everything else in Mogadishu was in chaos, but roadside stalls were still selling fresh bundles of *khat*, or *qat*, an amphetamine-like stimulant that gives chewers a small high. It was also an appetite suppressant, useful when food was scarce, according to Ajoos.

The *khat* is wrapped into a small bundle and chewed. It's legal in the Horn of Africa but there is a serious downside to the drug. At the very least it is psychologically addictive, and regular use can lead to insomnia and anxiety. Often it can make people feel more irritable, and even violent. I spoke to people in Somalia who thought the fact it was chewed by millions of people was holding them and the country back. So Iain, Shahida and I were in a bit of a moral quandary when the men told us we had to pay for their bundle.

'It's something they expect,' said Ajoos, who didn't chew. 'It's part of the contract with them. And you really don't want a group of gunmen looking after you who are grumpy and missing their fix.'

It was a winning argument. No doubt some armchair critics and BBC-haters would have a fit. But on the ground we had no choice. We paid for their drugs. What were we supposed to do? We were in Mogadishu, for goodness' sake. In any situation like that you have to make the rules up as you go along.

After a few days we were friendly with and fond of our guards. They were tough guys, but some of them were also lads just out of their teens. After we finished filming one day I presented a couple of them with BBC pens. They were just cheap rollerballs, but they had 'BBC' printed on the side, and the men were completely and totally charmed. It was as if they had never been given a present before.

One of them took his pen and wrote '2Pac', his nickname, on the front of his red beany hat, put the pen proudly into his breast pocket and turned it so the BBC sign faced out (where it remained for the rest of our stay), then laughed to Ajoos.

'He said he's been wanting to write his name on the hat for a year,' said Ajoos. 'I think you're in trouble now, Simon, they want to give you a special present.'

I scrambled to say I didn't want anything in return and that it was just a tiny gift. But it was too late. 2Pac presented me with a loaded Kalashnikov which he put over my shoulder.

'Mind the gap,' said Shahida dryly. She had grown up in the former Soviet Union and knew how to handle an AK47. When the safety catch is off there's a clear gap to indicate danger.

'Good point, Shazz,' I said.

I flicked the lever to safety. We politely took a couple of photos and then I went to hand the gun back.

'I don't think you understand, Simon,' said Ajoos earnestly. 'This is an ancient custom. You have given a gift, and now you must receive a gift in return. You would cause terrible offence if you gave it back. You will have to take the Kalashnikov with you to London.'

I blanched.

'Ajoos ... seriously ... I can't ...' I said. Then I paused. 'Hang on, you're taking the piss, aren't you?'

Ajoos's straight face crumbled. 'Yes, don't worry,' he laughed. 'Give it to me and I'll hide it back in the armoury. They'll never notice.'

The next day we were out again, driving north of Mogadishu to where local businessmen were trying to operate a rudimentary port away from warlords. As we drove through the outskirts of the city I had my helmet on my lap and my flak jacket propped up against the side of the vehicle as some protection against small-arms fire. We had decided against wearing the heavy jackets out on the streets for several reasons, but we kept them close at hand in case shooting broke out. Ajoos told us body armour was hard to get hold of in the city and thus extremely valuable to wealthy warlords. 'They will attack us and kill you just to get it,' he said.

As we drove along I was in the back of the lead technical

chatting with Ajoos and piping 'Mr Brightside' by the Killers through the car radio, loudly, from a transmitter on my iPod. 2Pac, who was in the back manning the mounted machine gun, banged on the roof and shouted to Ajoos, laughing.

'He says he wants to hear some Tupac or at least Eminem,' said Ajoos.

We slowed for a crossroads in a bombed-out area of the city, just as another gang in two technicals came to the junction down another road at the same moment. The other gang started screaming at our guys, and both groups locked and loaded their weapons and turned machine guns and anti-aircraft guns on each other.

For what seemed like an age the world stood still. The anti-aircraft gun on the other technical was pointing right at me. My body armour against the door would not have been the slightest protection. Rounds from an anti-aircraft gun would have shredded the armour, me and the vehicle.

The strangest sensation came over me. A sense of calm descended that I would never have expected. I told myself very quietly and very genuinely there was nothing I could do. Anything I did or said would almost certainly make things worse. It was a moment of acceptance. So I just sat there. Rock still. And I waited, to see if I would live or die.

Wise heads prevailed. The other gang drove off first. We sat there for just a second, as if bound by a spell. Ajoos spoke first.

'Well, let's go on then, shall we?' he said with a casual smile.

A day later we left Somalia on a cargo flight that took us north towards Somaliland. I felt a huge sense of relief when our plane was safely up in the air. It seemed we had been lucky. Other foreigners visiting Mogadishu around the same time were kidnapped. Tragically just a few months after we left, a brave and much-loved BBC producer called Kate Peyton was shot in the back while standing outside a guesthouse in Mogadishu, only hours after arriving in Somalia. She died from internal bleeding after being taken to a local hospital.

Landing in Somaliland everything felt different to Somalia. A smartly dressed immigration official stamped our passports. His presence and uniform were an immediate sign of order. Although rarely found on maps, Somaliland is home to roughly 4 million people. It borders the Gulf of Aden and sits next to Djibouti to the north-west and Ethiopia to the south and the west. Britain is the former colonial power and Somalilanders went to Britain's aid during the Second World War. Somalilanders still feel a strong attachment to the UK, and many struggle to understand why the government in London has not recognised their country.

The international status of many unrecognised states is tied up with geopolitics. One of the problems for Somaliland is that African states have collectively decided that, for better or worse, they will keep to colonial-era borders to avoid sparking wars across the continent as potentially dozens of minorities battle for their own states. The UK, I was told by a British diplomat, will not recognise Somaliland if no African state will recognise it first, to avoid accusations London behaves like a colonial power.

Somaliland faces an added complication because it has a potential port which could become a supply route for cargo to the Horn of Africa if the country was a full member of the UN. But neighbouring Djibouti already makes a fortune from its own deep-water port, so has a vested interest in blocking the recognition of Somaliland and preventing companies from trading with a potential rival.

As we drove into the sweltering capital Hargeisa, I chatted about the issue of recognition with Yusuf Abdi Gabobe, my local guide. He explained that Somaliland voluntarily joined with Somalia after independence from Britain in 1960, but when the relationship soured in the 1980s Somalilanders began campaigning and then battling for independence. Conflict erupted, and at least 50,000 men, women and children are thought to have died in Hargeisa alone as Somali forces and jets tried to quash the independence movement and bomb the city into submission. Up to 90 per cent of the city was destroyed by artillery and aerial bombing by aircraft flown by Zimbabwean mercenaries working for the Somali dictator Siad Barre. But in 1991 it was the Somali dictatorship that collapsed, plunging much of Somalia into decades of chaos. Somaliland then officially declared independence from Mogadishu and set up borders in line with what had previously been called British Somaliland. Yusuf, a towering figure of a man, had been a rebel leader fighting for Somaliland independence during the bitter conflict with Somalia.

Visiting Somaliland was a humbling lesson in survival and self-determination. Hargeisa was being rebuilt with little outside help, and refugees were returning from camps in Ethiopia. The streets bustled with activity, but I was trying to spot something small and understandable that I could point out to the camera, and by extension the viewers, which would illustrate in one moment the differences between chaotic Somalia and ordered, stable Somaliland. And then I spotted the symbol I had been seeking.

I asked Iain if he would follow me with the camera, and we hopped out of our car to film . . . at some traffic lights. Hardly the most surprising thing in cities around the world, but a shock to see in the Horn of Africa. In Mogadishu people had talked almost lovingly about the bright colours of traffic lights, which had all been destroyed long ago in fighting. Somalis told us that farmers and villagers would even trek into the centre of Mogadishu to see the traffic lights because they were so novel, and such a marvel. Their absence in Mogadishu was just a tiny example of the chaos of the city. Their presence in Hargeisa, and the fact drivers all obeyed them and stopped dutifully on red, was a contrasting sign of order. The reality of the whole state boiled down to a set of traffic lights at a particularly busy inter-section. I felt they were totemic.

Our driver had been a little too good at obeying the traffic regulations and vanished when the lights turned green, so I followed Yusuf as we walked a short distance across the city to where a Somali MiG jet which had bombed the city sat atop a poignant war memorial.

Yusuf explained that lack of recognition was hitting Somalil-and hard. It meant the self-declared state was having trouble securing any investment or foreign aid to help with a terrible drought. Tens of thousands of people were at risk of starvation. He took me to see Edna Adan Ismail, the extraordinary head of the maternity hospital in Hargeisa. She explained that even medical supplies could not be delivered because Somaliland had no international recognition.

'I really struggle to get international help here,' she said wearily. 'I have had volunteers from abroad, doctors, who want to come and help to train our nurses, but they can't even get insurance to come because the world says that we are part of Somalia.' As she gave me a tour, there was a shrill scream from another room, and Edna dashed off to help a mother giving birth.

Edna was a completely inspiring and amazing woman. She

was a nurse and midwife, but she was also the dynamic Foreign Minister of the country, and she took me to the President's office and walked me straight into a full cabinet meeting.

I backed out, we waited in our car for a while, and then had a meeting with the President, who was wearing an ill-fitting suit and said he was running the country on just a few million pounds a year, or 'whatever we can get'. Because nobody would recognise his government it could not get loans, which at least meant Somaliland was not burdened by foreign debt repayments.

The Somaliland Minister for Tourism saw us filming at the cabinet meeting and was elated he finally had a rare foreign visitor he could take to see his country's national treasures.

'Don't worry!' said the enthusiastic minister, as I reluctantly agreed to accompany him to some rock etchings recently discovered at Laas Ga'al outside Hargeisa. 'The drawings are beautiful, and it will just be a small detour from the road!'

We headed out on a dirt road bordered by low scrub and spreading acacia trees, then turned off into the bush. After bumping along a parched and pot-holed goat track for long enough for my bones to separate, I started to think my scepticism was justified. But we crested a hill, dodged wiry bushes on a wide plain, and finally scrambled over vast boulders to find exquisite rock paintings dating back thousands of years.

Even under the scorching sun, the paintings had strong, vibrant colours and stark outlines, showing the ancient inhabitants of the area worshipping long-horned cattle and venerating a pregnant cow. In a low cave further up the hill I found human figures dancing along the rock. There are paintings of dogs, camels, a giraffe, and the ancient herders of the region, presumably the people who painted the images. The whole site is an absolute treat. Laas Ga'al is probably the most significant Neolithic rock painting site in the whole of Africa. The rock art has been dated to 9000–3000 BC, but still looks as though it was painted last week.

For a brief moment I felt like an explorer finding hidden treasures, at a time when the entire world seems easy to reach on package holidays. Somaliland is proof there are still areas of the world off the beaten track which can excite and amaze. The territory does not feature on many tourist maps. In fact, it does not feature on many maps at all. According to the international community, Somaliland does not even exist.

Yusuf took us deeper into the mountains and then on to the port of Berbera. 'There are tracks along the coast west from here towards Djibouti, and mangroves, gorgeous islands and coral reef,' said Yusuf. 'If only you had a few more weeks we could head out along the coast. But let's go to the airport instead.'

It sounded like a poor alternative. We stopped at an old, dust-blown, abandoned airfield, driving in through a wonky, creaking gate and past a small hand-painted sign: 'Wellcome to Berbera International Air Port'. A set of passenger steps lay baking in the sun, covered in sand and muck. Yusuf took me up into the dilap-idated control tower, and we wiped the windows so we could see outside. It didn't look like much, but then Yusuf explained that at more than 4.5 kilometres, the runway was actually one of the longest in the world. I was stunned.

'It was built during the Cold War by the Soviet Union,' he told me. 'Moscow based heavy bombers here in Berbera, until the Soviets switched allegiance from Somalia to Ethiopia in the 1970s, and we asked the Soviets to leave.'

In their place the Americans arrived, and NASA decided to

use the airfield as an emergency landing strip for the space shuttle, apparently paying something like £30 million per year in rent. Yusuf could see that I looked completely disbelieving.

'It's true!' he said with a smile. 'It was just in case the shuttle had trouble on re-entry and couldn't make it around the planet and back to the US. You see, we have more surprises to share with you, Simon.'

We left and drove further into Berbera in our four-wheel-drive vehicles through the bush, when Yusuf suddenly stopped the car again and leapt out, motioning for me to join him.

'Quick, quick,' he said. 'Have a look at this beauty.'

I followed him for a short distance over to a colossal termite mound standing like a monolith at least six metres tall.

'These wonders were our friends when we were fighting in the bush for more than ten years,' he said, his eyes shining. 'When I was a guerrilla commander we could hide behind them and even rocket-propelled grenades could not get at us. One time we were attacked by the forces loyal to the Somali dictator Siad Barre in helicopter gunships and most of us were able to find protection behind the mounds.'

He slapped the side. 'Feel it, they're like solid concrete.'

Termite mounds are astonishing eco-systems with ventilation and natural air-conditioning systems. What you see above ground is just a fraction of what lies below the surface. They are like solid desert icebergs.

Yusuf was a softly spoken, unshockable man who I gradually realised had seen far too much horror. We paused a few hours further up the road, still in the bush, and prepared some food. I dug out a round of food ration packs for all of us and began heating them up. A heating element is put into a bag containing another sealed bag of stew or curry and then a small sachet of water is poured on top. The water causes a chemical reaction in the element that then heats the food.

Yusuf stood watching me as I prepared our meals. He wasn't an easy man to impress, but he couldn't contain himself.

'That is completely incredible,' he said. 'Incredible ... incredible ... How does it work? Oh, if only we had those with us when we were out in the bush, they would have made life so much more bearable. The food was one of the worst things about being a guerrilla fighter.'

We sat on the ground and had a picnic, with Yusuf still shaking his head and smiling as he ate each mouthful of the magic stew.

Somaliland made a huge impact on me. The place, unrecognised or not, was a revelation, with stability, democracy, a minister for tourism, women in parliament, a police force, and traffic lights. But it was the Somalilanders themselves who I found most impressive. They are still to this day determined and completely inspiring. Largely ignored by the world, they are building an independent state from scratch.

Sadly, it is still possible that war between Somalia and Somaliland could erupt again. But there is also a much more optimistic future for the country. Perhaps one day Somaliland will have its own seat at the United Nations, and tourists will flock to the rock paintings at Laas Ga'al, and to its stunning beaches to swim at the mouth of the Red Sea.

CHAPTER EIGHTEEN

Fishing with the President

I was genuinely gloomy about leaving Somaliland. We headed back home and I quickly repacked for the next trip to an unrecognised country on the edge of Europe. Transnistria, a sliver of a place between the former Soviet republics of Ukraine and Moldova, was an unofficial nation thought to be home to 400,000–700,000 people, depending on who was doing the counting.

After the Soviet Union collapsed two thirds of the people in the country that became Moldova were of Romanian descent and wanted to have closer ties with Romania and the West. The remaining third of the population wanted to keep their ties with Russia and Ukraine. There was a short but ferocious war and the land east of the Dniestr River became the unrecognised state of Transnistria.

The little state's campaign for recognition was not going well when I visited. The United Nations and the rest of the world said Transnistria was officially and legally part of Moldova. Only three other states had chosen to recognise Transnistria, and they were also unrecognised, so hardly counted. To get to the breakaway statelet I had to travel through Moldova, the mother country from which it had split, and I headed there with Shahida and Will Daws.

My first impression of Moldova as we drove out into the

251

countryside was that it was clearly staggeringly poor. I had a guidebook with me that talked about 'unspoilt landscapes', 'rural pastures', 'charming backwater', which I think translated as something like: 'grinding poverty', 'high unemployment', 'no development', 'most people have left'.

The statistics showed that many people in Moldova were earning less than £2 a day. I confess I had no idea such abject poverty could exist right on the doorstep of the European Union. We drove through the Moldovan countryside on roads of mud, passing villages so poor that buildings were barely standing. Most of the countryside was empty of people except for young children and the grandparents who looked after them.

Moldova was officially the poorest country in Europe. I was stunned by the conditions people were enduring. I have travelled through rural regions of Romania and Hungary, but they don't even get close to Moldova for poverty. I saw an elderly woman trying to pull a small wooden plough across a field like a two-legged donkey. We drove to one village that was in such poor repair, with roads pitted with rocks and potholes, that we had to get out of our rugged four-wheel drive and walk. People who remained in some communities were so utterly impoverished they had resorted to the most desperate methods possible to earn money.

In the heart of one village we walked up a steep muddy track, past broken fences until we came to a green metal fence with a small house, beyond which scrawny chickens were penned and dogs barked incessantly. My guide, local journalist Liliana Vitu, introduced me to three of the remaining men in the village who had sold one of their kidneys to foreign buyers desperate for a transplant.

They sold a kidney.

For an example of the reality of poverty, in its most basic form, it was utterly shocking. And on the edge of Europe? I was stunned.

The men showed me scars that ran from the base of their ribs almost to their armpits. Most had been paid less than £2,000. One man had used the money to buy a washing machine and some clothes for his children, another bought a cow and redecorated his house. As I spoke to them, I couldn't quite believe this was happening in the twenty-first century.

These poor, desperate people had done something extreme in a vain attempt to survive, in a country with no economy to speak of, and had then squandered the money they had been paid. All the men said they were experiencing sickness and weakness.

Walking through their village I started to wonder how Moldova could ever build a functioning economy. Huge areas of the country were the preserve of kids, grandparents, the sick and the weak. They were empty of young adults.

Around a million Moldovans were thought to have travelled abroad. There were only 3 million people remaining. Across much of the country there was almost no one left of working age. Most had fled in a desperate search for work in Europe or Russia.

For me it was a stark illustration of an aspect of the migration debate in Europe I had never previously considered. People inside the borders of the EU often discuss the pros and cons of migration into Europe based on a relatively selfish idea of what is good or bad for Europe. '*What do immigrants do for us?*' is often the tone of the debate.

Very rarely does anybody talk about the consequences for less-developed countries of seeing their ablest and fittest leaving in search of work. In ghost communities in Moldova I saw the effects. Moldova had lost an entire generation, and society was reeling and listless as a result.

I have since been in many other countries which have lost millions of people to migration, from the Philippines to Mexico, from Bangladesh to sub-Saharan Africa. Many of those left behind complain their brightest and best are being poached by the West through complicated immigration quotas, often so they can work as taxi drivers and pizza chefs, rather than staying at home to develop their own businesses and the national economy.

Take healthcare workers. The International Organisation on Migration (IOM) has concluded there are more Ethiopian doctors working in Chicago than in the whole of Ethiopia. One study found that an astonishing 77 per cent of physicians trained in Liberia were actually working in the US. More than half the doctors born in Sierra Leone, Tanzania, Mozambique, Angola and Liberia are now working in wealthy Organisation for Economic Cooperation and Development (OECD) countries.

In the UK more than a quarter of doctors received their primary training outside of Europe, and the main countries providing doctors to the UK from outside the EU include India, Pakistan, Nigeria, Egypt, Sri Lanka, Iraq and Sudan.

The money the UK saves by recruiting Ghanaian health workers may well exceed the money Britain gives Ghana in aid for health. African and East Asian states in particular spend a fortune on the education and training of nurses and doctors only to see European countries actively recruit them, often straight out of college. It is just one of a hundred ways poorer countries continue to subsidise wealthier nations. The NHS is especially dependent on migrant healthcare workers. The government Office for Budget Responsibility admits that without them the NHS would be in 'dire straits'. We should be paying more to the countries that train our doctors and nurses, compensating them for fixing our own skills shortage.

Consider what happens when your nation is drained of the young, able, middle-class professionals and the educated. In several countries in the Caribbean 70 per cent of people educated above high-school level have fled or left their countries for opportunities elsewhere. By one estimate Jamaica has lost 85 per cent of university educated workers. It is infinitely more difficult to run a state without a middle class and the tax revenue they generate. They help to pay for schooling, welfare and medical care. If they are absent the country is crippled.

I can understand why individuals leave, of course. But collectively the consequences can be a state that never stands on its own two feet.

Some economists say that increasing 'immigration flows', as they call them, could have enormous economic benefits. If the developed world took in enough immigrants to enlarge their workforce by just 1 per cent, they claim, the additional value created could be worth more to those migrants than all of the foreign aid payments in the world combined. I have no doubt that could well be true.

But a benefit to the relatively small number of people from developing countries who have migrated abroad does not necessarily mean benefit to the hundreds of millions left behind.

Other supporters of migration – large corporations, for example – say that countries like Moldova or Bangladesh receive huge sums in 'remittances', the sums sent home by migrants. But those remittances do not help to create communities; they often become what Australian Aboriginals call 'sit-down money', a welfare cheque received without any requirement to find work. Often they can help to entrench poverty by encouraging people in remote communities empty of employment to do little but drink, fester and wait for the next handout from their relative abroad.

I am not completely opposed to migration. I am not saying immigration is always a bad thing. I just think the debate in Western countries concentrates on the effect it has on us. We are selfish. There should be more discussion about the effects on the poorer, developing countries and communities that people are leaving. Because on the ground in rural Moldova, and in dozens of other places I have visited in the years since, the consequences are often tragic.

We went to visit the President of Moldova. You can do that when you're a BBC TV crew making a documentary about Transnistria. Along with the poverty, unemployment and migration, the breakaway state was perhaps the biggest issue affecting the nation. Liliana explained that President Vladimir Voronin's mother lived in Transnistria and for the past two years he had been unable to visit her because of the border dispute with the breakaway territory.

I feared my time with the President would involve a formal chat. But as we drove through a set of iron gates, arrived at the palatial presidential property and discovered that President Voronin wanted to take me fishing on his very own well-stocked lake. My only other memory of fishing was when I was twelve, and I slipped off a bank, fell into the River Piddle up to my neck, and then had to walk through the local village while people lined pavements to laugh at me. President Voronin helped exorcise my demons. A couple of ornate, gilded state chairs were set up on the bank by the lake for us to relax in, slices of watermelon were brought out, and the President tried to show me how to cast a line.

A lifelong Communist, Voronin was white-haired, in his sixties, and had been the head of a bread factory in a small Moldovan town before he entered politics. He still had the air of someone involved in provincial middle-management. I asked him what he thought about Transnistria and whether anything was going on there that the rest of Europe should be concerned about.

'It's a hole,' he said. 'I cannot go there. I cannot see my mother; the place is nothing more than a black hole of corruption and trafficking.' He was angry, but it was an oft-repeated speech.

'Moldova has a 480-kilometre border with the Ukraine and the section in Transnistria is not controlled, and via this there's uncontrolled migration, contraband, arms trafficking, the trafficking of human beings and drugs. These operations are being legitimised by the separatist regime. There are thirteen enterprises in Transnistria that are producing arms non-stop.'

At that moment the President broke off from the chat because his aide announced he had caught a fish. Then he asked me to join him on a tour of his wine cellar. It must have been a quiet day for the President, because he decided we needed to celebrate Moldovan national independence day, and went straight for vodka and his favourite cognac. He insisted we weren't about to get drunk.

'I'm just very proud of Moldovan cognac and I want to promote it,' he said.

We were all finishing a second bottle when his wife came in from the shops, complete with plastic carrier bags, told him to stop teasing and playing with the foreign film crew, and we staggered out.

You don't have to travel far to discover the exotic appeal of an unrecognised state. It is only around an hour by bus or car from the leafy Moldovan capital Chisinau to the border with Transnistria. Officially it was still part of Moldova and the border did not exist. But the reality on the ground was tanks, armed guards, bunkers, fortified positions, and reams of razor wire. I was surprised at how tense the situation was. We were visiting years after actual fighting had stopped, but each side feared it might erupt again at any moment. Just before we arrived Transnistria had upped the stakes by banning the teaching of Moldovan in schools, allowing only Russian. Moldova had responded with an economic blockade. If you looked at the situation on paper it would seem that tiny Transnistria could not survive the siege, but still they held out.

We showed our passports to surly guards and soldiers, then drove and walked through what was essentially a demilitarised zone before crossing into Transnistria. I had arrived in my second breakaway state and felt a gentle sense of elation.

Transnistria was quite the experience. I thought I had gone through a time warp. It was like visiting a Soviet-themed adventure park. In the capital Tiraspol the hammer-and-sickle emblem of the Soviet Union had pride of place outside many buildings, and a statue of Lenin dominated the street outside the House of Soviets.

My new guide Larissa, a teacher with a kindly soul, met us at the crossing. I asked whether the Soviet symbols meant people looked back fondly on the past.

'No, we just do not carry out war with monuments,' she said with a grin.

Moldovans had warned me hungry armed men roam the streets of Transnistria, but although the border was tense, the leafy streets of Tiraspol were full of cafés and restaurants. People sat outside on cheap plastic chairs as old cars chugged past. Fighting talk was limited to thoughts on political strife in neighbouring Ukraine and the impact on the price of *salo*, pig fat, a major Ukrainian export. Transnistrians were eating it covered with chocolate, partly as a joke, and partly I think to show how hard they were. I had to try it, just for research purposes. Sweet on the outside and extra salty on the inside, after a moment of chewing it just tasted like raw bacon rind. It was unappetising, but not quite as bad as it sounds.

Larissa spoke English well and was thoughtful, with well-considered views. She said she had no doubt that breaking away from Moldova and keeping ties with Russia was the right decision. She talked optimistically about the future. 'We are young,' she said, 'but there is work here for the people, and you can't say that about Moldova.'

Then she showed me her Transnistrian passport. It looked more convincing than my Somali diplomatic offering. I asked her who recognised it as a legitimate travel document.

'We do,' she said, and she laughed.

'Does anyone else?'

'No,' she said. 'Not yet.'

Transnistrians celebrated their National Independence Day while we visited, an event which bore a striking resemblance to old Soviet May Day parades. Small children in uniforms sang 'our army is the best army' with evident pride, and the army goose-stepped along the main road past a platform of officers awarded medals by the kilo. Having always wanted to visit Red Russia, I watched goggle-eyed.

But I also felt sorry for them. Years since they split, the ongoing tension between Moldova and Transnistria ensured both states were economically depressed and continued to suffer.

The President of Transnistria, Igor Smirnov, was happy to explain why independence was so important. 'It means the protection of all the generations that live here regardless of their nationality,' he told me. But then, realising that he had set himself up for a tricky follow-up question, he added that there were forty-six different nationalities in Transnistria and begged: 'Please don't ask me to list them all.'

There was a party atmosphere in Transnistria the day they celebrated independence. Cafés served great flagons of beer and we ate heartily. The rest of the time Transnistrian cafés were some of the trickiest places to eat on the planet.

Each one had a menu the length of a telephone directory, as if they were listing all the food available on the Eurasian land mass. We would request something, and the waiter would go to the kitchen and ask if it was available. Then they would return, shake their head almost imperceptibly, and say simply in Russian: '*Nyet.*' I like the people of the former Soviet Union and I missed them during the past few years while I was travelling in the tropics. I missed their hard shells and inner warmth. I missed their culture, their language, their resigned shrugs, and their ability to talk without moving their lips or using facial muscles. But ordering a meal in Transnistria became a right saga. After a couple of requests for meals were rejected we thought it best for the waiter to simply tell us what was available. He went off again, returning five minutes later.

'Chicken. And potatoes.'

The first time we ate a meal in Transnistria we saw our food being chased around the yard outside. We knew it was fresh but then we waited two hours for it to be served. Cafés in Transnistria, I can say with absolute certainty, are the slowest on Planet Earth. So the next day we tried to ring ahead. Despite assurances to the contrary, nothing was cooked until we arrived, and we waited another hour. The next day Dimitri went ahead to order, pay and browbeat them into cooking, but the chef walked out in a huff. Apparently, it was the custom for everyone to be sitting, waiting, before anyone would even start boiling water. The long, long waits gave time for repeated karaoke rehearsals of the uplifting Transnistrian anthem. In dark moments I can still hear it rattling around in my head.

Bulgaria and Romania were both waiting to join the European Union when I visited Transnistria. After they entered the bloc in 2007 that put the breakaway state right on the eastern edge of Europe. The EU is supposed to be a gathering of nations committed to improving life for all, but critics say it has failed to adequately press for reform and change in Transnistria and other post-Soviet 'frozen conflict' zones.

When I visited, Transnistria was thought to be a haven for smuggling. It certainly had a Wild West feel. Time and again we discovered that a business, stadium, restaurant or factory was run by a single mysterious firm controlled by former Red Army officers who seemed to have bottomless pockets and a penchant for flashy, top-of-the range vehicles.

International investigators claimed they were unsure what was going on, hardly surprising when there were no foreign embassies and few foreigners visiting the extraordinary little state. Rumours and undercover reports suggest it was a major producer of illegal arms, and the border with Ukraine was said to leak like a sieve. We drove to the south-east of Transnistria and I crossed the unguarded border on foot. I could see for myself how easy it would be for smugglers to traffic arms to the Black Sea port of Odessa and from there to anywhere on the planet.

One of the main reasons for making the series was to high-light the risks of leaving unrecognised countries isolated, and Transnistria was a classic example. Guns from Transnistria have turned up in conflicts around the world.

Russia was said to be calling the shots in Transnistria, so we drove north for a few hours and then crept through bushes to try and get shots of a secret Russian military base that was roughly half a mile away.

'They'll never see us over here,' I was blithely saying to Will Daws, who was filming behind the camera, when there was a squeal of tyres, a couple of old Ladas screeched up and four KGB heavies in trench coats jumped out. It was like a scene from a 1950s spy movie.

The KGB had never been disbanded in Transnistria, and we were detained, marched away, and trucked off to cells in the secret police headquarters. Perhaps I had seen too many Cold War thrillers, but I had visions of being held for years and having to write escape plans in blood using my toenails for nibs. We were taken from the cells individually and questioned. Over and over they asked in halting English what we were doing in Transnistria and why we were trying to film the base.

'Are we being arrested?' I asked the officer.

'No,' he said. 'You are being ...' he searched for the word, '*detained*.'

The way he said it left me feeling nervous. 'Arrest' was a procedure. 'Detained' was more open-ended.

Fortunately for the team and me, I'd been gassing away to my guide Larissa about how my family's solitary claim to fame was a distant link to the man who rebuilt much of London after the Great Fire.

'Not Sir Christopher Wren?' Her eyes had lit up.

'Yes,' I said, surprised. 'How did you know?'

'We studied London as a module in Soviet times: Buckingham Palace, Regent's Park, Saint Paul's Cathedral.' Larissa was supremely impressed. My local stock had risen dramatically.

Larissa heard we'd been detained and turned up at the KGB headquarters in the middle of the night, literally banging on the door and demanding to see the officer in charge.

'You cannot arrest these people,' she wailed at him. 'One of them is related to the Queen of England. You will bring terrible shame on Transnistria.'

There was a great banging of doors and clanking of keys. We all thought something awful was going to happen. Then a senior KGB officer appeared and apologised for the misunderstanding. 'Perhaps we can go for a drink to smooth this over,' he suggested. We were all released into the night and agents gave each of us KGB cap badges as souvenirs.

We left Transnistria in a hurry fearing the KGB would change their minds and seize our tapes. We separated them out between us, hid them in our bags and in our clothing, and left the territory in taxis, buses and cars, just to reduce the risk if one of us was stopped and detained. Again I was disappointed to leave. It was a crazy place, but edgy and fascinating. We escaped with a precious travel experience to share with viewers and I had a tale to bore my son with for years to come.

We headed east, across the Black Sea and Turkey towards the Caucasus, never the most stable part of the world, and Georgia, which had no less than three regions which broke away when the Soviet Union collapsed: Ajaria, South Ossetia and Abkhazia. In the ensuing conflicts thousands were killed and the whole region has suffered ever since.

Yet initially Georgia felt safe and impressive. For a couple of days we set the scene by exploring and filming ancient monasteries, old sulphur baths, trendy new bars in the capital Tbilisi, and ate meals with a population that delighted in drinking endless toasts to family, country, friends and football teams. Georgia gave the world a Golden Fleece and Stalin, who they commemorate with a museum. When our local guide vanished I was able to sit on Stalin's personal toilet and strike my own small blow against the veneration of a murdering madman. Then we drove back to the capital, and a meeting with the young Georgian President 'Misha' Saakashvili, who was trying to re-unify the whole country and drag it into the twenty-first century.

We were waiting for the President in his offices when someone said he was dashing outside to talk to a crowd of demonstrators, so we jumped into the same small lift. He was completely unfazed.

'Mr President, Simon from the BBC,' I said.

'Hi, how are you?' he responded, in American-accented English.

I asked him what was going on with South Ossetia, the main breakaway state in Georgia. 'It looks like Russia wants to stir up trouble on the border,' he said, 'but we are trying to keep things calm. We don't need any other bloody clash there.'

I asked him how difficult the situation was at that moment.

'It's a very small piece of territory,' he said, striding out of the lift and across the ground floor of the presidential offices, 'but it looks like for Russians it's kind of a Maginot line of defence, but

God knows for what interest. There is a chance there will be a clash, but we hope it won't happen.'

With two bodyguards, wearing obligatory sunglasses, he dived into the crowd and told them he was praying for peace every single night.

Emotions were running high on the border between Georgia and the breakaway region of South Ossetia, which had its own government and army. Just a day before we arrived there fifty Georgian soldiers had been taken captive by South Ossetian forces, who were being trained, backed and encouraged by the might of Russia. We tried to cross into South Ossetia but became trapped in a no-man's-land by Georgian soldiers who said we were not allowed to go forwards or backwards because of the risk of kidnap or detention by South Ossetian and Russian forces.

Moscow had placed 'peace-keepers' along the border. Georgians viewed them as 'piece-keepers' – desperately trying to keep the old Soviet Union alive. It was one of President Putin's early and successful attempts at meddling in a former Soviet state that wanted closer ties to the West.

We were only released from the no-man's-land when a Russian general, who said his forces were preventing fighting, agreed to chaperone us into the breakaway region. We crossed into South Ossetia, the land of the Ossetes, who told me they speak a different language to Georgians and are determined to remain independent.

President Putin was a hero in Ossetia. His poster was everywhere, looking down on the leafy streets of a tiny territory that seemed stuck in another 1970s Soviet past. Old Lada cars spluttered along on potholed roads, and gaunt, elderly civilians with hollow cheeks sold vegetables from baskets on overgrown pavements. Russia was not gifting them a marvellous alternative to rule by Georgia. The place was desperately poor.

The Ossetes were hugely suspicious of foreigners, partly because our minder kept telling people I was from London in America. After I explained London was on the edge of Europe, young soldiers shared a drunken birthday toast and vowed to fight and die rather than rejoin Georgia.

'We will never allow the Georgians to rule us, because throughout Ossetian history they have always tried to push us around,' said one young soldier, idly twirling a dagger around in his hands. 'We've never submitted to that, and we never will.'

The soldiers were drinking, but they were friendly and engaging, and they invited us to sit with them in an outdoor area behind a restaurant and let us film. I swapped tales from my travels for their stories of life on the front line, and then the youngster offered his dagger as a gift. I refused, but he insisted. I was genuinely touched and gave him my watch in return. I still use his knife as a letter opener.

Even after years of conflict with Georgia, the Ossetes were noticeably edgy. People were scared about the prospect of renewed fighting with Georgia. With some rudimentary Russian I nearly caused a riot in a local fruit market by accidentally insulting a female fruit seller while I was trying to buy some apples. Years of travel should have made me a paragon of diplomatic virtue, the very embodiment of the culturally sensitive adventurer. But my inadequate grasp of languages has repeatedly tripped me up. Sometimes a broad smile has got me out of trouble, and sometimes a rapid exit is the only available option. Employing a translator is no guarantee of social safety. 'I'm here to grasp your private parts,' was how an interpreter translated President Jimmy Carter's opening comment when visiting Poland.

The Ossetian market seller was livid. She was throwing apples at me and shouting to other stall-holders. Someone claimed I had asked if she had a penis. I had to be rescued by our furious Ossetian government minder, and I swore to stick to the most basic local phrases. It was an uncomfortable visit, and we were shadowed everywhere by the secret police.

Back in Georgia we found American and British troops training Georgian soldiers, and entire trains loaded with troops and tanks, waiting for the call to head to the front line. It was clear war could erupt between Georgia and South Ossetia at any time.

Heading west across Georgia an overnight train took us to the western Black Sea coast and Ajaria, a holiday destination and summer paradise with beaches that attracted tourists from across the former Soviet Union. It was rejoining Georgia, largely because of local anger at the former strongman dictator. His son would close the best road every night and race his Lamborghini up and down the seafront. Strangely, this did not go down well among locals earning £20 a month. They kicked out the strongman and were welcomed back into Georgia. But they still had a thing or two to learn about leadership: the new governor took us to a restaurant which was immediately cleared of other customers by henchmen who looked like extras from *The Sopranos*.

Abkhazia may well be a lovely place to visit, but we barely made it across the border before the Abkhaz government kicked us out. No Western government operates in Abkhazia, although organised crime gangs are thought to be based there.

All of the breakaway regions of the country were a shock, but perhaps the single most bizarre and chilling place I visited in the region was actually a former secret Soviet military base inside Georgia. The sprawling base had been abandoned when the Soviet Union collapsed, and even when I visited, more than ten years later, it still contained thousands of tons of almost completely unguarded high explosives in artillery shells and anti-aircraft munitions. A local scientist, who had taken it upon himself to rally some help from other retired experts and deactivate some of the weaponry, showed me into a corrugated-iron shed, locked by a single piece of string, inside which were 30,000 rusting shells still containing the military high-explosive TNT. He claimed that if any explosives at the base detonated, the chain reaction would destroy most of the hill the base was sitting on and register on seismic charts around much of the world.

Then to really put the fear of God up me, the scientist took me further up a grassy, overgrown hill and showed me dozens of rocket pods holding even more powerful surface-to-air missile systems. Each one contained, he told me, more than 200 kilograms of TNT.

'One can destroy almost anything, they are extremely powerful,' said the scientist. 'For example, a skyscraper, no problem.'

He was clearly frustrated, exhausted and worried. I asked him how easy it would be for someone to take out the explosive and use it in a terrorist weapon. He smiled wanly.

'Everything is inside,' he responded, 'that's why a small spark or static discharge will detonate them. You could detonate one with a small battery.'

I looked around at the edge of the base. There were fence posts, but no fences. The scientist told us that some houses in local villages had been destroyed when locals tried to extract explosives from some of the smaller artillery shells. He also said he had no money for petrol for a lawnmower, which meant long dry grass had grown around the missile systems, creating a real risk that a fire could detonate the weapons. Nobody was willing to cut the grass with a hand scythe because the area was infested with snakes. The situation was set to get worse.

'Soon, the base will be reclassified,' said the scientist. 'At the moment it has five guards, but soon it will no longer be a military base, so even those five guards will be removed, and the base will be completely and totally unguarded. Isn't this crazy?'

I had to agree.

Militants were active throughout the volatile region, but there wasn't even fencing around the base to protect the missiles from theft. I found it astonishing governments were warning us of the threat from terrorism, and troops were hunting for weapons of mass destruction in Iraq at the same time, yet so little was being done to safeguard powerful weapons abandoned in the former Soviet Union. The scientist had rung the US embassy to warn them the stockpile could be stolen, but nobody even bothered to return his calls.

I wanted to move on across the Caucasus mountains to breakaway Nagorno-Karabakh, a small, mountainous, landlocked region in the South Caucasus. But on the phone from London we had only been able to find one person there who spoke English and could act as an interpreter. His name was David, and he was on holiday visiting relatives. We had to delay our journey for a week until he returned, so instead we headed to Azerbaijan, which had gone to war over Nagorno-Karabakh.

Historically Nagorno-Karabkh had been mainly Armenian Christian, but Stalin, who was skilled at using division to control people, gave it to Azerbaijan, which is mainly Muslim.

After the Soviet collapse Azerbaijan and Armenia got their

independence. When Nagorno-Karabakh then wanted to become independent, neighbouring Armenia sent troops into battle and helped the Karabakh army push out local Muslim Azeris who had been living there for decades.

Both sides committed terrible atrocities during the conflict. When I visited, Azerbaijan was still officially at war with Armenia. With a young, passionate guide called Tural we started our journey on the Azeri front lines looking into Karabakh. Active conflict had halted, but it was still one of the world's forgotten hot spots. Azeri soldiers spoke of their fury at losing family homes just across the front lines. They seemed genuinely determined to get them back. Some still had keys to homes now occupied by Armenians. Ethnic Muslims were forced to flee, leaving towns and villages destroyed so there was no way they could return.

It might have been the twenty-first century in the rest of the world, but on both sides of the border between Karabakh and Azerbaijan young soldiers were still manning trenches. We had to sprint across the open ground of no-man's-land to avoid sniper fire. I heard shots, but nothing came close.

The conflict over Karabakh actually began in the dying years of the Soviet Union. Back in 1988 there were demonstrations in Karabakh and Armenia calling for unification. Then an Azeri march degenerated into a riot and clashes in which there were deaths and injuries on both sides. Azeris and Armenians had lived among each other for generations on both sides of the border, but more outbreaks of violence erupted and people began fleeing to safety, often running through the night with their families. Armenians fled back to Armenia, Azeris to Azerbaijan.

I remembered reading about the conflict and the war that

followed while still a teenager. Back then it had seemed like an unfathomable conflict in a very faraway corner of the world, in countries I could not understand involving people I could not comprehend. Now I was there. Talking with them. And their motivations were completely understandable. I could see clearly how a chain of individual events, dislikes, hatreds, connections and disconnections, had led to tragedy.

Reading about the situation from afar I had been tempted to criticise and condemn when I arrived. But it's all too easy for outsiders to misunderstand and underestimate the complexity of relationships and situations that lead to such conflict. Nagorno-Karabakh was one of my first real tastes of what I had always thought of as medieval hatred and tension. So often we don't understand situations and try to suggest or impose simplistic solutions. Yet the problems between the Armenians and Azeris had developed over generations. People from both sides might have got stuck in the past, but for them that past mattered. Understanding that was a starting point in my own attempt to try and fathom what had happened, and I reminded myself that Europeans were in no position to criticise, given the wars we had started and the conflict that raged across our land mass just a few decades before. Anyway, criticising wasn't my job, then or now. I wasn't there to cast simple aspersions. I was there to try and offer a balanced view of the situation, show an unrecognised state to the viewers, and encourage them to learn more about the chaos and tragedy that exists in our world.

We drove back into Azerbaijan and discovered there were still thousands of refugees from the war living in appalling conditions. Although the country has vast oil wealth, and once used to

supply half the world's oil, children and the elderly were surviving in rusty train carriages on a railway siding.

We walked among washing lines strung between the boxcars
like a community from the Great Depression. It was bitterly
cold and dozens of families were trying to survive with no electricity, no water and no heating.

Walking past one boxcar I heard children's voices and our
guide told me it housed a small school. Inside teenagers were
being taught with almost no resources. I spoke to one teenage
girl and asked her how long she had lived there.

'We came in 1993,' she said. 'I was very young, I don't remember before. This is the only home I remember.'

I struggled to comprehend. She had spent more than a decade
living in a railway car designed to carry freight. If I hadn't seen
it with my own eyes it would have been inconceivable. No one
was giving up hope of going home, but, as is often the case, refugees like this had become pawns in a bigger game. Azerbaijan
didn't want to assimilate the refugees into the country and give
them proper homes, because if they did they could no longer be
used as evidence of loss. Integration would be a tacit acceptance
that they were never going to get Nagorno-Karabakh back, and
the government and the country could never allow that. The
desire to maintain a hold over a breakaway state would keep
those refugees exactly where they were on a railway siding at the
border.

We drove on, feeling sombre. Everyone mentioned the war. We
stopped to grab something to eat in a wooden hut of a café that,
at one time, had been a brothel. A wandering minstrel came in to
sing us a melancholy song. He explained it was about the homeland
he had lost and longed for. The emotion was heartfelt.

The border between Azerbaijan and Karabakh was closed, so

to get there we took a monumental detour across the border into Georgia, passing through stunning snowy mountains and then on into Armenia.

The journey took a few days and the camera rolled most of the time because we knew just about anything could happen. Our car skidded off the road and had two punctures. We had a row with some truck drivers, spent hours listening to strange Azeri and Georgian music on cassettes, and ate plates of unidentifiable food at mountain truck stops. It was a challenging but brilliant adventure, so I was gutted when the programme was later put together and so little of the journey made it into the cut. But we only had thirty minutes and the other footage we had filmed was much stronger.

Finally we headed south over icy mountain passes and into Karabakh. A sign set above a snow-capped landscape bade us welcome. It was early evening and the moon was out. I felt snow crunch under my boots as I looked out at the disputed landscape. A twisting, empty road through the mountains led to Stepanakert, the capital, past eerie, burnt-out villages destroyed after the Azeris left.

In Soviet times Stepanakert, which sits on a high plateau, had been a provincial town under Azeri control. Now the only inhabitants were Armenian-Christian Karabakhians. It was a town stuck in a mindset of continual conflict. In the morning I was taken to visit a school, where young men were being trained to strip down a Kalashnikov blindfolded.

The scenery and churches of Karabakh were impressive, but it was difficult to visit without asking awkward questions. Before Karabakh declared independence from Azerbaijan its population was split between Azeris and Armenians. After the bloody war only a handful of Azeris remain.

Everyone in Karabakh had their own, very different take on the conflict and division. It was the other side of the story. But it was also another side of the truth. Two peoples can go to war and endure decades of conflict and division, but both can still be right. Both can still deserve our sympathy. We can go through the events that created the situation and identify who on each side made mistakes and who committed crimes, but when the end result is long-term suffering, everyone deserves understanding.

David took us back towards the border region, much of which had been mined. We were walking through a gully at the side of a road when we saw the skeleton of a cow. Its back legs had been blown off. Then someone screamed: 'Don't move, we're in a minefield!' I froze rigid. We were there for a few moments, calling to each other and trying to reassure everyone that we would be all right. We knew how to get out of a minefield but it is, of course, exceptionally dangerous and takes hours. Then we heard a vehicle pull up on the road above the gully, and an army officer in a camouflage uniform appeared.

'Don't worry,' he said, 'there are only tank mines here, so your weight will not detonate them.'

We retraced our steps. Very carefully.

David took us to see the work of the magnificent British charity, the HALO Trust, which runs demining operations around the world, has cleared vast areas of mines and saved countless lives. They were working hard to clear mines in Nagorno-Karabakh and a former British Army officer showed us a plot they were surveying. I wanted a closer look so he lent me a flak jacket and a thick curved perspex mask supposed to deflect at least some of a blast.

Walking towards the minefield was nerve-wracking. One of the teams was working close to a village. They told me pigs occasionally wandered onto mines, sometimes when deminers were working in the same area. The HALO deminers explained to me that whenever they saw pigs or other animals straying into a minefield they would have to suspend their work and retreat, rapidly.

There are hundreds of different types of landmines. Some only detonate after they have been trodden on three times, or ten. Some explode immediately with a blast directed upwards. Some are designed to leap half a metre into the air before blasting hundreds of ball bearings around a huge radius, severing limbs and turning attacking soldiers into casualties that become a drain on their colleagues. Others will spray ball bearings at head height over an area the size of a football pitch. One mine detonation can cause others to explode, like dominoes. They are astonishing works of evil, and they can sit in the ground for a decade or much longer, just waiting for the unwary to stray across their path.

We got down on our hands and knees and crawled to the edge of the minefield, ready for them to begin demining, poking very slowly through the ground with plastic spikes designed to identify but not trigger a mine. Whenever they found something they would need to place a marker on the ground and then, very slowly, excavate the area to remove the deadly threat. I was learning all about this while we were on the ground right on the edge of the minefield, when suddenly we realised there were people, villagers, actually walking through the minefield in front of us. One of them was carrying their shopping bags. I couldn't believe anyone could be so stupid. They had crossed into a clearly marked minefield.

I did just about the exact opposite of what I was supposed to do. Rather than burying my body in the ground, or leaping up and running away to find hard cover, I stood up and started shouting at the villagers.

'What are you doing?!' I said, in English, rather unhelpfully. 'Go back, go back!'

In fairness, other people were roaring at them as well.

Rather than standing stock-still and begging for help, the villagers just looked irritated. They actually wandered over to our position, causing me to raise my hands to the heavens in despair.

'What are they doing?!' I said in vain to the lead HALO deminer.

'It's very tricky, because they can live somewhere like this for years and perhaps nobody gets injured and so they stop being afraid of the minefield and become blasé about it,' he said. 'We often find people letting their cattle wander through areas that we know and they know are littered with ERW [explosive remnants of war], or using the minefield as a short-cut to get to shops or even school.'

He was despairing, and I really felt for him. His team were already risking their lives on demining operations, and they also had to deal with foolhardy local villagers. What a task.

Despite the willingness of people in Nagorno-Karabkh to wander through minefields, they seemed to be a surprisingly long-lived people. My guide David took me to a cemetery high in the mountains where we found headstones of both men and women who had lived to become centenarians. David was convinced people from the region lived longer than anyone else on the planet. It sounded unbelievable when first suggested, but then I found a headstone in the cemetery for someone who died aged 115.

One other gravestone indicated the plot contained a husband,

and had space ready for the wife, whose date of birth was already inscribed on the headstone. But there was no date of death, and David said she was still alive. I stared at the date, did a quick calculation, never my strong point, and realised that if she were still alive she would be 120. It is most likely she had been displaced in the conflict and never made it to her resting place, but David was convinced she was still alive. 'If we had international recognition,' he said proudly, 'then everyone would know people in Nagorno-Karabakh live longer than anywhere else in the world.'

In the years since I have heard similar claims in other mountainous regions of the world. Perhaps it's the fresh air, perhaps it is the organic mulberry vodka people kept pouring down our throats, or perhaps it is the fact mountain people are forever walking up and down the hills, and exercise keeps them fit and healthy. Whatever it is, I think someone should investigate.

We left the cemetery and drove back to the plateau. I suggested we should finish our time in Nagorno-Karabakh on the front line. We took another long drive up into the mountains and hiked to a remote outpost manned by young men, boys really, and looked out to the Azeri trenches in the distance where we'd been just under two weeks before. It all felt very sad and remote.

Although international recognition seems highly unlikely, wealthy Armenian exiles in the United States still provide massive funding to encourage the Karabakh government's claims for independence. This annoys many Armenians, who are sick of the conflict dominating their lives and draining their government budget.

There seems no easy end to the situation. In 2016 dozens were killed and a helicopter gunship and a tank were destroyed in ongoing clashes between Azeri and Armenian forces battling over Nagorno-Karabakh. One day full-scale conflict may erupt again, causing huge problems for the supply of oil from Azerbaijan and the Caspian region to the outside world. Perhaps it's only when oil pipelines are switched off and petrol prices in the West rise as a result that the rest of the world will wake up to the ongoing crisis of breakaway states.

CHAPTER NINETEEN

The 'Golden Age' of Travel

Failing all else, surely the threat of World War Three should alert people to the risks surrounding unrecognised nations.

We left the Caucasus and headed to the Far East. Lack of international recognition is not limited to poor countries. The island of Taiwan has one of the most powerful economies in the world and it has been the tenth largest trade partner of the US, but it has no seat at the United Nations and no major state recognises it as a proper country. It is the wealthiest and most powerful unrecognised nation on the planet, the ultimate place that doesn't exist.

When Chinese Nationalists were defeated by Mao's Communists they fled to Taiwan and took over. Taiwan has since become a stable democracy, but Beijing views Taiwan as a renegade province, wants it back, and has repeatedly said it will use extreme force if necessary. Successive US presidents have said they will support, protect and even defend Taiwan.

Everything hinges on recognition. For the past forty years both Beijing and the authorities in Taipei, the Taiwanese capital, have had a tacit understanding that Taiwan is actually part of China. Taiwan exists in a strange diplomatic limbo where it takes part in events like the World Cup and the Olympic Games, but generally uses a name like 'Chinese Taipei', which China will accept, rather than 'Taiwan', which would suggest it is a state, and might provoke fury or worse from China.

Despite sometimes flirting with the idea of declaring independence, Taiwan has never gone the whole hog. In return China has held back its vast army from invading and taking the island. But China has said, repeatedly, that it will go to war, against anyone and anything, even the US, if Taiwan tries to split itself permanently away from China.

It all sounds quite extreme. I wanted to visit Taiwan and see what all the fuss was about. First, of course, I had to visit China.

We flew into Beijing in the mid-2000s when it was a building site. The country was going through the most spectacular and profound transition imaginable, as it transformed from a nation of poverty and peasantry to an economic powerhouse. I had never visited China before, and I felt a sense of awe. For all the human rights abuses, the decades of suffering and starvation, the Chinese government was now lifting more people out of extreme poverty than any other leadership in world history. It was a stunning time to visit.

With a young guide called Rock, who seemed pretty relaxed for a guy who was taking the BBC around a state with all-powerful authoritarian rule, we started our journey by heading to one of the symbolic centres of Chinese power: Tiananmen Square, where demonstrators had been massacred in 1989. Guards did try to stop us filming, but in fairness they let us continue after checking our permits.

Tiananmen Square is colossal. It's where Mao Zedong proclaimed the founding of the People's Republic of China in 1949. Visiting from abroad, and seeing it for the first time, I felt like a witness from a very small, distant land. China seemed so huge, its population so vast. Even at twenty to nine in the morning, hundreds of Chinese visitors were queueing to see Mao in his tomb, and revolutionary and Communist propaganda statues and slogans still dominated public spaces.

But much was changing. We found a Rolls-Royce showroom, something completely unimaginable just a few years before. Then we went to the main antiques market and found piles of Mao memorabilia. In the past he had to be venerated. By the time I was there, he had become for many a curiosity, even a figure for amusement, with his image on clocks and hip-flasks. In a dusty shop I found and bought a poster dating back to the time of the Cultural Revolution which had a slogan that said, effectively, 'We must recover Taiwan! We must get it back!' It was classic state propaganda imagery, with five sturdy male military figures carrying a red flag and a picture of Mao. But there was something slightly worrying about it as well. A country that had retained such a focus on one issue for so long would surely find it hard to simply let it go.

There are no direct flights from Beijing to Taipei, so we flew there via Hong Kong, met up with a guide and translator called Sen-lun Yu, and travelled on to the tiny Taiwanese island of Kinmen, just off the Chinese coast. Taiwanese soldiers on the island fought a twenty-year artillery duel with the Chinese. During one forty-four-day period the Chinese lobbed 474,000 artillery shells at Kinmen. Eventually both sides came to a gentleman's agreement to bombard each other on alternate days. For more than a decade the two sides agreed the Chinese would bombard on Monday, Wednesday and Friday, and the Taiwanese would return fire on Tuesday, Thursday and Saturday. On Sunday everyone took the day off.

Then the Taiwanese built the world's largest neon sign and the world's loudest loudspeakers on Kinmen and bombarded the mainland with propaganda. They released balloons designed to carry anti-Communist propaganda pamphlets into China, and a few more bizarre offerings: one balloon that apparently drifted to Israel was found to contain see-through underwear. Times have changed and local shops now melt old artillery shell casings into kitchen knives for visiting tourists. I still have a set in my kitchen drawers.

We drove to the coastline which remains the front line against possible invasion. A multitude of signs warned of mines in the sand, but our driver said it was safe so we made our way down to the beach. Just a few miles away the south-east Chinese city of Xiamen was clearly visible through the haze. Sen-lun Yu was a little overwhelmed. She had never seen China before.

I asked her what she had been told about the Chinese when she was growing up and her reply said much about the nature of propaganda.

'Here we grow bananas and we get to eat bananas, and over there they only get to eat the skins of bananas,' she said. It was comical to hear, but telling all the same.

I asked Sen-lun what sort of messages the loudspeakers had been broadcasting to China.

'They used to say, "Taiwan is a treasure island, we are free China, we will come to save you from hell,"' she told me with a smile.

Thanks to Sen-lun's skills of persuasion, we were allowed to board a Taiwanese coastguard cutter. Chinese fishing boats were encroaching into what the coastguard said were Taiwanese waters, and they were being turned back.

But what completely fascinated me were boatloads of Chinese tourists on packed pleasure cruises who had come out to have a look at an island, and an enormous propaganda sign on a hillside, which they had previously only seen from afar or in news bulletins. The sign had the snappy line 'Three Principles of the People Unites China', and was a slogan the Taiwanese used to represent their belief in nationalism, democracy and the livelihood of the people. The principles were said to be the basis of Taiwanese prosperity and featured in the first line of the Taiwanese anthem.

The coastguard crew were grumpily telling the boats to turn around and head back to China, never appearing to realise how ironic it was that until recently they had been desperately trying to convince the Chinese that life was so much better on the capitalist side of the strait. The pleasure cruises were right next to us and turning so fast it was as if their crews were pulling handbrake turns, and the Chinese tourists on board were waving enthusiastically at us and the stony Taiwanese crew on our boat. I actually became a little emotional seeing their eager, excited faces, and the coastguard captain looked at me, baffled, and asked if something was wrong.

I knew they were a symptom of profound change, and the vanguard of a Chinese tourist revolution. Tens, perhaps hundreds, of millions of people across on the mainland were deciding they wanted to do what much of the rest of the world had been doing for ages, and get out and explore. On my journeys since then I have seen an ever-growing number of Chinese tourists just about everywhere.

I watched them for ages, really feeling the joy of people who had rarely had the opportunity to travel, before it was time for us to leave and we headed to the Taiwanese capital.

The city is completely dominated by Taipei 101, then the tallest building in the world. It hadn't fully opened when I visited, and there was still a smell of fresh paint inside. But we were allowed to take a superfast lift to the top, saw a giant ball on a pendulum that was supposed to balance the tower during an earthquake, and then emerged blinking into the light on top of the building, so high up we could see planes flying beneath us.

I loved Taipei. For me it was a great mix of bling and grime, of culture and excess. The city has some of the finest restaurants in the world, but instead of filling ourselves somewhere classy, we went for noodles in a night market which was also selling medical remedies made from honey mixed with cobra blood. A sign in English said: 'The snakes sold and cooked at this store are definitely not protected animals. Welcome and taste!' Clearly some other concerned travellers had been there before us.

Taiwanese cities felt like cleaner versions of locations in *Blade Runner*. Neon signs lit skyscrapers and the night market, while girls from the Chinese mainland sat outside obvious brothels.

To give you an idea of the options we would consider as a team when heading somewhere for filming, and the research I would put together as the presenter, I have dug out a document buried on my computer with the title 'Taiwan things2do'. Four pages long and 2,457 words of scribbled notes in total, it stands up reasonably well to scrutiny many years later, and includes simple notes for me to remember for 'PTCs' (pieces to camera, where I look directly down the lens and talk to the viewer):

> *Mainland China is a one-party state. Taiwan is a functioning democracy. China locks up anybody who threatens Communist party rule. Taiwan is alive with combative politics and a lively free media.*

Thoughts about what we could do:

> *Be good if we could try to show how an advanced breakaway state/ unrecognised nation develops and matures: e.g. musicians sing about*

Taiwan and political repression in the Taiwanese language (which used to be banned!).

We ticked that box when Sen-lun took me to see a Taiwanese boy band, who sang of their pride at being Taiwanese, not ethnic Chinese like their parents.

There were also quick notes on what was changing in Taiwan:

And the first passports with the word Taiwan on the cover have been issued.

Some background stats:

According to an annual poll taken by Taipei's Chengchi University, the proportion of Taiwan's residents who consider themselves exclusively Chinese has plummeted to 10 per cent from 26 per cent in 1992, while the number who think of themselves as exclusively 'Taiwanese' has jumped to 42 per cent from 17 per cent.

And the sort of imaginative wish-list things you can only request at short notice if you are filming a documentary for the BBC:

Very keen to go on 1 of Taiwan's 2 combat-ready subs. They're seen as being crucial to defending the island and the US is planning to sell Taiwan more of them – much to China's fury.

My favourite line, however, is the first:

Is it possible for us to meet the President?? Perhaps he could take us for a Taiwanese meal?? Worth a try.

We never managed to wring a meal out of the Taiwanese President, but he did fly us to see a firework concert in Taiwanese Air Force One, then refused to speak to us and dumped us in a muddy field. I still have a couple of souvenir Air Force One sick bags in my van.

We had a series of strange encounters and experiences in Taiwan, but one of the most memorable was visiting what used to be the biggest school in the world, with more than 5,000 pupils. The children would arrive before 8 a.m., clean the school, raise the Taiwanese flag – yes, they do have one – then be drilled like little soldiers and march back to their classes after an outdoor assembly.

Taiwan is a huge success story. After the Second World War it was one of the poorer countries in Asia. In the decades that followed it built a super-high-tech economy and became one of the top twenty economies. Taiwanese firms make 90 per cent of the world's laptops. Its success has been partly built on the back of one of the finest education systems in the world. When I last visited it was ranked fourth in the world for maths teaching and second in the world for science teaching. It is an astonishing achievement, partly down to huge investment in education, and partly down to the quality of the teachers – who all have PhDs, and deserve the bow they are given by children at the start of each lesson, even at primary school.

Children at the school were motivated, and encouraged to be competitive, but they were not robots. They were cheeky and fun, leaping around in front of our camera and gurning into the lens. They knew when they could have fun, and when they had to be serious. So how on earth did the teachers keep them in line?

I asked the head teacher, a surprisingly relaxed and friendly woman in a pink suit who carried two walkie-talkies, and was in charge of maintaining order.

'It's like controlling a line of Taiwanese donkeys,' she said, with an honesty that instantly made me smile. 'They're all connected to each other by ropes, so you just have to know which one to pull and the rest will follow.'

All too soon it was time to leave Taiwan, and come to the end of the *Places That Don't Exist* series. I thought back to my time across the water in mainland China. We had travelled west out of Beijing to visit a section of the Great Wall of China. We puffed our way to the top of a hill on a broad section of steps. It was breathtaking, of course, quite literally. I was amazed by the height of each step, which meant even I had to lift my foot almost to my waist to climb up. Were the ancient Chinese giants? The view out was spectacular, but I was more taken by the view when I turned around, and the words of a guide. 'Everyone thinks that the Great Wall was just built to keep bandits out,' he said to me. 'But the wall was also built to control movement of people, and to try to unify the country within.'

That last bit was crucial. For a large part of its history China was split into fiefdoms. For hundreds of years Chinese leaders believed one of their greatest challenges was to keep the country together, and the people, who are mainly Han Chinese but also come from dozens of other ethnic groups, as one. The fear for generations has been that if Taiwan was allowed to declare independence and break from the motherland, then other provinces might try to follow. Only by unifying the people, leaders have said, can China remain strong.

It was a realisation that helped to shape my thoughts about China, a country that I think many of us still get very wrong, labouring under the misconception the Chinese are automatons broken by decades of Communism who do the bidding of their masters almost without question. Our image of them is often still as little more than units of production on a factory line, churning out plastic consumer goods for eager buyers in the West. If we think any more of them it is usually as money-grabbing *nouveau riche*. It is a perception that is completely unfair.

From the first time I visited China I met men and women who were strikingly individual and eccentric. Since China began to open up millions have turned back to interests which reveal their depths. They have become intellectuals, Buddhists, vegans, enthusiastic pet owners and artists. Often it is not easy under the heavy hand of one-party rule, but still culture endures. How could it be any other way when their history stretches back thousands of years? The Communist period is barely a moment in the overall history of an ancient civilisation.

I've had far too many experiences getting slightly drunk with Chinese tourists singing karaoke on ferry boats on the Yangtze, or meeting experts on the architecture of Iceland or the work of Banksy, to find the country anything other than captivating.

I remember one moment when we were in a far-flung part of the country in a city which was rapidly becoming a megalopolis. We were walking back from a distant restaurant, heading for the godforsaken hotel the BBC had booked us into, and I could hear jazz saxophone playing on a radio. We were a bit lost and went around a corner or two and the music became louder and louder. Then I realised it was coming from the basement of an office complex. Idly looking in as we passed, I suddenly saw a security guard sitting inside in front of banks of

CCTV screens he was supposed to be monitoring. He was crammed into the cubicle, but he was rocking back in his chair, wearing a pair of *Blues Brothers* sunglasses and playing a polished saxophone like a 1920s Harlem master. It was a perfect travel discovery.

Life has changed spectacularly fast in China, of course – more dramatically and quickly than anyone thought possible. And perhaps the authorities in China are not always the terrifying human rights abusers many of us might imagine. Filming in another remote city we stopped our cars outside a major Buddhist temple. We didn't realise at first but our drivers had parked illegally and were partially blocking the entrance to a fire station. As we stood a short distance away filming the temple a stern policeman appeared, but didn't bash the drivers around with a truncheon. Instead as he was walking towards the vehicles he produced a handy-cam and started filming the parking violation, presumably as evidence for a fine or prosecution. I was surprised. In turn, the drivers, far from being in fear of this agent of the authoritarian state, attempted to stand in front of him and his camera to stop the filming. The interaction was similar to what you might find someone doing to a traffic warden in the UK.

I am not saying the Chinese police are representatives of a benevolent state, or could give lessons in community policing to a Swedish village cop. But I think we still swiftly criticise China without adequately acknowledging the country has lifted more people out of poverty in the last generation than has ever been achieved anywhere in the world. By contrast I think India, for example, often gets an easy ride despite being a place of appalling poverty and suffering. I have seen situations in India that would result in howls of outrage if they were happening in

China and result in aid appeals if they were happening in sub-Saharan Africa.

As we were getting a parking ticket in China next to the temple, despite the loud protestations of our drivers, I noticed a large permanent sign on the wall nearby which our translator (when he had also stopped shouting at the police officers) interpreted for us: 'I'm your district police chief, and if you have a problem please get in touch.' The police chief was a woman, as were both her deputies, who were also pictured underneath. Three female law enforcement officers in charge of the borough of a massive city, complete with their names, direct phone numbers as well as their email addresses. That police plaque was not evidence of a faceless bureaucracy. It might not be Denmark, which remains one of my benchmarks for an inclusive and well-run society, but it was hardly *1984*.

Yet there are of course many lines that cannot be crossed in China. You certainly wouldn't want to be an opposition activist, or a bookseller offering anti-Party material. Amnesty International is clear: 'Freedom of expression is severely restricted in China and anyone who speaks out against the authorities faces harassment, arrest and detention. Torture is widespread across the country and justice is elusive for many.' Investigating corruption is forbidden, as is questioning the rule of the Party or China's ownership of Taiwan.

Back in the mid-2000s in Beijing before heading to Taiwan I took some time out to wander around the magnificent Forbidden City, which was home to the emperors and their households for almost 500 years. Then I did something I try never to do in my programmes: I went to see a government man in a suit.

'Taiwan has never been a country,' said the senior official, who had the task of leading Chinese policy on Taiwan. 'It is still not a country. The Chinese people will not allow Taiwan to be separated from the Motherland. The Chinese people will safeguard their sovereignty and territorial integrity and we have the ability to break any intention to make Taiwan independent.'

It was couched in a bit of official-speak, but not much. The sentiment was strong. But how far would China go? I wondered. I asked him whether the Chinese government was concerned that a conflict between China and Taiwan might involve the United States.

'I don't believe the American people will be prepared to spill their blood for Taiwanese independence,' he said.

For many years Chinese plans for the invasion of Taiwan were jokingly referred to as 'the million-man swim', because the Chinese navy was so weak compared to the Taiwanese forces. In the last decade, however, China has upgraded and rebuilt a powerful military machine, complete with aircraft carrier and submarines.

Chinese policy back in the mid-2000s was to get Taiwan back, and it remains the policy now. Nobody should be under any illusions. China is still ready and willing to go to war over Taiwan.

Visiting places that don't exist left me wide-eyed. They are quite literally off the map, with eccentric customs, the energy of upstarts, and with patriotic locals desperate for the rest of the world to recognise their existence. It had been a series of incredible journeys and adventures.

Going to Taiwan, in particular, made me realise I could make a travelogue exploring the light and shade of life almost anywhere. It wasn't a style that only worked in a country that was dark, poverty-stricken or at war.

We just needed to find moments that were quirky and

countered a prejudice or revealed something telling about a place. Often that could come from a jokey interaction with someone. But it could also come from something I spotted and identified to the camera. In Taipei, for example, I realised that telephone junction boxes were works of art: local artists had been commissioned to paint murals on the street-side green boxes. A place that can think about beautifying street furniture is clearly at an advanced stage of development.

Taiwan might be better run than Switzerland, but there was still darkness to explore, as there is everywhere. Wherever I go now part of my aim is to look for the alternative to whatever stereotype dominates the perception of a place. This could be something positive or even fun in a troubled country, perhaps playing *kabaddi* in poor Bangladesh; or the opposite in an affluent country, such as discovering a dark rubbish island in the otherwise paradise world of the Maldives. The point is to overturn preconceptions, starting with my own.

Taiwan worked for me as a destination for a documentary because I explored the place with my eyes open. If I had gone there just looking at history, or landscapes, there would have been fewer dimensions to the journey. Getting off the beaten track and learning more about the places we visit – both the light and the shade – always makes for a more interesting experience, a more rounded adventure. I don't think travellers need to ignore darkness. I haven't been anywhere where people won't talk about issues or problems. For most people it's cathartic to share with outsiders.

Other travellers might not be mad keen to copy some of my hairier journeys, but I still think many could benefit from injecting a few elements into their next holiday. Apart from exploring the light and the shade, my trips have been memorable, for me at least, because they combine adventure with a clear plan and destination.

More of us should try turning a break into a proper adventure with a healthy dose of purpose and meaning. It almost guarantees a lifetime of memories. You could follow a river from source to sea or start a trip in one location and then head to another, exploring along the way. Taking chances is often where the best memories are, and the richest rewards in life come from a bit of risk-taking. We can all benefit from pushing ourselves, our partners, friends or family, out of our respective comfort zones. On a holiday that can be as simple as not wasting your life lying horizontal by a swimming pool. Personally, on any trip I try to push myself a little and follow a simple set of rules: go to strange places, take chances, ask questions, do things that are exciting, eat strange foreign food, and dive into the culture of the world and embrace risk.

A proper adventure is now more possible than ever before. You can go almost anywhere and do almost anything. We are often sold a vision of the world as a dangerous and frightening place. In reality the world is friendly and astonishingly hospitable. And the further you go from the tourist traps the warmer the welcome and the more authentic and unforgettable the experience. Some people think the 'Golden Age' of travel was when steam wafted from trains, crystal clinked in dining cars, and air stewardesses wore long white gloves. I think the real Golden Age of travel is actually now, when it is cheaper and safer than ever. It's also a guaranteed way of tingling your senses, enhancing your life and gifting you a huge stock of memories, encounters and experiences.

CHAPTER TWENTY

Exorcism at the Monastery

I came back from filming *Places That Don't Exist* and began plotting a new adventure, this time around the equator. It was a much longer, more ambitious journey than I had attempted before, and the first programme we shot did not end well. I spent a couple of weeks sleeping and recovering from malaria, and a couple more considering whether to continue the journey. Anya and I talked about it not just in terms of career options, but from the perspective of my health. I'd had a brush with death and I felt I would never be the same again. She wanted me to take at least a moment to consider the future.

As I mooched around, friends and family came to see me, offering commiserations about my illness, and then ribbed me about my trips as if they were holidays.

I started talking about the hardship, the dangers, and the endless pieces of heavy camera kit which daily need to be lugged in and out of four-wheel drives and dodgy hotels. 'These journeys really aren't holidays,' I said earnestly.

Then I regaled them with tales of sleepless nights in godforsaken villages, scuzzy hotels and even unmade beds in part-time brothels. I offered up a couple of recent experiences, like the joy of sleeping head to toe with colleagues in a tiny African hut, where the smell from our pile of unwashed sweaty clothes was enough to ward off all local insect life.

I moved on to the Groundhog Day experience of eating identical meagre meals together with three colleagues day after day and week after week. I droned on about one of the most difficult aspects of filming while travelling: the fact we're constantly on the move. On every journey I make there are always half a dozen places where I would love to pause to savour the surroundings. Filming in Bukhara, for example, I would have given anything for a chance to relax for a few days and explore. If I was travelling for pleasure I could simply have decided to halt the trip and unwind. But on filming trips we have the briefest of stops to shoot, then we're back on the road.

I say 'road'. On many trips, roads were often just connected potholes. Travelling for months meant I was spending large chunks of my life being bounced around in small cars. The result was backache and spinal pain that earned me a loyalty card from my local osteopath. Finally, I would tell friends and family about the bureaucracy and paperwork. It's an aspect of the journey we never show on TV, simply because it is hideously boring. But the meetings we have to attend and forms we have to complete just to be allowed into a country to film are enough to try the patience of a particularly calm nun.

But who was I kidding? Filming trips certainly aren't a holiday, but they are still a glorious treat. Filming for the BBC opens doors. I have seen and done things and gone to places most folk can only imagine. I have met some of the most incredible and inspiring people on the planet. Filming a TV series while on a journey is one of the most spectacular ways to travel. It is enlightening, entertaining, and it provides a purpose and reason for adventure.

How could I turn my back on the madness? How could I turn my back on the light and shade? Even the first part of

Equator had been magnificent. I spoke to the BBC about my illness and what should happen next. A lot of time and money had been spent planning *Equator* and they were keen for the journey to continue. But they were still concerned for my health. It was up to me. I thought about it briefly, but I knew there was no way I could turn my back on a chance of adventure and experiences, or the near-guarantee of meeting people I would remember forever.

Within two months of returning home in the aftermath of malaria, I was flying back south from London to continue my journey following the equator eastwards across Africa. It would become one of the most humbling journeys of my life.

I felt fragile and mortal. I had no idea if I would sicken again, and I was flying to the Democratic Republic of Congo, one of the most dangerous countries in the world, a nation the size of Western Europe, where medical cover was extremely limited.

But the team were brilliant. Sophie Todd, the producer-director who helped save my life in Gabon, had agreed to take me back on the road. A tough and adventurous sort ready for a challenge, Sophie was joined by an assistant producer called Jamie Berry, a great shooter who was young but enthusiastic and rarely fazed.

We arrived into Kinshasa, capital of the DRC, and together met up with Brian Green, a South African war cameraman who had flown in from his home in Johannesburg. Straight from the off it was clear Brian was a bit of a card, in the best possible way. Witty, brave and resourceful, Brian had dodged bullets and artillery shells during the Bosnian War, was marvellous at using humour to dilute tricky situations and would amuse us all by slipping into the kitchens of slow cafés to help cook the food when we were in a rush. He owned a shopping centre in South

Africa but loved the excitement of an adventure and the chance to record a moment of history.

We had a briefing chat in Kinshasa with officials from the United Nations, who seemed determined to put the fear of God into us. They explained there was still fighting in the east of the DRC. Following the equator would take us through an active conflict zone, but first we went north towards the small city of Mbandaka in a tiny Cessna Caravan plane flown by a missionary called Dan from Colorado.

Flying through blue skies we tracked along the vast Congo River, a mirror for low, fluffy cotton-wool clouds. It was just a tiny corner of the DRC, the largest country in sub-Saharan Africa, but it was breathtaking. Endless green forest stretched in every direction, broken only occasionally by remote villages and dirt tracks. My eyes were glued to the view, my mind following every slope to a peak and every curve along the river. Everything was fascinating; everything was wondrous. To be a stranger in a strange world such as this, as travellers have for thousands of years, keeps wonder alive. It exercises astonishment, even awe.

I looked out of the window to the west, towards Congo-Brazzaville, a separate country, and also crossed by the equator line. The Ebola outbreak in Congo-Brazzaville had actually worsened since I was in Gabon, and we had no option but to avoid the country altogether and land on the outskirts of Mbandaka in DRC. The moment I stepped off the plane I knew I was back on the equator. I had forgotten how hot it could be. The sun was merciless.

By this point in the mid-2000s I had explored several dozen countries, recognised or otherwise. But everywhere new still felt different and surprising. Each country still does today. I have never lost the sense I am doing something exceptional. Perhaps the reality of my past is part of the reason. Hardly travelling when I was younger, let alone exploring exotically, helps ensure these experiences feel remarkable as an adult. I have never felt jaded. On each new journey I sense possibility, discovery, and most especially in a country like DRC, enormous challenge.

Emery Makumeno, a wonderful, warm and softly spoken fixer, was to be our guide and translator in the DRC. Somehow he had managed to find us four-wheel-drive vehicles in one of the poorest areas of Africa, and we set off to find a place to stay.

Mbandaka, like the rest of the country, was desperately, appallingly poor. There were hundreds of people walking and some cycling on the dirt roads, but very few cars, and those were mostly UN vehicles travelling in convoys. There were no hotels to speak of, and no running water or public electricity.

The DRC was, and remains, in a desperate state. Two wars had ravaged the country. They were often described as civil wars, but they involved forces from nine countries and perhaps two dozen armed groups. They were Africa's world wars. The death toll was simply astonishing. By the time I visited in the mid-2000s at least 4 million people had died since 1998.

We stopped in the street in central Mbandaka and I looked around. I had been focused too closely on my own selfish recovery and personal journey. Suddenly the reality of where I was hit home. There was a dirt road, busy with people walking and cycling past, balancing metal pots on their heads and long pieces of thin timber on shoulders. To the sides were old one-storey concrete buildings and shanty huts, in front of which weary women ran basic stalls selling vegetables, clothes and single-use sachets of washing powder and shampoo.

It might sound perfectly pleasant, but there is rarely anything romantic about poverty. Most people had next to nothing.

Children looked ragged and malnourished. The country was staggering from crisis to crisis. Some there told us it was cursed.

Yet there were few obvious scars of conflict. No bullet holes like I had seen everywhere in Somalia. Often the weapons of choice during the conflict in the DRC, as neighbouring ethnic groups attacked and hacked at each other, were machetes.

We found rooms in a spooky, semi-abandoned monastery. At dusk we lit candles next to our wooden beds and incense coils to drive away mosquitoes. I dug out my travel kit, covered myself in natural repellent, screwed my mozzie net into the ceiling and unrolled a black plastic sheet and sleeping mat. Then I grabbed my head torch and went off to find a toilet.

If you really want to feel like you've travelled and experienced a completely different culture, you need to bid farewell to bleach and flushing loos. A bit of personal discomfort actually helps to create priceless travel experiences guaranteed to linger in the memory. Travelling abroad and realising it is all a bit mucky helps put our own lives into context and reminds us how lucky we are to have running water at home.

But the toilet in the monastery was astonishing. Round the side of the main building I followed the remains of a path to a derelict outhouse with a small platform and a huge pit. The fumes were so overwhelming and so combustible I nearly collapsed into the black swamp.

For sheer danger that experience competes strongly with a coastal village in Indonesia I reached later on my equator journey. I was shown to a drop toilet in a small outhouse made of rotting branches perched precariously over the sea. It was low tide, and as I attempted to let nature take its course an entire pack of enormous, ravenous pigs fought their way up through the hole in the floor, their sharp teeth snapping at my undercarriage. Children watching outside giggled, but I very nearly lost more than my dignity.

I can hardly complain. Experiencing and briefly enduring the reality of life has been an education. That night at the monastery scores of local villagers began to gather in the overgrown grounds. At first we thought it was for a church service. Then the darkness was pierced by a series of bloodcurdling screams, flaming torches were lit, and a terrifying exorcism began. It all came as something of a shock. We wanted to start filming.

'No, that would not be a good idea,' said Emery calmly. 'I think we should try to find a way of locking our doors.'

When the sun rose every one of the villagers had vanished. Sophie and Jamie did some yoga in the grounds, which made all of us feel much better, before we set off for a community on the equator that had suffered during Congo's endless fighting. I wanted to see what life was like in the aftermath of the deadliest conflict on the planet since World War Two.

Beyond Mbandaka we passed an old colonial mansion that had long since succumbed to the jungle. Surrounded by grassland, trees had taken root in verandas before twisting around pillars and porticoes to break through tiles on the roof. It was close to the Botanical Garden of Eala, once a lush and tended reserve home to thousands of trees, flowers, shrubs and bushes. But that was long ago. Many of the trees had been felled for firewood and what was left was neglected and astonishingly overgrown. Standing by the entrance track the reserve had an end-of-the-world feel, as if civilisation had vanished and left just a few survivors.

I spotted a lone figure walking slowly towards us. He was carrying a bundle of thin pieces of firewood across his stooping shoulders. Brian grabbed the camera to get a shot of him approaching. He was barefoot, tiny, ancient, and wearing just a ragged pair of old knee-length shorts. I sidled up to him as he drew level.

'How far have you come?' I said to him as Emery translated.

'About four kilometres.'

'That's a long way.'

'Yes,' he replied through Emery. 'And I still have a way to go yet.'

Emery and I helped him with his load so he could rest for a couple of minutes.

He said his name was Ngozi. He was so skinny his ribs were visible. His arms looked wizened and wasted.

'Thank you,' he said, as he shook my hand. '*Merci beaucoup.*'

'It's heavy,' I told him. 'It was heavy for me and all I did was lift it down from your shoulders.'

'It is heavy,' he said, stretching his old limbs, 'but that's the price I pay in order to survive.'

We sat on a rock and he laid the machete he used to cut the wood across his knees. Bright-eyed and smiling, he seemed completely unperturbed by our presence or the camera. It was as if he had been expecting us. Like it was fate our paths had crossed.

'Do you mind if I ask you a cheeky question?' I said to him.

'Not at all.'

'How old are you, Ngozi?'

He smiled. 'Sixty-eight. I look older because I work so hard. I'm not strong any more. Carrying so much wood makes me weak.'

'What do you do with the wood?'

'I pick it from the forest and then I take it to the market and I sell it. Sometimes it can take a whole day, working from dawn to dusk. Everything I get for my survival comes from the forest.'

I asked him how much money he would get for the wood he had been carrying. He thought for just a moment. Then told me he would earn perhaps 400 francs per day. Emery did the calculations, checked with Ngozi, then turned to me. It was roughly 42 pence. Per day. I was horrified, but I tried to make sure it didn't show.

'It's not enough to buy the food I need,' said Ngozi thoughtfully. 'But it's all I can get for the wood. This is what I have to do in order to support myself.'

I shook his hand again and thanked him for talking to us. It was just a brief moment. But it lives with me. How could it not? There is hardly a day that goes past when I do not think of Ngozi or the other humbling souls I met on that trip. This was the journey, more than any before or since, that helped convince me of both the personal value of an adventure, which at its best should challenge, enlighten and fulfil, and the merit of taking a camera to a remote part of the world.

Capturing a sense of how our fellow humans, our brothers and sisters, struggle to survive in parts of the world enduring conflict and poverty can be a potent reminder of reality for those watching in less blighted corners. I still believe it has value. Even years after this series aired I would be stopped by a viewer who would sidle close or put their hand on my arm to convey the sharing of an experience and tell me they also remembered Ngozi. A young woman once sought me out to say she watched this journey on the television, changed her university course to study remote medicine and was about to become the only doctor in a faraway refugee camp. She was telling me the ripple of the programmes had an effect. Making a television series is surely not enough, but at least it is something.

Emery wanted us to see a village called Ngamba-Kinshasa,

where a school teacher was waiting to talk to us. To get there we had to journey up the Congo River. We stopped at a busy jetty, watched in amazement as a man walked past with a small crocodile on his head, then hired a long dugout canoe fixed with an outboard motor.

We set off with a breeze coming off the muddy water and locals bathing close to the banks. They were waving and chanting as we passed them, so I waved back.

'They're taunting you, Simon,' said Emery, laughing.

'What are they saying, then?'

'It's a song. *White man – your breath stinks.*'

We pulled alongside a huge barge. In a country with only 300 miles of paved roads, the river was the lifeline and main thoroughfare, and barges carried basic trade and people wanting to move from place to place. This barge was completely rammed with travellers. It looked like an entire village was living aboard, under tarpaulins strung up on poles.

'Have you done that, Emery?' I asked him, smiling away rather naively as if nothing could be more pleasant than a barge trip on the Congo.

'Travelled on the barges? Of course, many times.'

I gazed across the water to where the people on one massive barge were all but spilling over the sides and asked him how long he would have to wait until a barge was ready to leave.

'Minimum is a month,' Emery said.

'A month?' I was incredulous. My smile vanished.

'Maximum is three months.'

I couldn't believe it.

'Conditions are terrible,' he told me. 'You can have four or five hundred people and only two toilets for all of them.'

I was silent for a while after that. The DRC often left me

numb. You can read about a place as much as you like, but only by going and seeing can you truly appreciate both the beauty and the tragedy. The DRC had both in epic quantities.

It was explorer Henry Morton Stanley, he of 'Dr Livingstone, I presume' fame, who really helped begin the subjugation of the people of the Congo basin. Under the colonial rule of King Leopold II of Belgium 5–10 million people died in what is now the DRC. Some historians argue it is the hidden holocaust.

Independence from Belgium was no salvation. The country set sail on its own with just a couple of dozen graduates in the entire country and not a single person with a university degree in law, medicine or engineering. The Belgians had prevented almost anyone from getting an education.

Just as you can't run a country if all the educated people leave, so the DRC then floundered. A dictator called Mobutu Sese Seko took over, ran a kleptocracy for thirty-two years and deliberately didn't build any roads so nobody could attack him in the capital. He milked the country for personal wealth and created a culture that enrichment through the state was standard. Corruption remains endemic.

Today there is enough fertile land in the DRC to feed the entire continent and enough hydroelectric potential to power most of it as well. But the DRC is astonishingly poor.

Finally, we arrived by canoe into the village of Ngamba-Kinshasa, a simple settlement of wood-and-thatch houses built on stilts, and pulled our boat up onto the bank, next to fishermen who were mending small nets using random pieces of string.

Jose, a young teacher from the community, took us to see the basic school. He said he hadn't been paid by the state in months but was still trying to give some kind of education to the next generation.

'There's no money, but I do the best I can,' he said. He led me through a church which doubled as a school. The floor was open planking with no desks, just rough pews for kids to sit on.

'There are no books,' he admitted sadly, 'no tables where they can write, they just rest the paper on their thighs.'

'How many children are there?' I asked him.

'Sixty. They're split into different forms, first and second because of the different ages. I place one form on this side, another on this side and so on. We have nothing, and we need everything, blackboard, books, chalk.'

We visited Jose's home where he and his wife were not only trying to raise three children of their own, but three more children of family members who had died of disease, including malaria. Jose's youngest son Johnson, who was just a year old, had also contracted the disease. I felt my heart wrench. There were no German doctors who could rush round to see them.

This was the harsh reality of poverty, corruption, and life in the DRC. An astonishing 60 per cent of children were dying before their fifth birthday. Even those who survived into their teens faced enormous challenges from afflictions such as malaria. Life expectancy for a man was just forty-two years.

We flew further along the Congo river with the help of Dan from the Mission Aviation Fellowship (MAF). With his crisp white shirt, moustache and pre-flight clipboard checks, Dan seemed slightly out of place in the jungle. I asked him whether he felt he had a calling to be in the DRC. He laughed and said if he didn't there would be no reason to be there. 'I'm not getting paid enough to do this,' he added.

I have always been taken by a line used by Archbishop Desmond Tutu about the arrival of Christianity on the continent: 'When the missionaries came to Africa they had the Bible and we had the land. They said "Let us pray." We closed our eyes. When we opened them, we had the Bible and they had the land.'

Even in recent decades other missionaries in other parts of the continent have done wicked and appalling things in Africa, reportedly only agreeing to help people in one area if they would be tattooed with a cross on their forehead, ensuring their annihilation when persecutors returned to town. But MAF pilots seemed completely selfless, shuttling missionaries but also lepers, cancer patients, the injured and anyone needing urgent help around the DRC and other areas of the world lacking infrastructure and roads. You can book a flight via their website. Dan didn't lecture or hector us about faith. But he did slip a couple of leaflets into my bag.

Dan was one of the few people prepared to fly into the east of the DRC despite the ongoing conflict.

'What's the situation like there at the moment?' I asked as I sat in the co-pilot's seat with grasslands and waterways unfolding beneath me.

'Flare-ups,' he said. 'One after the other, there's continual fighting. The Ugandans keep coming across the border. There's the Hutu and the Tutsis who are always fighting it out. The cattle people fight with the farmers. It's anarchy.'

DRC was a collapsed state. The United Nations was the life support.

Dan flew us to a UN base just north of the equator and we landed on tarmac surrounded by a multitude of helicopters used to ferry thousands of troops around the east. The UN was running the largest peacekeeping operation in the world in

DRC to prevent the country slipping back into a devastating regional war. They were trying to disarm well-armed militia groups and also train the nascent Congolese army, which still had a terrible reputation.

As we drove to our lodgings we passed a troop of Congolese soldiers exercising in the middle of town. Dressed all in black they looked more than a little menacing. People moved swiftly out of their way. Emery summed up the local feeling.

'It's all right in the middle of town here,' he said. 'Lots of people around and the UN soldiers are everywhere.' His voice was low as if he was worried someone might overhear. 'In the middle of the bush, though – if we met them there – I wouldn't be anything like as happy.'

'Why?'

At first, he seemed a little reluctant to answer. 'It's common knowledge. The army, or some of them at least, rob the population.'

Much of the fighting had been about gold and diamonds. The DRC was and is fantastically rich in mineral deposits. I wanted to visit a gold mine, but all the roads were blocked or too dangerous even with an armed escort. But the United Nations agreed to take us on a UN helicopter flight to a mine. A detachment of Pakistani soldiers came along for our protection.

As we came in to land I could see more soldiers in pale-blue UN helmets guarding the strip to make sure we didn't come under attack from militia groups with rocket-propelled grenades. We lurched through the bush in the back of Land Rovers to reach a lucrative mine which had changed hands on five separate occasions during the war.

It was an astonishing sight. In a vast pit of mud and water, perhaps a mile long by half a mile wide, hundreds and hundreds of men, women and children toiled, up to their waists and often deeper. The work was often impossibly hard. Passing heavy pans of sludge and mud from hand to hand they would then tip it out and purify it over a water bed padded with carpet that would hold small flecks of gold.

There was very little machinery. Almost everything was done by hand. The mine was under the control of a powerful local militia which charged miners a daily fee to work there. If anyone found any gold the militia would then take a hefty commission. It all looked, sounded and smelt absolutely horrific.

I asked one of the miners whether he thought gold had been a blessing or a curse for the DRC.

His answer chastened me. He said that people were poor, but at least with the mine they could earn a little money. Without the gold, he said, life would be unbearable.

I took a photograph in that mine of a youngster standing on the rim, in front of a vast hole in which tiny bodies look like insects. I have the photo on the wall in my office. I see it every day, and it reminds me not just of the humbling endurance of the Congolese, or their apparently eternal suffering, but also how sheer bloody lucky I am to not be working for twelve hours a day, seven days a week, up to my waist or my neck in sucking mud and filth.

The Pakistani UN force invited us to their base for dinner that night. It was a matter of honour for them that we ate well.

There was no alcohol on offer, of course, but we talked late into the night and they spoke with horror and wonder about the state of the DRC. Men from the deserts of Balochistan, they said they were astonished to discover when they arrived that people in the region were starving.

'This is a place where you drop a seed in the ground and by the next year there is a tree,' said one captain. Gradually the Pakistanis realised they were dealing with an entire society that had been traumatised by endless and apocalyptic conflict. People had lost touch with fundamental skills and leadership was completely absent. Refugees began gathering around their base begging for help and advice, so men from the deserts of Pakistan began offering crash courses in smallholding. By the time I visited there were vegetable stalls lining the roads near their base, and malnutrition rates, in their area at least, had fallen dramatically.

Each time I have visited a UN military contingent they have gone out of their way to both protect and feed us. Elsewhere in the DRC a contingent of Moroccan UN soldiers were especially proud of their food, and had spices, dried apricots, fruit and meat flown in weekly. 'Our own special aid flight,' one of their senior officers said with a smile. The best UN food I have eaten was, perhaps a little predictably, a meal with an Italian force. They had flown in not just fresh garlic and vegetables, but pasta, cheese, wine and their own chef.

But a posting with the UN in the DRC was no cushy job. When I visited in the mid-2000s there were 17,000 UN troops working not just as peacekeepers, but peace enforcers, author- ised to fight warring factions. Dozens of UN soldiers had been killed and they were taking no chances when out on patrol.

The next day we headed out with the Pakistanis on a patrol that is often described as 'force projection', a show of power designed to intimidate enemies and reassure friends. Driving around flanked by UN armoured cars with mounted machine guns was nerve-wracking. Attacks with RPGs were still worry- ingly common.

We were taken to a district where an astonishing 50,000 had

died in fighting between different ethnic groups battling over land that one side wanted to use for crops and the other to graze their cattle. Whole communities had been wiped out. The UN dropped us off in the village of Nizi, where locals from the Hema tribe told me they had been attacked by the neighbouring Lendus. The village chief took Emery and me to see a mass grave where victims had been buried.

'How many are there?' I asked as I looked out over a forest of wooden crosses.

'One hundred and fourteen. All killed in one attack.' His eyes narrowed at the memory. 'They were mostly women and children.'

'How did it happen?' I asked him.

He took a moment before he responded. 'Early morning, just as the sun was coming up they attacked the village with machetes.' He pointed into the distance, towards the Lendu village from where the attackers had appeared. 'They massacred women and children, hacked them down wherever they came upon them.'

An older man appeared, clearly traumatised. He struggled to contain his emotions as he described the attack. He escaped with his life, but his arms and hands bore the scars of machetes and his right ear and head had been split with a heavy blow.

'They tried to hack me to death,' he told me. 'I don't know how I survived.'

'How many members of your family did you lose?'

'All of them. They killed my wife and all my children. There is no one left, the Lendus took everyone from me.'

Emery and I were both deeply moved by the suffering we heard in the village. We had a quiet hug after meeting that poor man, before we headed back into the town of Bunia in search of a reflective beer. On the dirt road outside our guesthouse was a bar with a sign at the door showing a crossed-out sub-machine gun and the legend 'Pas d'armes / No weapons'. It was perfect. We sat outside and Emery, as decent a human being as you will find on this planet, told me he was optimistic about the future. He showed me his voter registration card for upcoming elections and said he would guard it with his life.

Emery had faith in the democratic process. In the years that followed the President of the DRC, Joseph Kabila, secured repeat terms in office in 2006 and 2011, then refused to leave when his term expired in December 2016. Further fighting has erupted in the north-east, with more suffering and tens of thousands forced to flee. Meanwhile in Mbandaka there have been Ebola outbreaks even within the town. It seems the people of the DRC must continue to endure the endless consequences of climate, colonial rule, conflict and sapping corruption.

CHAPTER TWENTY-ONE

The Open Prison

We flew east to Uganda, and then travelled on overland to Kenya, the most stable African country on the equator, where my guide Michael Kaloki has since become a firm favourite on repeated trips. Keep your ears open for his name, because he often pops up on the radio. Tall, thoughtful, and the sort of bloke who keeps a pen in his pocket, partly to chew and partly to make notes on anything that interests him, Michael is also one of Kenya's (unsurprisingly few) ice-carving champions.

'How on earth did you discover ice-carving?' I asked him when another colleague mentioned his slightly eccentric skill. Michael remains much too modest to brag.

'I was a journalism student in Canada,' he said, 'and I happened to see the winter carnival in Toronto.' Michael was captivated by enormous, glistening, almost transparent sculptures. Back in Kenya he persuaded a friend who sculpted more traditionally in stone and wood to turn to ice and they found tools to use on small blocks they produced from home freezers. Eventually they were allowed to use a walk-in freezer at a hotel in Nairobi to practise, and Michael has since represented Kenya at ice festivals in Canada, Finland and in a competition on the sidelines of the Turin Winter Olympics.

With Michael leading us, we set off across Kenya, keeping our eyes peeled for anything odd or interesting that might be happening. We didn't have to go far. Michael heard about a village close to the equator that was holding a weekend festival. Some traditional circumcisers would be attending. The rite was performed in Kenya on some boys aged around twelve as part of their transition to manhood. I wasn't sure if I was looking forward to it or not, but we tracked along the equator until we were driving through the outskirts of the community, and we found huge bulls being marshalled through the streets by groups of men wielding sticks, clubs and long spears. Obviously Brian, as an intrepid war cameraman, was out of our vehicle in a shot, racing towards the action. He was carrying a 14-kilogram camera on his shoulder, but I still struggled to keep up. We managed to get in front of the bulls and I asked Michael what on earth was going on.

'It's a bull fight,' he said.

We made our way beyond a series of broken-down buildings to a spacious patch of grass that seemed to form the bull-fighting arena. The animals looked confused and not even slightly itching for a fight. One guy appeared to be baiting his bull with a pair of hand-held bells that resembled maracas.

'He's psyching him up,' Michael said as my eyes took in the scene. Another bull was half hidden in a crowd of chanting men.

At that point a man wearing a long pink dress and a gorilla mask pulled me into the throng, past another bloke who had what appeared to be a dead rat on his head.

'Can someone explain what the hell is going on?' I said somewhat plaintively.

Michael came puffing towards me and said that it was the local tradition for people at bull fights to wear animal skins: their costumes were supposed to protect them. I raised a cynical eyebrow, but then the gorilla-man drew me towards two bulls that were being pushed closer together to lock horns.

'How do you know who wins?' I shouted over the chaos to gorilla-man.

'Eh?' He could barely hear me.

'How do you know who wins?'

'When one of the bulls runs off.'

As he was speaking the contest came to an abrupt end. A giant black-and-white bull saw off a brown bull, which turned tail and ran with everyone whooping and chasing after it. It was, I should point out, nothing like a Spanish bull fight where razor-sharp spears are thrust into an agitated beast. The Kenyan version is nothing to celebrate, in my view, but was still a much less violent affair. Two bulls would push and shove at each other for a moment or two, and then one would run away. That was it. The crowd, many of whom were drunk or at least jolly, seemed much more at risk.

I watched as the owner of the winning bull was hoisted onto shoulders and carried around the arena and onto the road. A few minutes later we had a quick chat. He was clearly delighted at the prospect of a victory payout.

'The loser gets a little too,' he said. 'In the old days the winner would get a sheep and the loser would still get a cockerel.'

'It's just a bit of country fun really,' said Michael with a smile. So long as nobody gets seriously hurt.

Amid all the chaos Michael spotted one of the circumcisers we were supposed to be meeting – a young guy wearing a brown shirt, an animal skin and a massive wig, with his face and arms painted with leopard spots.

'Seriously, Michael?'

'That's him.

'Would you trust him with your todger?' I said to Brian. 'I wouldn't.'

Just a moment later another of the bulls turned during a fight and raced off through the crowd, catching a young man on his leg. Chaos turned to bedlam.

People were attempting to drive off the bull with shouts and chants as another man with a megaphone tried to marshal the crowd.

'Can someone please put the boy into a vehicle and take him to hospital?' he begged. The boy was bleeding from a loosely tied bandage.

'What's happened?' I asked one of the men carrying him.

'He's broken his leg.'

We had the only suitable car, a large four-wheel-drive vehicle used for game-spotting on safaris, so Michael intervened and volunteered our transport.

And that is how, ten minutes later, I found myself in the surreal situation of sitting in the back of a makeshift ambulance with a lad called Magnus who had been injured by a rampaging bull, a Kenyan ice-carving champion, a South African war cameraman and two knife-wielding traditional circumcisers dressed in animal skins.

Michael had dragged the circumcisers along with us on the way to the hospital, and they helped us lift the lad out onto a hospital gurney. Rather ironically, he was the son of the chairman of the bullfighting association. Nurses in starched uniforms took him away, and we went for a chat in a bar with the circumcisers. The older of the two was called Thomas and he brandished a rusty-looking blade as he explained the procedure. I listened intently, sitting with my hands fisted in my lap and a grimace on my face.

'Thomas, that sounds really painful.'

'That's how he becomes a man,' the circumciser assured me. 'Then he can sit with the other men.'

'Are you very busy?' I said. 'Do you do the procedure a lot?'

He nodded. 'We can circumcise a hundred boys an hour.'

'A hundred?' I said. 'Don't they mind you working so quickly?'

'That's the way it's done. You can become crazy.'

Now I was really mind-blown. 'What do you mean?' I said, shaking my head with a strained smile. 'What do you mean, you can become crazy?'

'There is singing, it's frantic.' Thomas was wild-eyed. 'It gets into your head. You're in a frenzy and just continue to cut, cut, cut.'

Legs crossed, I'd heard enough. We gave the circumcisers a lift home, then drove on along the equator towards Kenya's Lake Nakuru National Park. It was said to be home to the most fabulous bird spectacle in the world. How could we resist?

The lake itself is relatively small and shallow, but that helps to keep the water warm all year round, which feeds the growth of algae, which in turn is the major draw for a vast population of flamingos.

As we hopped out of our vehicles we were met with an almost perfect filming moment. Brian was thrilled. I was in raptures. In the foreground were buffalo and rhino, even a hyena trotting along with a bird in its mouth for breakfast. Behind them, around them, above them and almost everywhere, in fact, were perhaps a million flamingos which had gathered in huge numbers at the lake edge but then seemed to reach right across the water like a scattering of pink petals.

This was the Kenya travellers wanted to see; this was wildlife and landscape in all its splendour.

We drove up to a vantage point over the lake called Baboon Cliff, which gifted a panoramic view of the lake, but also gave me a series of understandings and insights that inform me to this day.

Thousands of photographs have been taken from Baboon Cliff, almost all of them showing the wildlife of the park. Documentaries have been shot in Nakuru showing animals roaming majestically free. Indeed, down below I watched a giraffe out for a stroll around the edge of the lake, its stilt-length legs looking as though they were moving in slow motion.

But turn eyes and cameras just slightly to the north, and there in clear sight is the busy town of Nakuru, a home to more than 300,000 people.

I was stunned at the proximity of park and people. And at that moment I saw through the fantasies and illusions of advertisers and documentary makers, who for years with their careful shots and photographs have peddled an idea that Lake Nakuru and much of the planet is still properly wild. A bubble suddenly popped in my head.

At first glance Lake Nakuru might appear to be a wilderness, but in reality it was a managed park, controlled by humans and at risk from humans, who were right at its borders.

It was another moment where the journey became an education. I was learning every hour of every day on the road. Even here, while watching a giraffe out for a morning amble.

Countless times in the years since I have been confronted by the reality that we have been lied to for decades. By advertisers? Well, that's hardly surprising. But documentary makers have also gone to extraordinary lengths to create wildlife porn that bears no relation to reality.

While filming in Madagascar a few years after travelling

around the equator I visited Berenty, a tiny wildlife reserve that has featured in numerous nature documentaries and become synonymous with iconic lemurs. Unique to Madagascar, lemurs are the descendants of primates that travelled across the Indian Ocean from the mainland millions of years ago on rafts or logs. They are stunning and delightful creatures loved by all. Documentaries about them are hugely successful and sold around the world. Chances are, if you have seen a documentary about lemurs filmed in Madagascar, then it was at least part-shot in Berenty, even right around the offices, bungalows and restaurant of the reserve, with cameramen straining to keep the buildings out of shot.

The founders of Berenty cleared huge areas of forest and left just a token sanctuary that now provides habitat for a small number of lemurs. The reserve is only the size of a London park, and is surrounded by a huge expanse of agricultural land. When I visited, tens of thousands of acres around Berenty were being used to grow sisal, some of it apparently destined to become environmentally friendly packaging for Europe.

Yet often TV programmes about places like Berenty or Nakuru completely fail to show that reality, or the truth about what we humans have done and are doing to our world. The producer of one wildlife film on Madagascar told my colleague their team had been given explicit instructions to just make their programmes look good and avoid mention of deforestation and destruction. Partly as a result, I fear, many viewers do not fully understand just how humans are transforming and ravaging Planet Earth.

Because my brief from the outset has been to mix elements of both beauty and darkness, light and shade, we haven't needed to follow the same rulebook. Sitting up there on Baboon Cliff after wallowing in the beauty of the lake we were able to pan our cameras across to point at Nakuru town. We mentioned the proximity of the buildings, and then later went into the urban centre to film and hammer home the point that humans are right on the borders of wild areas, nibbling away at their edges, and posing a fundamental threat to the wildlife within.

Steve, a senior ranger from the Kenya Wildlife Service, then gifted me more understanding. He explained that Nakuru was being surrounded by a 50-mile-long electric fence, not to keep the wildlife in, but to keep the humans out. Farmers had tried to encroach on the park looking for more land, and poachers were a constant threat.

'This is our Ark,' said the ranger, holding his arms out as if he wanted to hug it. It was a light-hearted comment, but he was so right. The national parks of Africa and marine reserves around the world, which are basically national parks in the sea, have indeed become wildlife Arks. They are our last chance of protecting iconic life.

I was mulling all this over on Baboon Cliff, as good a place as any for moments of revelation, when Steve pointed towards the park entrance.

'Look,' he said. 'Here come the guests.'

It was early in the morning. Three car-loads of tourists were arriving at the park on a game drive. They headed straight for the edge of the lake, then hopped out to start snapping away at the glorious scene.

Steve was smiling.

'You think of them as guests?' I said. 'That's very positive.'

'Of course. They pay our wages,' he said with a laugh.

It was another light-bulb moment. Of course, tourism *can* be a powerful force for good. *This is what I love about these journeys,* I thought. *This is the reason to go back on the road after a brush with malaria, and to keep on travelling as long as I possibly can.* From the comfort of home, I used to imagine that tourism could only be a disaster for the environment. But up there on Baboon Cliff I realised national parks and marine protected areas are incredibly dependent on money from travellers. Entrance fees from tourists pay for guides, guards, patrol boats, salaries, uniforms and electric fences. If we don't visit national parks and marine protected areas around the world, and pay our entrance fees, those wildlife Arks will be poached to annihilation, turned into palm-oil plantations, or fished to death, or logged.

When I talk to guides and rangers in places like Nakuru I invariably discover either they or their parents were poachers or hunters before they started working in the park. By creating a park, and then providing jobs and salaries to local communities, we give economic incentives to people to protect what all of us surely want to preserve. It is something absolutely critical that travellers can do to help protect iconic life.

If you doubt the role you can play, take a look at the small-print 'About' section on the Kenya Wildlife Service website. Their mission statement, as daft as those things sometimes are, is profound: 'To save the last great species and places on earth for humanity'. And how do they do that? They collect fees and charges in parks, money from filming and hotels, then they plough that back into parks and for 'benefit sharing with communities living in wildlife areas'.

I am, of course, completely aware of the environmental consequences of travel. All our holidays and adventures, whether for hedonism or political enlightenment, have a deep impact on the planet. Forests are logged and marshes are drained to provide land or materials for more hotels and resorts. Planting trees to offset carbon emissions from our long-haul flights just legitimises our unsustainable lifestyles. But almost everything about our Western lifestyles is environmentally catastrophic. I remember paling when I read one study that estimated each and every Google search uses the energy it would take to boil two cups of water.

Just to be absolutely clear, I believe we are in a struggle for the future that I would liken to the Second World War for importance. The human and environmental challenges that I see around the globe are urgent and critical. We absolutely have to give a damn, and campaign, fight, demonstrate and agitate for profound change and immediate and dramatic environmental protections.

Yet tourism doesn't just have to be about exploiting and ruining. When it is managed sustainably and meaningfully it can really help to protect and preserve a place. So get up, get out there, and experience the best this world has to offer. Seek out authentic and immersive holiday experiences, something you will be able to look back on and remember forever. And pay your entrance fee for a park or a day pass for a marine park and know that you are helping to preserve some of the greatest wildlife on the planet.

My time in Kenya was supposed to be coming to an end. I was due to travel on along the equator to the coast of southern Somalia, where the African leg of the adventure would finish. In the distance ahead were journeys following the equator across southern Asia, and then from the Galapagos across South America to the mouth of the Amazon.

But at dawn on the morning of our flight to Somalia we were

told heavy fighting had broken out in the very area we were due to visit. The BBC High Risk team said they were sorry but there was no way they could authorise our trip.

So instead I decided to fly along the equator as far as I could, to get as close as possible to the border with Somalia. It was to be a decision that, in a positive way, has deeply affected my life, shaping my travels in the years since.

Right on the equator in eastern Kenya are the Dadaab refugee camps. We pottered through the skies in a tiny plane, flying above endless rusty-coloured desert scrub and low brush, then dropped down towards a landing strip in the middle of nowhere.

All around the land was flat, arid, and devoid of obvious features save for a dusty road, and a vast encampment of myriad huts, tents and makeshift shelters. This, at the time, was the largest refugee camp in the world, a home to hundreds of thousands of refugees from the relentless fighting across the border in Somalia.

We landed, met up with UNHCR, the United Nations refugee agency, who ran the camp and were very used to flighty television crews passing through their world, and then went to find new arrivals who had just made a long trek to the camp and were waiting to be processed by the UN.

It was tragic and pitiful. There were families with absolutely nothing to their names, squatting in the dirt waiting for someone to help them. I spoke to a woman who had fled fresh fighting in Mogadishu.

'Why did you come here?' I asked her.

She spread her palms in a hopeless gesture. 'The fighting was very bad. The worst I've ever seen.'

'Are you here with your family?'

'Some of them.' Her face masked immense pain. 'I had to leave two of my children behind.'

I was stunned, trying to imagine how appalling that must have been.

'I could not bring them,' she told me. 'I don't know what's become of them.'

She was absolutely desperate. My heart broke for her.

'We were attacked,' she went on. 'I lost them in the fighting. I don't know what happened to them. I had to flee. I brought my other children but I don't know where those two are. I had no choice but to leave.'

She told me her group had walked for almost three full weeks to get to the camp. Along the way their meagre supply of food ran out and there was nothing to survive on but rainwater. I had been to Somalia. I had some small sense of the violence they had fled. I knew the world had largely forgotten them. They were victims of a conflict that the region, let alone the West, no longer had any time for. I wondered how long they would remain there, on the edge of nowhere, with no way out, no hope and nothing to look forward to.

And then I met Fatima, a young Somali woman, aged twenty-three, who had been in the camp for an astonishing seventeen years. I was instantly reminded of the families and children living in railway boxcars near the border of unrecognised Nagorno-Karabakh. Both prisons, in their own way. Fatima was calm, assured and gentle. She appeared to be so worldly it was hard to believe she had never lived anywhere but this desert camp. She led me to her home, a simple hut made from saplings of acacia with a roughly fenced yard, and we sat down together to talk.

'Fatima,' I said, 'have you really been here for most of your life?'

'That's right.'

I asked her if she thought she would ever go home to Somalia. She replied clearly: no.

Would you want to? I wondered.

No, she said, never. 'Because I know the problems, I know that my people have been killed there.'

Fatima and thousands of other refugees in the camp did not want to return to Somalia, they wanted to integrate into Kenya. But the Kenyan government was concerned their presence would destabilise communities near the Somali border and as a consequence would not let them move deeper into the country to settle or work.

What that meant, Fatima explained, was that no one from the camp was allowed to travel more than twelve miles from the perimeter. They were stuck there. Fatima was literate, well educated, fluent in English and bursting with capability and promise. It was a positive camp run by caring aid workers, but it was also a forgotten prison. She was trapped in the desert, unable to go home because of conflict and chronic instability in her home country and forbidden from travelling more than a few miles from the camp by the Kenyan government.

While she was stuck, I was moving on, the fundamental difference between us just the place and circumstances of our birth. Backpack over my shoulder, I walked with her to the edge of the camp.

'This feels so wrong,' I told her. 'I'm leaving. I have a British passport which gifts me freedom and a chance to travel. I'm on a journey that will take me around the world and yet you're stuck here.'

Fatima gazed out across the empty landscape.

'We call this an open prison, that's what we normally tell

people,' she said, 'where we're free to go just so far and no further. The nearest town is 90 kilometres away and to get there you have to have a vehicle. We don't have cars and, even if we did, the police would stop us and ask to see our ID cards. We don't have ID cards so they would know we came from the camp and we'd be sent straight back.'

Fatima had only left the camp twice. Once for a meeting of youth leaders in the town, and once for a volleyball game, of all things. Apart from that, for nearly two decades, she had been stuck out in the desert.

Meeting Fatima hit me like a bolt. I had spent the last couple of months being treated and recovering from malaria and then pondering whether to continue the journey of a lifetime. Yet here was someone denied the most basic freedom of movement. Unable to go home because of conflict in Somalia, Fatima had spent almost her entire life trapped in a tiny patch of desert. Her story haunts me. I remember her every single time I reach for my passport.

Before we met I had felt the compelling joy of travel, but Fatima was tangible proof that travel was still an extraordinary luxury, and an intense privilege. Those of us who can fly must never forget how lucky we are, and that travel is still the preserve of a fortunate minority. Standing with Fatima I thought back to my own dear grandmother, who first sparked my love of discovery with her magical mystery tours in her adapted car. Both women had been trapped by circumstance, while my renewed health and passport now gifted me a licence to explore.

In that moment, I knew I never wanted to stop travelling, and discovering. I knew that for as long as I could I needed to use each journey to enrich my mind, heart and life. I would take chances, go to strange places, and dive into the culture of the world. And I would never take it for granted.

'Thank you for showing us around,' I said to Fatima.

'You're very welcome,' she said. 'Thank you to you and your team. I really appreciate you coming and seeing my home.'

We both smiled. I had a lump in my throat.

My travels along the equator in Africa were coming to an end. But my journeys around the world were just beginning.

Acknowledgements

I would like to thank Robert Kirby and Rosemary Scoular, my lovely agents at United Agents, who encouraged me to put fingers to keyboard to make this book a reality. Rupert Lancaster, the charitable publisher at Hodder and Stoughton, has been badgering me for years to tell a few more tales about my life and travels, so must also share some of the credit and the responsibility. Huge thanks also to Cameron Myers at Hodder, and Natalia Lucas and Kate Walsh at UA.

Jeff Gulvin helped tease out and structure my stories and did much of the initial heavy-lifting for the book. Friends and family carried me along the way, as they have done through so much of life, especially my mum Cindy and my brother James, who both racked their brains to recall and discuss events and moments from what initially felt like a distant past.

This book covers more than three decades of my life, and sadly I cannot express gratitude to everyone who has guided me along the way. You would be reading a phone directory. But to all who have nudged, inspired and encouraged me I thank you from the depths of my heart. Most of all my thanks go to Anya, my wife and partner in life, who has tolerated, supported and inspired me since the day we met, and to our wonderful son Jake, who fills us both with joy and purpose, and to whom I dedicate this book. Love you son.

An invitation from the publisher

Join us at www.hodder.co.uk, or follow us
on Twitter @hodderbooks to be a part of
our community of people who love the very
best in books and reading.

Whether you want to discover more about a book
or an author, watch trailers and interviews, have the
chance to win early limited editions, or simply browse
our expert readers' selection of the very best books,
we think you'll find what you're looking for.

And if you don't, that's the place to tell us what's missing.

We love what we do, and we'd love you to be a part of it.

www.hodder.co.uk

@hodderbooks

HodderBooks

HodderBooks